The Brook
Necropolis
Railway

by
John M. Clarke

LONDON NECROPOLIS & NATIONAL MAUSOLEUM COMPANY

MORTUIS QUIES VIVIS SALUS

THE OAKWOOD PRESS

© Oakwood Press & John M. Clarke 2006

British Library Cataloguing in Publication Data
A Record for this book is available from the British Library
ISBN 0 85361 655 8
ISBN 978 0 85361 655 9

First published 1983
Second enlarged edition 1988
Third revised and enlarged edition 1995
Fourth revised and enlarged edition 2006

Typeset by Oakwood Graphics.
Repro by PKmediaworks, Cranborne, Dorset.
Printed by

Dedicated to my Mother
Who started me on this journey

Title page: The great seal of the LNC. The motto may be translated as 'A healthy life and death'. *Author*

Pull-out: Map of Brookwood Cemetery. The illustrations show (reading clockwise) the second Anglican chapel, a view along St Mark's Avenue, the Roman Catholic chapel, the Nonconformist chapel, and a view of St George's Avenue. *Author's Collection*

Published by The Oakwood Press (Usk), P.O. Box 13, Usk, Mon., NP15 1YS.
E-mail: sales@oakwoodpress.co.uk
Website: www.oakwoodpress.co.uk

Contents

London and South Western Ry. 787

From

TO

Brookwood

Preface

'People are dying to get into Brookwood Cemetery.'
(Music Hall joke)

The London Necropolis Company was unique in providing continuous railway funeral traffic for 87 years. This book aims to provide a history of the service.

Prior to 1983, when this book first appeared, there was very little information about the funeral trains. Undoubtedly the nature of the traffic contributed to this lack of information. The aversion of modern society to the importance of death and dying meant a polite disinterest surrounded the subject. The destruction of the Necropolis Company's London terminus during the last war, with the assumption of the loss of its records, provided another and more substantial excuse. Consequently inaccuracies, errors, and 'myths' found their way into print. One book stated that 'the engines were adorned with evergreens'; whilst I have been told that all the locomotives used for the service were painted white and that the driver and fireman were suitably dressed in mourning, complete with top hat and gloves!*

I have written this account in what I hope is a logical and straightforward way. The introductory chapter briefly outlines London's burial problem in the mid-19th century, and how the Necropolis scheme evolved from this. This is essential in order to understand why the service began, although it can be skipped by those wholly interested in the railway details. It is based on my unpublished undergraduate dissertation *Cemeteries in Conflict: the Disposal of the Dead in Nineteenth Century London 1849-1854*, which covers this material in greater detail. Chapter Two discusses the development and changes that took place to the two private Necropolis termini, whilst Chapter Three covers the cemetery end, including the branch, the cemetery stations, and Brookwood station. Chapter Four brings all these elements together, explaining how the Necropolis Company operated its funerals by railway. Chapter Five continues this theme by considering a series of special trains operated from time to time by the company, and a few incidents that occurred during the lifetime of the service. Chapter Six then studies the stock used for the Necropolis train over the years, and Chapter Seven looks at the fare structure and the tickets used. Finally, Chapter Eight rounds off the account with an evaluation of the system and the service.

I have often been asked how I became interested in the line. It was by pure accident. One summer I was reading about the Great War of 1914-18, and was moved by the great sacrifices in human life that were made, often with seemingly trivial results. On my mother's suggestion, I visited the military section of Brookwood Cemetery to form some impression of the unintelligible numbers that fell during those terrible times. After musing amongst the sombre, uniformly ranked headstones, I wandered aimlessly, and chanced upon a low brick wall which I recognised at once as the remains of a railway platform. I thought this quite incongruous, if not bizarre, and thereafter I was driven by sheer curiosity to discover as much as I could about the cemetery's railway line.

---

* Some of these errors appear to originate from Basil Copper's gothic thriller *Necropolis* (*see Appendix Five*).

Contrary to popular misconception, the cemetery continues to change and develop, as further burials take place. During the past 20 years five major changes have taken place along the route of the cemetery railway. The first is the use of the trackbed in the former unconsecrated section (now formally named 'Railway Avenue') as the site of a number of substantial family graves. The most notable of these is the magnificent mausoleum commemorating HH Sharif Al-Hussein Ben Ali (died 1998), situated opposite the platform of North station. Second is the decision by the owners of the Najmee Baag burial ground, which incorporates the former nonconformist chapel and the site of North station, to plant leylandii around the boundary of their plot. In time this will result in the destruction of the remains of the platform of North station, and it is a shame the community did not plant these trees further across the platform site. Third is the major office development adjacent to the cemetery entrance off Cemetery Pales, site of the former Superintendent's office. This area was sold off as a consequence of the 1975 Brookwood Cemetery Act, a piece of private legislation which allowed the then cemetery owners to sell land within the cemetery boundary. Woking Borough Council subsequently allowed the site to be dramatically redeveloped with a devastating impact on the cemetery landscape which has also resulted in the death of all the mature trees surrounding this site. Fourth is the Ismaili Cemetery which is located on plot 71 and which will in time extend along the former trackbed up to plot 74. Some of the buildings associated with the Ismaili Cemetery have been constructed on the former trackbed. Fifth is the site of South station. Owned by the St Edward Brotherhood since 1982, the monks have planning permission to build a new Brotherhood House on the site of the station courtyard. The architecture has been sympathetically designed to mirror that of the St Edward Church nearby, and a building appeal is currently underway. Part of the planning consent. requires that the station platform is fully restored, that the foundations of South station are marked out, that interpretation boards will be erected for the convenience of visitors, and that a small museum will be created in the original Church of England chapel.

It seems incredible that this book first appeared more than 20 years ago. It is even more remarkable that new, substantial sources of information continue to be identified. These have resulted in a number of major changes to this edition. Chief amongst these are the several donations of material made to the Surrey History Centre in Woking. The most important is Mark Wealthy's collection of material on the London Necropolis Company, some of which I first looked at over 25 years ago, and which is now available for inspection. Part of this collection covers the details of Necropolis Company tickets issued from 1922-41, and allows a much clearer picture of the Necropolis train's usage during this period. Also of note has been the appearance of my own substantial guide to the cemetery, *London's Necropolis: A Guide to Brookwood Cemetery* (Sutton Publishing, 2004), published to celebrate the 150th anniversary of Brookwood Cemetery. The appearance of this major work has also meant the identification of further sources of information, some of which have been exploited for this new edition.

In 1983 I wondered if any new information would emerge on the London Necropolis Company's railway funeral service. In fact there was much more to discover. Three further editions have made full use of the quality and quantity of new information unearthed since 1983. Even this new edition, however definitive it may appear, cannot be regarded as the final statement on this curious railway service. I would still welcome any further information on the Necropolis train and ask that material be forwarded to me, c/o the publishers.

For this edition I am indebted (as always) to the cemetery owners, Ramadan and Diane Guney, for allowing me access to the registers and for their unfailing hospitality, interest and support. I should also like to thank Dr Brian Parsons for allowing me to quote from his recently published history of Woking Crematorium *Committed to the Cleansing Flame: The Development of Cremation in Nineteenth Century England* (Spire Books, 2005); he has also read much of the revised manuscript and made many valuable suggestions. Mr George Lambert, sometime Superintendent of the London Necropolis, offered valuable insights into the company's operations during the latter period of the railway funeral business. I should also like to thank former staff at the Cemetery Office: Mr D. Dally, the General Manager and subsequent owner of the site, and his two secretaries, Miss E.M. Iggulden (later Mrs Maeder) and Mrs Jackson.

I am grateful to HarperCollins Publishers for permission to quote from *A Traveller's Life* by Eric Newby (London, HarperCollins Publishers, 1982). The extract from *My Early Life* by Sir Winston Churchill is reproduced with permission of Curtis Brown Ltd, London, on behalf of The Estate of Sir Winston S. Churchill and is Copyright The Estate of Sir Winston S. Churchill 1930. I am indebted to Basil Copper for permission to quote sections from his gothic thriller *Necropolis*, which was commissioned for and first published in hardback by Arkham House Publishers Inc., USA, 1980, and is Copyright Basil Copper 1980 (all rights reserved).

For help with additional information and photographs for this and previous editions I would like to thank: Mr Akehurst, Father Alexis and other members of the St Edward Brotherhood, David and Sêan Barber, Jennie Bisset, Mr H.V. Borley, Mr H.C. Casserley, David Charlesworth, Mr C. Chivers, Richard and Rosemary Christophers, Barry Clarke, Tina Cockett, Mrs M. Cockram, Mr T. Coleman, Mr B. Copper, Dr E. Course, David and Lynne Cowley, Mr D. Cullum, Mrs G. Dalgleish, Lyndon Davies, Mr & Mrs Dendy, Kevin Desmond, Edward Evans, Mr David Fairhurst, Mr J.N. Faulkner, Mr F. Foote, Mr E. Foster, Mr D.G. Geldard, Mr R. Gillam, Mr C.R. Gordon Stuart, Mr D. Gould, Mrs J. Graveson, Mr P.A. Harding, Mr M. Harvey, Steve Hayes, Derek & Sheila Heasman, Mr A.L. Hillman, Margaret Hobbs, Mr C. Hobson, Mr D. Hoodless, John and Karen Humpage, Ian Hutchinson, Mr A.A. Jackson, Mr M. King, Mr P. Kingston, Mr N.C. Langridge, Mr D. Latimer, Maurice C. Lawson, Pat Lowry, Mary Lucas, Michael Mehta, Mr R. Molock, Dr Chris Molyneaux, Anthony Montan, Janet Nixon, Jon Nuttall, Mr J.H. Otto, Mr M. Passmore, Mr G.A. Payne, Vicky Pollard, Julian Pooley, Tanya Jane Richards, Mr R.C. Riley, Mr R.F. Roberts, Mr S. Rumble, Mr J.E. Shelbourn, Mrs Gwen Spencer, Mr L.E. Squance, Minister Haruhisa Takeuchi, Mr P. Temple, Marilyn Scott, Terry Stamp, Jo Toogood, Mr H. Tumilty, Mr A.M. Urry, Stan Verrinder, Iain Wakeford, Mark Wealthy, David Weatherill, Gordon Weddell, Mr S. White, Mr E. Wingfield, and Mr P. Woods.

I would like to thank the staff at the following libraries and institutions for their unfailing help: the Bodleian Library, Farnborough Library, the Guildford Institute, the Guildford Muniments Room, Lambeth Library, the Lightbox (formerly the Woking Galleries), the National Railway Museum, the National Archives (Kew), the Surrey History Centre, the Transport Ticket Society, the University Library Cambridge, the Westminster Central Reference Library, and Woking Library. The Historical Model Railway Society, the Southern Railways Group, and the South Western Circle, have also been only too ready to give advice and information.

John M. Clarke
Mytchett, Surrey;
Sheffield,
and Surbiton
1983-2006

Typical travel 'warrant' issued by the Borough of Southwark for the Necropolis train. It authorises the issue of two third class mourner tickets for a pauper funeral.

Southwark Local Studies Library

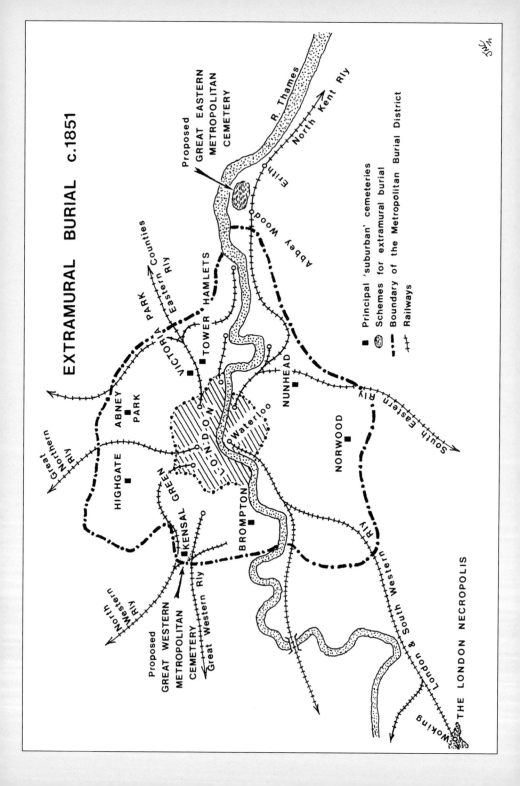

EXTRAMURAL BURIAL c.1851

Proposed GREAT EASTERN METROPOLITAN CEMETERY

R. Thames

North Kent Rly

Erith

Abbey Wood

Eastern Counties Rly

VICTORIA PARK

TOWER HAMLETS

ABNEY PARK

Great Northern Rly

HIGHGATE

L·O·N·D·O·N

Waterloo

NUNHEAD

NORWOOD

South Eastern Rly

KENSAL GREEN

BROMPTON

North Western Rly

Proposed GREAT WESTERN METROPOLITAN CEMETERY

Great Western Rly

London & South Western Rly

Woking

THE LONDON NECROPOLIS

■ Principal 'suburban' cemeteries
◉ Schemes for extramural burial
━·━· Boundary of the Metropolitan Burial District
╄╄╄ Railways

Chapter One

Historical Background to the Necropolis Service

'It was fitting enough that the largest city in the world should have the largest cemetery in the world.'
(The Times)

The 'London Necropolis' was intended to become London's only cemetery by providing enough land to contain all the metropolitan dead for an almost indefinite period. It was established to solve the capital's interments problem, caused by a chronic lack of burial space amid a rapidly growing population. The metropolitan community had more than doubled in the first half of the 19th century, from just under one million people in 1801, to over two and a quarter million by 1851; there was a corresponding increase in annual burials, from 49,900 in 1838, to 55,500 in 1851. But in spite of London's growth, from 44,800 acres in 1838, to 78,000 acres by 1851, the total area of burying grounds remained relatively stable at under 300 acres, resulting in acute burial congestion.

The consequences of this situation were horrific. The sanctity and permanence of grave spaces was rarely respected, and graves were continually re-used, the contents broken through, unearthed, and scattered over the ground. Alternatively, vast pits were excavated, involving the desecration of many previously buried corpses, into which any number of new bodies would be ruthlessly crammed. Debris of the previous occupants of graves was either burned or collected for the second-hand 'coffin furniture' market. Scraps of coffin wood were used for household fuel in poor neighbourhoods, whilst many tons of human bones were shipped from London to the North each year, to be crushed and used as fertilizer.

In addition to these repugnant modes of interment, many contemporary medical experts believed exhalations from the improperly and inadequately buried dead poisoned the air, rendering it harmful to life. Those living adjacent to graveyards, usually the poorest classes, were especially at risk. Decomposition also led to the contamination of drinking wells, springs, and water courses.

No radical, comprehensive or worthwhile solution was attempted until the cholera epidemic of 1848-9, which resulted in 14,601 deaths in London alone, and exacerbated the interments problem almost to saturation point. Two main schemes, both designed to relieve this intolerable pressure on the burying grounds, evolved from this crisis of congestion. One was an unsuccessful Government enterprise which attempted to place the administration of all metropolitan burials under the supervision of a public burial board. Two 'national' cemeteries would be opened (one based on an enlarged Kensal Green Cemetery and to be called the 'Great Western Metropolitan Cemetery', the other to be opened near Abbey Wood and called the 'Great Eastern Metropolitan Cemetery') and managed by this board. Thenceforth all the overcrowded burying grounds would be closed, and all interments channelled into the two public cemeteries. This project failed to mature because of flaws in the

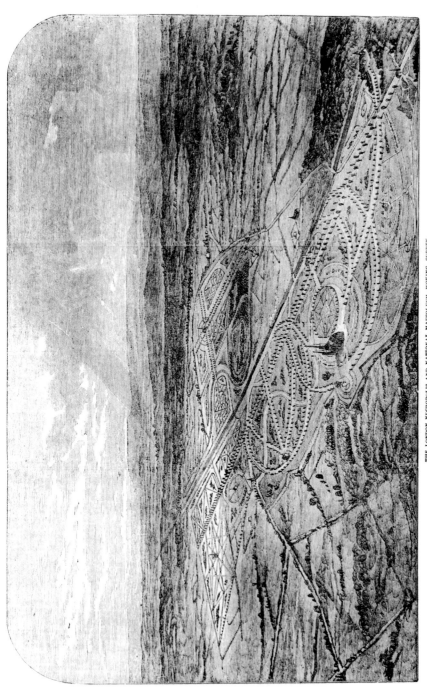

THE LONDON NECROPOLIS AND NATIONAL MAUSOLEUM, WOKING, SURREY.

An engraving of Henry Abraham's proposed London Necropolis and National Mausoleum, 1852. The area depicted stretches from what is now Hook Heath and Star Hill (*foreground*), to the present-day Brookwood Cemetery (*left of centre*). Note how the LSWR runs through the site.   *The Illustrated London News*

Metropolitan Interments Act (1850), its dependence on a central monopoly for success, the scepticism of the Treasury concerning its viability, and the resentment engendered by its interference with private enterprise. All this, and the rise of the second scheme, led the Government to reconsider the propriety of the measure in 1852.

The other plan was the London Necropolis, devised by Sir Richard Broun and Mr Richard Sprye at the end of 1849. This project was intended to solve the burials problem by itself. The cemetery, to be situated beyond any possible future extension of London, at Woking in Surrey, could never endanger the public health of the capital, whilst its vast area would provide ample capacity for the anticipated volume of metropolitan dead for many years to come. The site could be reached cheaply and conveniently only by railway, hence the vital role of the London & South Western Railway (LSWR) to the success of the enterprise, for the promoters were counting upon the cheapness of land (hence of interments) and economy of transit to attract sufficient custom to the Necropolis. This scheme transcended all the disadvantages of intramural burial: a site that would not become engulfed by London; cheap, common land; and inexpensive, rapid rail transit from central London to the cemetery. In his original Prospectus for the plan Sir Richard Broun explained that:

> A grand and complete system of extramural metropolitan sepulture ought to embrace the following features:
>
> *1st.* An area of ground so distant as to be beyond any possible future extension of the Capital, sufficiently large to allow of its sub-division, not only into spacious distinct portions for the burial of each sect of the Christian Public, but also, if desired and deemed expedient, into as many separate compartments as there are parishes within London and its suburbs.
>
> *2nd.* The administration of the Company's affairs upon liberal principles . . .
>
> *And 3rd.* A Mausoleum Church, with funeral chapels, private mausolea, vaults, and catacombs, large enough to contain, not only the thousands of coffins now lying within our numerous Metropolitan Churches, but also the coffins of all such dying in London, in this and future generations.

The huge area proposed – upwards of 1,500 acres - was carefully calculated. Broun estimated the 200 or so London burial grounds amounted to about 218 acres, whilst the existing 'suburban' cemeteries added a further 282 acres, making a total of about 500 acres. It had been estimated that around 1,500,000 burials had been forced into the lesser area during the previous 30 years, whilst the 'suburban' cemeteries were primarily designed for the burial of the better-off. Assuming that one acre of land could accommodate a maximum of 3,887 coffins laid side by side in a single layer, the proposed London Necropolis could accommodate 5,830,500 bodies. Moreover, if the London Necropolis attracted around 50,000 burials a year, it would take 118 years to fill.* But Broun realised

---

* By contrast, the Directors of Kensal Green Cemetery reckoned on accommodating 133,000 graves in the seven acres allocated for pauper burials, with each grave containing ten coffins. This is equivalent to 1,900 graves per acre (with one coffin in each) but 19,000 coffins per acre at the rate intended by the Directors. On this arithmetic, the proposed London Necropolis would accommodate 2,850,000 coffins in a single layer, or 28,500,000 bodies with ten coffins per grave. In fact the LNC was limited by its Act of Parliament to one coffin per grave (save next of kin), a restriction not applied to existing cemetery companies.

⚜ THE LONDON NECROPOLIS. ⚜

BROOKWOOD CEMETERY, WOKING, SURREY.

THIS LOVELY CEMETERY, situated at Brookwood, near Woking, is the largest in England, the most complete in all its arrangements, and unanimously admitted to be an *ideal* burying-ground. It consists of 500 acres of beautifully-wooded land, with large expanses of heather and rhododendrons, and surrounded by charming scenery.

The grounds have been laid out with the utmost regard to order and perfection; trees, flowers and winding paths diversifying the view, and avoiding the monotony of ordinary burial-places.

This Cemetery was established in 1850, being the outcome of a movement which led, and is still leading, to the closing of over-crowded London graveyards.

The Company has a private Railway Station in London, the entrance to which is from Westminster Bridge Road. When within its gates a funeral party is shut out from public gaze, and in forty minutes reaches the Unconsecrated portion of the Cemetery, where there is another Station, with well-appointed waiting-rooms.

After a short stoppage, the train runs direct through the charming grounds to the Consecrated portion, where similar accommodation is provided.

At each Station the train is met by the Superintendent and his staff of trained assistants, ready to bear the Coffin to one of the Chapels, and thence to the Grave.

Adjoining the Superintendent's house there are Monumental Masonry Works and Show Rooms, where designs can be inspected and estimates obtained.

There are also extensive greenhouses, where supplies of flowers and shrubs can always be had; and graves can be planted and attended to at moderate charges.

No more simple, complete, and reverential mode of burial can be imagined.

Relatives may leave their loved ones in this quiet spot, feeling that here indeed is a veritable

 GOD'S ACRE. ᔦ

"In the absence of any ameliorations whatever of our present cemeterial system being obtainable, it is plainly to the interest of every class, high and low, to avoid the seething suburban cemeteries and to bury their dead at Woking."—FRANCIS SEYMOUR HADEN.

A description of the cemetery from a LNC brochure of 1899.

that families would want to be buried together. So, allowing for husband and wife, or mother and child, to be buried in the same grave, he calculated it would take upwards of 350 years to fill the cemetery, without disturbing the humblest of burials. The definitive answer was provided by Dr John Sutherland of the Home Office in February 1855, when he confirmed that 'an area of twelve hundred acres will be sufficient to accommodate the present interments of the metropolis in perpetuity one body in a grave, with power to re-open in ten years'.

Broun saw his scheme as the means for clean, decent and efficient burial for all Londoners, even its paupers:

> This City of the Dead at Woking is intended by me to be throughout all future generations a ... grand and befitting gathering place for the metropolitan mortality of a mighty nation; a last home and bed of rest where the ashes of the high and low, the mighty and the weak, the learned and the ignorant, the wicked and the good, the idle and the industrious, in one vast co-mingled heap may repose together. A Necropolis which shall not merely stand out in wide relief from the category of small cemeteries with which public enterprise and taste have surrounded the metropolis, but eclipse in grandeur, in uniqueness, in extent, in perfection, all places of sepulture throughout the world.

Railway Funerals

Broun realised that a cemetery situated over 23 miles from London would seem 'over distant', but use of the railway meant the site could be reached cheaply and conveniently. He asserted that this made the proposed necropolis nearer to the centre of London than any one of the eight suburban cemeteries. Broun argued that a hearse and carriage from Somerset House to Kensal Green or Norwood cemeteries could take 'several hours' and cost somewhere between £5 to £10. But he calculated that the railway would take 30-40 minutes and cost 'a few shillings' each for mourners, and less than 6d. each for coffins. Only the railway provided a ready, cheap and convenient method of access to Woking; hence the vital role of the LSWR to the success of the enterprise.

Broun's idea to use the railway was not original, although he may be credited with giving the idea a new impetus which resulted in its realisation at Brookwood and several other cemeteries.* John Claudius Loudon (1783-1843), the influential landscape gardener and horticultural writer, appears to have been the first person to suggest the idea of large extramural cemeteries close to railway lines. As early as 1829 he wrote in *The Gardener's Magazine* of his idea to create cemeteries 'of some hundreds of acres each . . . on the poorest soil, and planted as an arboretum'. In 1830, in the same journal, he elaborated further:

> A railroad and locomotive engine might convey corpses thither once a day, and company [i.e. visitors] at all hours. Those who had near relations buried in the arboretum, should be free of it for seven years; all others should pay a shilling each . . . the poor soil would become enriched and the trees would thrive; and at half the burial fees now taken the establishment would pay.

---

* See Appendix Seven for a brief survey of these.

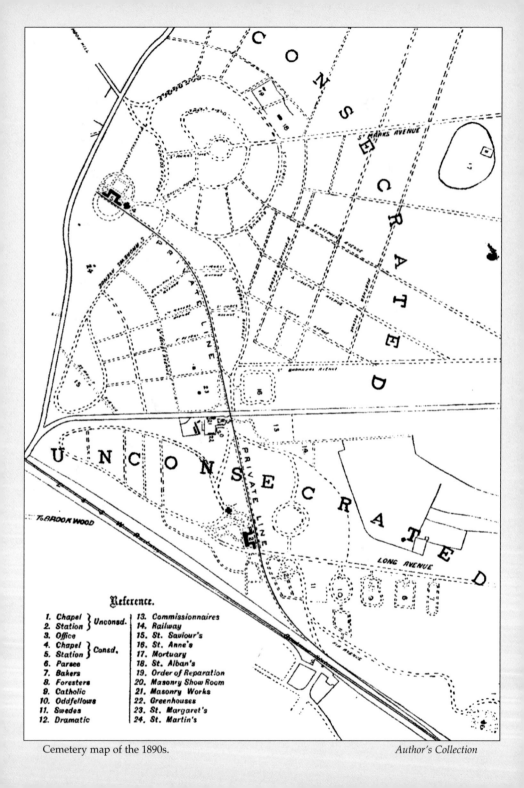

In his *On the Laying Out, Planting, and Managing of Cemeteries* (1843), Loudon suggested the purchase of common land at Woking where the soil was suitable for cemetery purposes, and where all kinds of evergreens would thrive:

> We see no objection to taking land for temporary cemeteries at a considerable distance from a town, provided it were on the line of a railway, as for example, at Bagshot Heath; . . . There are thousands of acres of the poorest gravely soil, which the Southampton railway passes through, that at present do not rent for more than 3s. or 4s. an acre, which would afford a cemetery sufficient for all the poor of London, and the rich also, for ages to come; and the same may be said of some thousands of acres not far from the Thames, in the neighbourhood of Chertsey.

Similarly, in 1842, a contributor to *The Westminster Review* noted that most of the main lines from London passed through areas suitable for the foundation of new burial grounds, especially around Wimbledon and beyond Kensington. In 1849 the sanitary reformer Dr George Alfred Walker (1807-1884) suggested the use of such land for cemetery purposes. He mentioned in particular Woking Common on the LSWR, using Nine Elms station, and High Beach or Wanstead Flats on the Eastern Counties Railway, as suitable examples. In 1850, a 'Bill for promoting extramural interments' was proposed, based on the idea of allowing railway companies to purchase and hold land for the purpose of forming cemeteries. This never became law because many MPs feared it would encourage the railway companies to divert attention from their proper and legitimate function. But it was Broun who put all these elements together, published his *Synopsis of the London Necropolis and National Mausoleum at Woking* (1851), and set about promoting a company to carry out his scheme.

Not everyone agreed with Broun's exploitation of the railways in promoting more sanitary burials. For instance, the Bishop of London was against using railways for funeral traffic. His verdict was:

> . . . I consider it improper . . . At present we are not sufficiently habituated to that mode of travelling not to consider the hurry and bustle connected with it as inconsistent with the solemnity of a Christian funeral.

He also found the idea of assembling a number of funerals from widely different social backgrounds in the same conveyance 'offensive', and believed that this would shock and injure the feelings of the bereaved. When asked his opinion concerning the carriage of more than one coffin 'at the same time, in one and the same conveyance', the Bishop replied:

> . . . my impression is that they [the bereaved] would object . . . It might sometimes happen that persons of opposite characters might be carried in the same conveyance; for instance, the body of some profligate spendthrift might be placed in a conveyance with the body of some respectable member of the church, which would shock the feelings of his friends; and however poor they might be, I think they would feel a pride that their relations should not be conveyed to the place of interment in the same carriage with the body of such a man.*

---

* These views are included to suggest an alternative interpretation of the proposed system of railway funerals. The Bishop of London's observations were made before a Select Committee of the House of Commons in 1842 where he was not commenting on the Necropolis scheme but was expressing his own opinion to certain questions put to him.

Shareholders of the LSWR were also concerned at reports of the railway's involvement with a cemetery company, and what this might mean in terms of concessions made to the Necropolis company, how the funeral trains would be operated, and how these trains might interfere with ordinary railway traffic. At the shareholders' meeting held at Nine Elms station in August 1852, criticisms were voiced by Mr Herepath about the secrecy surrounding these arrangements which were subsequently reported in *The Times*:

> Mr HEREPATH said he had been informed . . . that the secretary interfered a great deal with the board (hear, hear), and that he had without consulting the board made certain arrangements with the Woking Cemetery Company, and that he had stated before Parliament that the board were perfectly agreeable to the establishment of the company.
> THE CHAIRMAN [Mr W. Chaplin] said the fact respecting the Necropolis Company was that the board about a year ago had come to a resolution that the establishment of that company would be beneficial to the railway, and they saw enough of the elements of the traffic to satisfy them that it would be remunerative, and the secretary was instructed to deal with that subject. The railway company were pledged to no thing; they were not to give up land or anything to that company, with the exception of one train in the day at a certain price, all other matters to be paid for at a price to be decided.

Later, in 1859, when the Necropolis scheme had been operating for five years, *Punch* queried the whole practice of 'the Railway System of Interment' by commenting on the wastage involved by railway speculations:

> We see a Burial Company advertises to those who stand in need of it, that it pursues what it calls 'the Railway System of Interment'. What this puzzling phrase may mean it very much perplexes us to guess. We have very often heard of railways having killed people, but we never before learnt that they undertook to bury them. Yet when one hears it said they have a 'system of interment', one cannot but suppose the practice must be frequent with them. . . . Railways . . . have buried heaps of money, there is no denying that; and they have also caused interment of the hopes of many shareholders. These burials have been generally performed at railroad speed; . . . they usually have proved to be the most costly ceremonials, and have been known to drain the very deepest pockets. . . . We must confess ourselves completely at a loss to see its merits; and if they wish to gain a good name with the public, we think the less that burial companies are 'distinguished' by it, the better.*

The Private Act of Parliament

The Necropolis scheme was launched by a private Act of Parliament which received the Royal Assent on 30th June, 1852. It incorporated The London Necropolis and National Mausoleum Company (LNC),† and provided for a cemetery near Woking, and all the necessary provisions pertaining to this. Due to the important role of the LSWR, it was made a party to the Act. The railway

---

* The Editor of *Punch* had a short memory since the journal commended the Necropolis scheme (or at least its tariff for funerals) in 1854 (*see Chapter Seven*).
† This remained the proper legal title of the company until it was changed to the simpler form 'The London Necropolis Company' in 1927. I have used the latter title throughout this book.

company would not only provide 'the most convenient mode of transit' but also hoped to make some £40,000 a year from the additional traffic.* The Act set out guidelines for agreements between the two companies for station accommodation at London and Woking, the arrangements for the conveyance of corpses, attendants, and mourners, and fixed the maximum charges that could be levied. It bound the LSWR to the maximum rates for the funeral traffic but not to the detailed arrangements for the carriage of corpses and mourners. These arrangements were to last forever without reference to the shareholders of the railway company. The Secretary of the LSWR justified this (in 1852) by stating:

> . . . it is perfectly in [the Directors'] interest to do so; it is obvious the cemetery is likely to produce a vast amount of traffic from persons who will for years come to visit the spot, and frequent the Churchyard [sic]; and I can conceive of no duty more obvious for the Directors than to make the best bargain they can with the Cemetery Company without consulting their proprietors.

The traffic arrangements between the two companies had been discussed at various dates from 1852 onwards and several draft tariffs discussed. The final 'arrangements', agreed without apparent documentation, were concluded at a meeting between Mr Scott (Traffic Manager, LSWR) and Richard Churchill (Secretary of the LNC)† and reported to the Directors of the LNC on 30th October, 1854, when the final 'draft tariffs' were also approved. The LSWR's solicitors admitted in 1890 that no formal written agreements were in existence for the junction (or any junction) at Brookwood, the railway into the cemetery, and also for the LSWR's conveyance of corpses and mourners from London to Woking and into the cemetery. None of these were binding in any way on either company under the terms of the 1852 Act. The solicitors concluded that much of the business conducted with the LNC was performed 'on the basis of an implied contract'.

Broun and Sprye had, even before the Act became law, lost control over the execution of their plan. They had intended to sell the rights of the scheme to four people (or 'provisional trustees') they chose to establish the LNC. By a 'deed of agreement' (1st April, 1851), Broun and Sprye were to obtain considerable benefits from the sale of the scheme to their trustees, amounting to £20,000. However, the 'provisional trustees' (amongst them William Voules who effectively acted as Chairman of the 'company')# ignored any understanding with the promoters, and went on to found the company on their own. Early in 1851 the trustees appointed their own officers and Directors, whilst on 3rd October, 1851 the trustees signed the LNC's 'deed of settlement', which stated that 'the said several Persons [the trustees] . . . had agreed to form

---

* The Directors of the LSWR must have been disappointed by the actual revenue from operating the Necropolis train (*see Appendix Two*).

† Richard Churchill (dates not known) was appointed Secretary by the 'provisional trustees' at the end of 1850, and was confirmed in post by the committee of enquiry at the end of 1853 (*see below*). He remained as Secretary until his resignation in May 1870.

William James Voules (dates not known) was sometime Poor Law Commissioner. He was 'nominated' Deputy Chairman at the end of 1850.

a Joint Stock Company'. It ignored the contribution of Broun and Sprye, the 'deed of agreement', and sealed the independence of the LNC. It was the trustees, not Broun and Sprye, who secured the passage of the Act in June 1852.

Yet Voules' group of Directors were also unable to complete the scheme. During 1852-53, despite negotiations with some of the metropolitan parishes and the planned opening of the London Necropolis in May 1853, the scheme stagnated. Essentially, Voules and his Directors failed to convince enough people to invest money in their extramural enterprise. The shortage of share capital meant money to purchase the site from Lord Onslow could not be identified or raised in loans. Valuable time was lost, public confidence in the company collapsed, and it seemed the plan would suffer the same ignominious failure as the General Board of Health's project. Nevertheless it is possible to compare Broun's scheme with that proposed by the first Architect to the LNC, Henry Robert Abraham, and with the final and successful evolution of the plan (see Chapter Three). Early in 1853, a few Directors were obliged to resign, Voules included, for their inability to pay calls on shares. By July 1853, the Directors were forced by an extraordinary general meeting, popular criticism, pressure, and the prospects afforded by the threat of a further cholera epidemic, to form a 'Committee of Enquiry'. This committee investigated 'the state and affairs' of the LNC. Its subsequent report, issued in September 1853, was unanimously approved by the shareholders. The company was reformed, including the expulsion of all four trustees, resulting in a new Board of Directors who instilled a spirit of confidence and efficiency of action.

The Necropolis scheme was finally established in 1854. During that year a private terminus was constructed just outside Waterloo, and a private branch line (it was more like a long siding) built into the Necropolis that was formed at Brookwood. The cemetery was consecrated on 7th November, 1854, and opened to the public a week later on 13th November, when the funeral trains began their sombre service. As *The Spectator* reported on the following day:

> The question of suburban interment is settled. It has not been accomplished by the Board of Health. . . . at last London is rescued from this abode of death; . . . and by the opening of the cemetery at Woking we are secured ample burial space for generations yet to come.
>
> . . . The novelty of the railway train is to have the newer novelty of the funeral train. Once a day the black line will leave the metropolis for Woking; the station will put on a funeral aspect, and death will take its turn amid the busiest traffic of life.

Chapter Two

The London Termini

'This station is probably unique.'
(The Globe)

The London terminus of the LNC was a vital centre for its business, from which funerals were arranged and conveyed to the cemetery. Eventually, and logically, it became the main headquarters of the LNC and the centre for its metropolitan business.

It was Sir Richard Broun who suggested Waterloo for the site of the Necropolis terminus. He believed it was the most conveniently located of all the London termini:

It is not overcrowded at any time with goods and passenger traffic. It has spacious arches capable of being easily fitted up to receive bodies *in transitu* to Woking. It is reachable from all parts of the metropolis north of the Thames by three bridges. It is surrounded by open streets, in which there is nothing approaching to thoroughfare. And it lies so near to the river that boats may be employed to collect at little trouble and expense nearly one half of the annual mortality.

Furthermore, the journey to Woking on the LSWR passed near to 'comforting scenery':

Again, whilst several of the lines on leaving town run for a length of way over the tops of houses - or through long dark tunnels or deep cuttings - into vicinities which are *terrae incognitae*, the South Western Railway train scarcely passes the palatial buildings of Westminster and Lambeth until it emerges upon Battersea Fields, and passes in rotation the beautiful vicinities of Wimbledon Park, Richmond Park, Hampton Court, Bushey Park, Claremont Park, and Oatlands.

But above all, in the immediate vicinity of Waterloo, there were several eligible sites for the LNC's 'reception station'. In particular, the arches of the LSWR's viaduct, which constituted its metropolitan extension from Nine Elms to Waterloo, provided a cheap and spacious depository for coffins awaiting transit to Woking.

This economy style terminus appealed at first to the LNC. During the Committee stages of the Bill, the convenience of these arches was explicitly mentioned, and the LSWR, which had few alternative uses for them, was also interested. At this stage their 'crypt-like' appearance was seen as peculiarly advantageous, and it was suggested that coffins could be raised, by lifts, through the crown of the arches, and placed unseen into the hearse carriages at rail level, which would incorporate sliding hatches in their floors.

At this time too, it was believed that one station would be inadequate to cope with the anticipated volume of traffic. Waterloo was the most suitable for the LNC's needs, and may even have provided the location for another private terminus, yet sites elsewhere were also considered. Vauxhall was eventually

The interior of the original York Street station train shed 1854-1877. The blank western wall is on the left, beyond which lay the L&SWR's lines into Waterloo. The LNC's two private lines are in the centre. Note how the platform (*right*) is incorporated into the structure of the main building.

Author's Collection

The Waterloo 'A' box and the York Street station *c*.1867. The exterior of the LNC's private terminus is on the extreme right. *By courtesy of the National Railway Museum*

judged unsuitable because there were no sidings (or room) for spare carriages; but Nine Elms, by now used for goods traffic only, offered possibilities for a second terminus. The fact that no passengers now used it (save for the Royal Family on occasion) was advantageous, spare land was available, and it had the further attraction of an immediate connection with the Thames. Thus the LNC's Act provided for termini at Waterloo and Nine Elms. In April 1853, Henry Robert Abraham (then the LNC's Architect) produced plans showing the site of 'a Station at Nine Elms and his report thereon' and was ordered by the Board of Directors to enter into negotiations for the purchase of the necessary land. But this proposal came to nothing. A few weeks later Abraham was requested to stop all work for the LNC and the company began an action for professional negligence against him. Abraham responded by suing the LNC for the non-payment of his fees.*

The York Street Station (1854-1902)

In early 1854, when the LNC returned to the matter of its London terminus, the overwhelming advantages of Waterloo, coupled with the novelty of the venture and the buildings required, made the company choose an area between the Westminster Bridge Road and York Street. This proved to be the location of the first private Necropolis terminus. The arrangements for the construction of a 'station and works' just outside Waterloo began in March 1854. The site required included land adjoining the LSWR's viaduct along with the adjacent arches under the railway. Sir William Cubitt (the LNC's Consulting Engineer) was invited to negotiate with William Tite (the LSWR's Architect) to take the matter forward.

The site selected for the terminus was immediately to the east of the down line of the LSWR. It was bounded on the north by York Street (now Leake Street), on the east by the backs of various houses and shops, and on the south by the Westminster Bridge Road. Strictly speaking, the main entrance to the station was on this road, but it will be referred to as 'the York Street station' to avoid confusion with the second one, which will be described later.

By May 1854, Tite had completed his plans for the new station. Once approved, he was requested to obtain tenders for its construction. The tenders were considered at a meeting of the LNC's Board of Directors on 23rd May, when Messrs Nicholsons were awarded the contract. Work started shortly afterwards. Tite made several alterations to his original plans, as suggested by the Directors, and these were approved in June 1854. Tite was also requested to estimate the difference in cost between having the LNC's offices built over the new station premises, or having the houses leased by the LNC at Nos. 1-3 Church Row, York Street, converted instead. In July, it was decided to alter these houses into offices.

The station was completed in October 1854 at a cost of £23,231 14s. 4d. Its design was ingenious in exploiting an extremely awkward location. The main part of the building was three storeys high. The ground floor consisted of two large living rooms for the station caretaker; a grand entrance hall and staircase for mourners attending the better classes of funerals; two mortuaries, which

---

* Abraham claimed £7,000 compensation and after arbitration was awarded £3,159 plus costs (24th March, 1854).

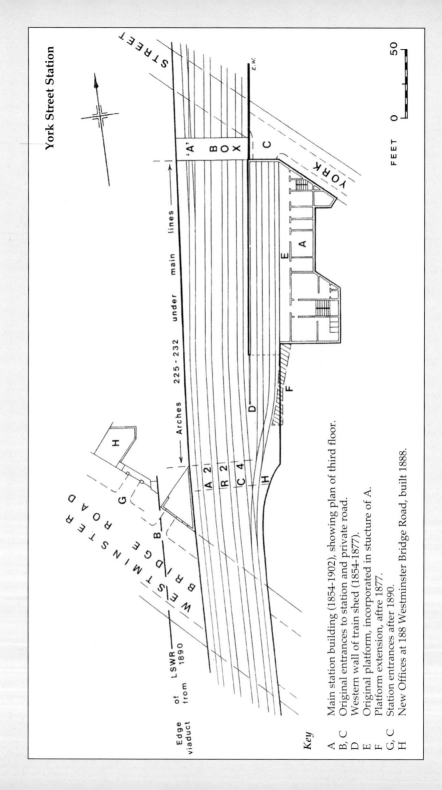

York Street Station

E.W.

STREET

YORK

Arches 225 - 232 under main lines

Edge of viaduct
LSWR from 1890

WESTMINSTER BRIDGE ROAD

'A'
BOX
C

A 2
R 2
C 4
H

B
G

H

A
E
C

D

F

FEET 0 50

Key

A   Main station building (1854-1902), showing plan of third floor.
B, C   Original entrances to station and private road.
D   Western wall of train shed (1854-1877).
E   Original platform, incorporated in stucture of A.
F   Platform extension, aftre 1877.
G, C   Station entrances after 1890.
H   New Offices at 188 Westminster Bridge Road, built 1888.

occupied the greater part of this floor; and another entrance hall with staircase for those attending the lowest classes of funerals. Both staircases were lit by skylights. The next floor contained a series of waiting rooms for 2nd and 3rd class mourners, toilets, a Boardroom, and the funerary workshops. The top floor, which was on a level with the railway, consisted of eight or nine 1st class waiting rooms, toilets, and the private platform.

This station was described in more detail in an article which appeared in *The Leisure Hour* for 1856:

> An archway of variegated brickwork leads from the Westminster [Bridge] Road into the station of the Necropolis Company. . . . From thence the narrow roadway, descending for some space between high walls, or rather sides of buildings on either side, brings hearses, carriages, and those on foot, on to the wide pavement of the station. . . . Across this pavement, which is as scrupulously bright and clean as a cathedral floor, the dead are lifted from their respective hearses into the seclusion of places purposely provided; and the vehicles drive on to the gate of the exit at the further end. On to this pavement, or platform, many office windows look, some of them made cheerful by bright-flowered plants. On this level are the range of third class waiting rooms, well and appropriately furnished. A massive and handsome staircase of stone leads to the next floor, which is devoted to the use of second class funerals; it then ascends to the third floor, level with the railway platform, and on which lie the first class reception and waiting-rooms. With the most trifling difference, the various class rooms are furnished precisely alike; to the honour of the Necropolis Company, it has been the first to strip the necessary ceremonies annexed to death and the grave of an invidious distinction of rank. There is the same privacy, the same quietude, the same respect for poor as well as rich. . . . If the sun be shining, it pours down through the lofty glass roof; it lies upon the wide and spotless pavement; it lights the pleasant windows of rooms and offices; it rests on planks and flowers upon the window-ledges; it casts no shadow on the massive tender [i.e. hearse carriage], waiting to convey the dead, nor on carriages that may convey the most touching and profound of human grief.

Sarah Tooley, who in 1898 travelled on the Necropolis train to witness a cremation at Woking, described the 'handsome staircase, decorated with palms and evergreens', and the 'suite of spacious waiting-rooms' of the York Street station. Elsewhere, *The Undertakers' Journal* noted a large room adjacent to the mortuary packed with over 300 ready-made coffins. These were kept 'in case of emergency', and an official of the LNC went on to explain that should a guest die in an hotel, and the landlord wished to keep it quiet, 'we are notified, and in the middle of the night we come for the corpse, and take it away in one of our ready-made wooden overcoats'.

Coffin lifts, worked by a 6 hp steam engine, otherwise referred to as the 'steam lift', linked all the floors. However at some stage the steam mechanism may have failed and was never repaired or replaced. An article published in *The Undertakers' Journal* in 1898 referred to the lift being worked by hand:

> . . . and the man who works it bears, through the nature of his occupation, an extraordinary similitude to Charon ferrying the dead across the Styx. The operation is a painfully slow one, but, as may be divined, nobody is in any hurry. Charon, therefore, has many opportunities to stop and blow, cull out the most interesting items in his *Daily Mail*, and even smoke a cigarette.

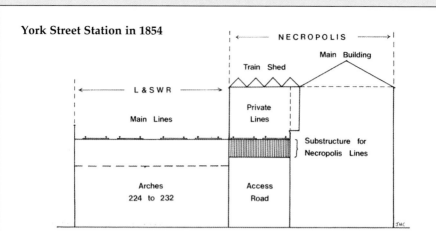

York Street Station in 1854

NECROPOLIS

Main Building

Train Shed

L & S W R

Main Lines

Private Lines

Substructure for Necropolis Lines

Arches 224 to 232

Access Road

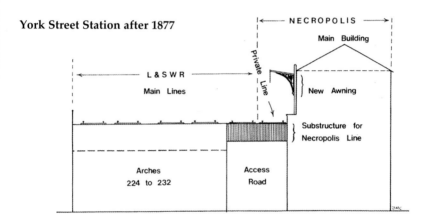

York Street Station after 1877

NECROPOLIS

Main Building

Private Line

L & S W R

Main Lines

New Awning

Substructure for Necropolis Line

Arches 224 to 232

Access Road

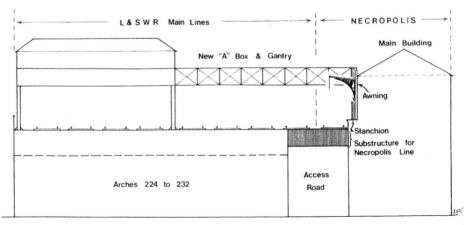

York Street Station after 1890

L & S W R Main Lines

NECROPOLIS

Main Building

New "A" Box & Gantry

Awning

Stanchion

Substructure for Necropolis Line

Arches 224 to 232

Access Road

Diagrams showing changes to the York Street station 1854-1890.

This main building was separated from the LSWR's viaduct, upon which its main lines into Waterloo were constructed, by the LNC's private access road. This ran from the Westminster Bridge Road, under the railway via arch 224, then turned north and ran parallel to the LSWR between the Necropolis building and the viaduct, past arches 225 to 232, and finally joined York Street. The access road enabled mourners to arrive conveniently and discreetly at the station, and also meant that no carriage or hearse would have to stop in a public road. The exit into York Street meant there was no problem in reversing out, for carriages could enter from one street and pass out at the other.

The Westminster Bridge Road entrance (often referred to as designed 'in the Norman style') was more elaborately arranged than that in York Street because it was always regarded as the 'main' entrance. Whilst both entrances consisted of a gated archway, that facing the Westminster Bridge Road was of ornamental red brick and tile, with elaborate iron gates by Messrs Bailey; gates which had been exhibited in 1851 (*see overleaf*).

Above this private road, and between the Necropolis building and the LSWR's viaduct, was a structure of iron girders and wooden beams which provided the necessary support for the LNC's private lines. The space for these was not available on the LSWR's viaduct, which was already filled with its four main lines. This constricted location was to be of great importance in the future development of the LNC's station. Glass slabs laid between the lines provided light to the private driveway below.

Unlike any later developments, the two private lines were enclosed by a train shed (*see page 20*). Its northern wall, facing Waterloo, was pierced by louvres, but the western wall was blank, though relieved by blind arches, to protect mourners from the idle stares of enginemen or ordinary passengers travelling on the LSWR. The exterior of this wall is shown on page 20. The hipped roof was extensively glazed, resulting in a well-lit, yet secluded station, apt for its purpose. Only one of the tracks served the platform; the other was probably used to store spare stock.

The train shed was removed at the end of 1877, and was the first major change to the private station. In 1874, a Bill promoted by the LSWR had sought, amongst other things, to 'enlarge and improve' Waterloo. The company had hoped to gain the westernmost (or outer) set of rails from the LNC, to ease traffic movements in and out of Waterloo. But due to the special nature of the LNC's business the LSWR was unable to achieve this by the Act alone, and suitable agreements between the two companies had to be drawn up.

The first of these was sealed in 1875. By this agreement, the LSWR could take over the LNC's outer private line after one month's written notice of its intention to do so. But in doing this, the company would have to replace the existing Necropolis train shed with a single line one. In return the LNC gained exclusive ownership of the land it had leased from the LSWR since 1854. The LNC also ceased to be responsible for the maintenance of the substructure supporting its two tracks. This issue had been causing friction between the two companies for some time, as the LSWR had increasingly been using the outer private line as a siding for light engines. This, in turn, had impaired the timber substructure, because water from the locomotives percolated down from track level. Now the LSWR accepted the task of maintaining this structure.

The Waterloo 'A' box and the Necropolis private station (*extreme right*) *c*.1884. This shows the first (narrow) awning valence provided in 1877 after the removal of the train shed, one of the early 'type II' or 'type III' hearse vans, and a LSWR 19 ft 10 in. four-wheeled second apparently in two-tone livery with crest. *By courtesy of the National Railway Museum*

The Westminster Bridge Road entrance to the Necropolis station in the early 1890s. The new company offices at 188 Westminster Bridge Road are on the left. The wooden screen with 'CEMETERY STATION' was added to the arch (No. 224) as part of the agreement over the new 'A' box stanchion. The splendid gates were designed by Messrs Bailey for the Great Exhibition; their subsequent fate is unknown. *Author's Collection*

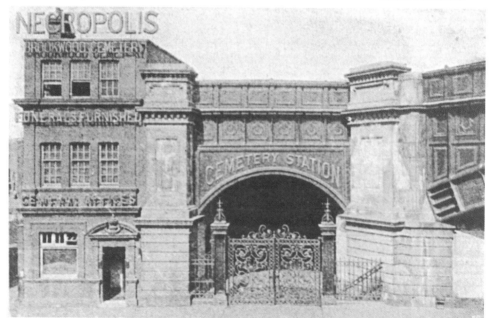

Other agreements followed in 1876 and 1877. In return for a better interest in the Necropolis station site (a 999 year lease), the LNC allowed the LSWR easier access to the outer line by the removal of the western wall of the private train shed - and its roof. But instead of replacing this with a smaller timber train shed, the LSWR provided the LNC with a modest platform awning, incorporating specially designed cast-iron cantilevers with the initials 'LNC'. This awning, which had a narrow valance with the words 'THE LONDON NECROPOLIS COMPANY' painted in bold capitals, is shown in opposite. In addition the Necropolis platform was extended, to compensate for the loss of the other siding. Communication with the down main line was ensured at all times during these alterations, so that the LNC's business was not impaired. The railway company also took steps (which proved inadequate) to prevent the percolation of water onto the access road below.

Further alterations took place in 1885 when Mr Jacomb, Engineer to the LSWR, proposed certain changes to the entrance on the Westminster Bridge Road. These were approved by the Directors of the LNC subject to the railway company lining all of the walls of the arch under the railway with white glazed bricks, and that the entrance on the Westminster Bridge Road should be 'made as ornamental as before'.

In 1887 an internal report by the LNC recommended a number of improvements to the station premises. These included more white glazed bricks for the walls of the arches, and further comment about the 'dropping of water from the Necropolis line of rails between the Westminster Bridge Road and York Street'. In April 1888, it was agreed that a 'reasonable time' should be fixed for completing these alterations and improvements. At the end of 1888 the shareholders of the LNC were informed that:

> [the LSWR] have at their own cost repaired and painted their abutting premises and rectified their drainage. They have also at their own cost commenced to line with white glazed tiles the archway approach to the Necropolis Station [i.e. via the Westminster Bridge Road], and have painted the ceiling of the Necropolis Company's drive and so dispelled the gloom which formerly existed.

The last major changes to this station took place in 1889-90. In connection with the resignalling of Waterloo, an enlarged 'A' signal box gantry was required to span all the approach roads into the LSWR's terminus. The width of this was so great that one of the iron stanchions supporting the gantry had to rest on the Waterloo end of the Necropolis platform. Permission to do this was granted by the LNC in 1889. In return the LSWR agreed to clad the LNC's gloomy entrance archway (number 224, which provided access to the Westminster Bridge Road) with white glazed bricks, and also add a wooden screen to the top of the arch. The LSWR also leased a small plot of land to the LNC just to the west of this entrance, so that new offices, numbered 188 Westminster Bridge Road, could be erected. This office block was designed by the LNC's General Manager, Mr Tubbs.*

It appears the LSWR also rebuilt the LNC's awning because by 1892 the valance depth had been increased to about twice its original dimension. This

---

* Cyril Bazett Tubbs (1858-1927), who joined the LNC in 1887 and served as General Manager from 1890-1919. He was a Director of the LNC from 1914-27.

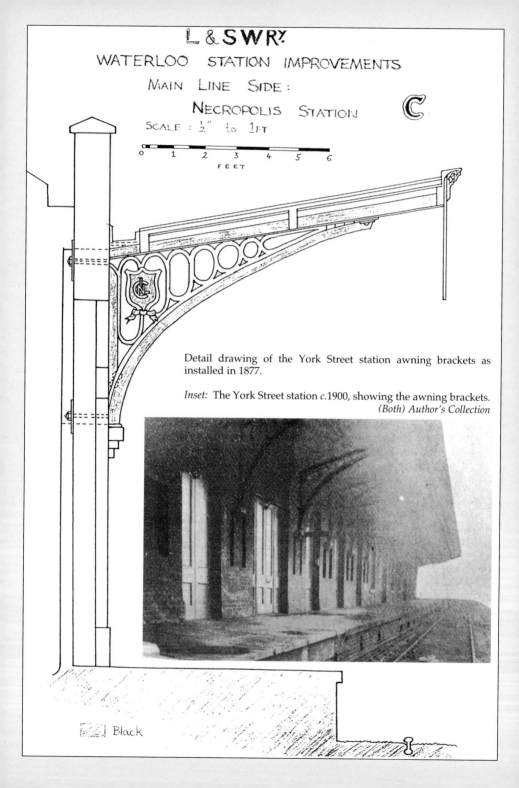

L & SWRY

WATERLOO STATION IMPROVEMENTS

MAIN LINE SIDE:

NECROPOLIS STATION

C

SCALE : ½" to 1FT

0 1 2 3 4 5 6
FEET

Detail drawing of the York Street station awning brackets as installed in 1877.

Inset: The York Street station *c.*1900, showing the awning brackets.
(Both) Author's Collection

Black

A section of the platform building in the York Street station. Designed by William Tite with the assistance of Sir William Cubitt, this is the only detail drawing of the first Necropolis terminus building known to the author. It shows one of the first class waiting rooms and the first (narrow) awning valance.   *Author's Collection*

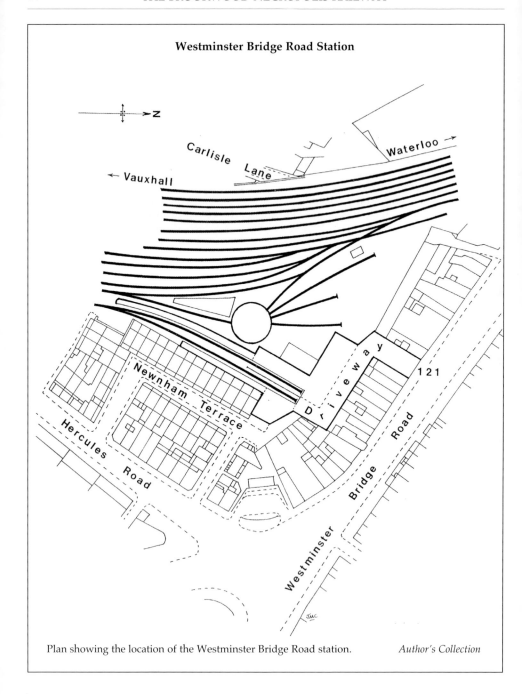

Plan showing the location of the Westminster Bridge Road station.   *Author's Collection*

was exploited by the LNC as a useful advertisement hoarding and included slogans like:

> Private station. Brookwood Cemetery, Woking: this cemetery is the largest and most beautiful in the world. Offices and show rooms, 188 Westminster Bridge Road . . . Arrangements in connection with funerals carried out for this or any other cemetery. Funerals on improved principles to suit all classes (*see page 134*).

The location of the York Street station determined its fate, for all the changes described above were symptomatic of the strategic location of the Necropolis station outside Waterloo. If the LSWR intended to further expand and enlarge Waterloo, then at some stage it would be necessary for the LNC's station to be removed completely. It was during the 1890s that this became increasingly obvious to both companies. The removal of the York Street station was inevitable once the Officers and Directors of the LSWR determined to improve and enlarge the facilities at Waterloo. This was achieved under Parliamentary powers secured between 1898-1900 and involved - amongst many other things - the construction of a new Necropolis terminus before the York Street station could be demolished to make way for the new works.

The Westminster Bridge Road Station (1902-1941)

At first the LSWR only appeared interested in gaining running powers through the Necropolis station, but little was done one way or the other until 1896. In October of that year plans were sent to the LNC showing two proposed stations that the LSWR would be prepared to provide for the LNC's future use. The LNC agreed to this in principle, but insisted on several important conditions. These were: that the company would be granted a perpetual, rent free lease on the new premises; that the details of the station would be decided by the LNC; that new stock would be provided for the Necropolis train; and that new traffic arrangements would be agreed, including free transit of appliances for use in the cemetery, and no limit to the number of mourners using the service.

The LSWR at first refused to meet these 'excessive' demands. The company suggested arbitration, but underestimated the strength of the LNC's position. The site of the York Street station was vital for the necessary widening of the approaches into Waterloo. Moreover, the LNC had a 999 year lease on its existing premises, and it could petition against the Bill that the LSWR required to accomplish its plan (the LNC had been very successful in this respect in the past). Alternatively, the LNC could oblige the LSWR to remove the stanchion for the 'A' signal box from its platform, because there was a clause to this effect in the 1889 agreement. The LNC's strength was shown by its high demands, which were all attained.

An agreement dated May 1899 sealed the fate of the York Street station. Not only did the LSWR agree to construct a new Necropolis station and offices to plans previously agreed to by Mr Tubbs and Mr Andrews (the LSWR's Engineer), but also to the rest of the LNC's demands. There would be a 999 year lease at a nominal rent; £12,000 in compensation for the loss of the old station

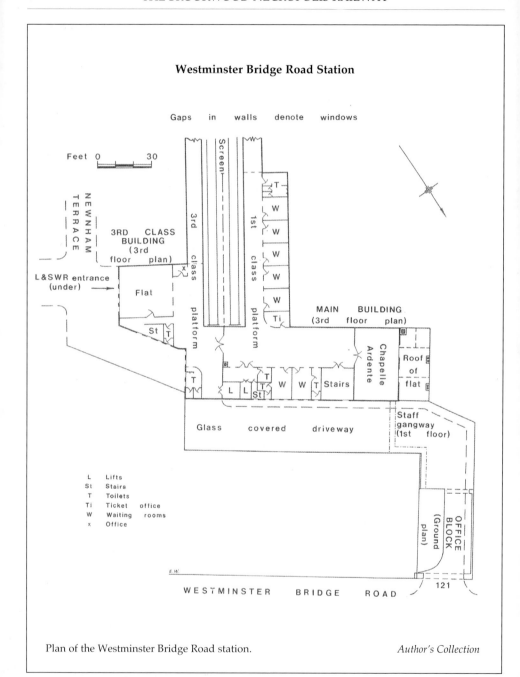

Plan of the Westminster Bridge Road station.   *Author's Collection*

and the transfer of the headquarters of the company; a new train would be provided; there would be no limit on the number of mourners travelling by the Necropolis train; fares would cover the journey from Waterloo (Necropolis) to Brookwood or the cemetery stations; and mourners could return by any train to Clapham Junction, Vauxhall, or Waterloo.

The site for the new station, off the Westminster Bridge Road, seems to have been chosen in 1896. It was further south from Waterloo than the York Street station, and on the opposite side of the road (and railway) from the offices at No. 188. The site was basically 'S' shaped, with the top 'leg' abutting upon the Westminster Bridge Road to the north-east. The other, longer, 'leg' stretched away from the main road to the south-west, and lay between Newnham Terrace (to the south-east), and the locomotive facilities known as 'the beach' (to the west). Between these two 'legs' lay the central portion of the site, behind the houses facing the main road. Most of the necessary land was purchased by the LSWR in 1899 for £5,500. The contractors used for the construction of the new station complex were Perry & Company, but work did not commence until the summer of 1900. The total cost of the station (excluding land) was £43,494, of which the LNC had to pay £1,500 for extra fittings and furnishings in excess of the originally agreed specification.

The York Street station continued in use until the new premises were completed. The LNC agreed to the removal of the stop block in the old station, which effectively gave the LSWR running rights through the station.

The new Necropolis terminus was completed by 8th February, 1902 since Godfrey Knight, Secretary of the LSWR, wrote to the Board of Trade requesting 'permission from the Board of Trade to bring the same [i.e. the station] into use prior to inspection on the understanding that any requirements of the Inspecting Officer will be duly complied with'. Clearly the LSWR wanted the LNC to move into its new station as soon as possible so the old station could be demolished. The first AGM of the LNC in its new station premises took place on 11th February, 1902. On the same day Major J.W. Pringle, who was appointed to undertake the official inspection, noted 'I see no objection - as the works are ready' but requested an appointment be made for his visit. This took place on 23rd February when he observed that:

> Access to the new station is obtained from the down main line, through an old siding connection which lies immediately south of Waterloo 'B' signal cabin. An up passenger train proceeding to the new station has to be shunted from the up main local to the down main line over an existing crossover road. The arrangement is not very satisfactory, but it appears to be the best available, and the crossover points have been provided with a facing point lock and bar and a ground signal. . . . The additional interlocking is correct with one exception namely:- Nos. 92 and 93 levers should interlock.
>
> I tested the new steel work by which the extension is carried over Allen Street & Homer Street, and also the steel viaduct work under & adjoining the new station. The girders & troughing proved stiff under test load & have sufficient theoretical strength.

Major Pringle also enquired on the power to the passenger lift and whether the main staircase to the platform was to be fitted with a handrail. The LSWR

The entrance to the Westminster Bridge Road station in 1902. The driveway, which ran through the station complex, can be clearly seen.

Author's Collection

replied on 12th March that the lifts were worked by electricity and that a handrail had been fitted to the staircase.

The new station stood at 121 Westminster Bridge Road. Here there was a tall, four-storeyed building, which contained the main offices of the LNC. This part of the station was completed in 1900, for this date appears in the terracotta decorative panel above the upper storey windows. At the bottom was an impressive archway leading to the driveway that passed through the station. This office building has survived, and is now the sole remnant of this unique station. The various offices contained here were described in *The Undertakers' Journal* in 1903:

> . . . on passing through the massive doors, one finds oneself confronted with a noble staircase, which at once prepares one for the striking character of the various apartments on the upper floors. The stairs, balustrades, and panelling are of the finest English oak, and the effect here, as throughout the building where the same wood is employed, is rich and pleasing to a degree. On the ground floor itself is an Enquiry Office and a charming little Waiting Room . . . On the first floor is the General Office and Counting House, with the Manager's Office opening thereon, a charming room furnished with the same sympathy that is conspicuous everywhere. Adjoining this room is another, which serves as an Order Office, and opens onto the stairway by a private door. A capacious Strong Room absorbs the remaining space on this floor, and we ascend by a further flight of stairs to the well-appointed Board Room. On the same landing is a splendid light apartment where draughtsmen are at work on the various plans and maps in connection with the Company's Estate at Woking; and off this is the private office of the Company's Architect and Estate Agent, who has himself designed the Buildings and Railway Station which form the subject of this article [i.e. Mr Tubbs].

From this description it should be noted that the decoration selected was 'modern' in the sense that the LNC wished to avoid the gloomy and oppressive decor that was typical of many metropolitan funeral directors at this time. The company chose light oak panelling, (and in the case of the entrance red brick and warm terracotta) and avoided the use of black anywhere in its offices. In its brochures, the LNC referred to the 'pleasing artistic effect' of these decorations, designed so that 'no additional gloom should be imposed' on the gathering mourners.

The private roadway, after passing under the office building, turned sharply to the left, and ran parallel with the Westminster Bridge Road under a glass canopy. The driveway had walls lined with white glazed bricks and was decorated with palms and bay trees. The road continued into Newnham Terrace and Hercules Road. This roadway was designed to give anything but a morbid effect and, with the separate exit into Newnham Terrace, ensured that however large the number of mourners alighting here, there would be no delay or overcrowding (*see page 36*).

The ground floor of this part of the station included mortuaries ('severely plain, but light and scrupulously clean, these Mortuaries are a fitting resting place till the time of interment'), stores, a boiler room, part of the caretaker's flat, and the stairs and lifts up to platform level. The correspondent from *The Undertakers' Journal* described the main staircase as:

The glass-covered driveway in the Westminster Bridge Road station *c.*1902. The entrance from the Westminster Bridge Road was to the right of the picture, at the far end of the drive. The doorways in the main building on the left led into (*from left to right*) the passenger lift, two private mortuaries, the main staircase to the platform, the stores, and the station caretaker's flat.

M. Wealthy Collection

The glass-covered driveway in the Westminster Bridge Road station *c.*1902. This view is taken in the opposite direction to and shows the exit into Newnham Terrace at the far end. The doorways in the main building on the left led into (*from left to right*) the passenger lift (note the open doors), two private mortuaries, the main staircase to the platform, and the stores.

Reproduced by permission of Surrey History Service

. . . one of the handsomest wrought-iron staircases in London, leading to the platform above. The staircase is lighted by large and boldly-designed windows, or, when the weather is foggy, by a massive electrolier which dispels the gloom.

The first floor consisted of workshops and finishing rooms, and the remainder of the caretaker's flat. The top floor was adjacent to the private platforms. From the main staircase, one stepped out onto the extreme right-hand end of the glass-covered, first class platform. Just to the right was the doorway to the '*Chapelle Ardente*', the special chapel which provided a private resting place for coffins in the most ostentatious surroundings. It also provided a place where those who were unable to attend the actual funeral could assist in the first part of the service at the Necropolis station (*see page 40*). *The Undertakers' Journal* described the chapel in more detail:

On the right-hand side of the platform is a most sumptuous Private Chapel, with a handsome oak catafalque in the centre, and oak stalls for the clergy and congregation. The Chapel is heavily carpeted, and the walls treated in bronze and green. In building this Chapel the Company were providing what experience taught them to be frequently needed: a place where those who are unable to attend the actual funeral could assist in the first part of the service at the London Station of the Necropolis. Beyond this, the want has frequently been felt of a *Chapelle Ardente* of sufficiently imposing character, where a coffin might lie in a certain degree of state until the time of burial. Altogether the Chapel forms a very striking feature of the new Station, and there is little doubt that it is much appreciated by those who desire refined and beautiful surroundings for their beloved dead.

To the left, along the platform were private waiting rooms, toilets, and the lift doors. Opposite these stretched the longer, 1st class platform, with its adjacent row of waiting rooms and the ticket office. The correspondent from *The Undertakers' Journal* described the 1st class waiting rooms in more detail:

These Waiting Rooms - one of which is reserved for each funeral - are furnished with light oak, upholstered in Morocco, and the floors laid with choice parqueterie, so that the whole effect is most artistic, and no additional gloom is imposed on a gathering necessarily sad.

This part of the station also had a glazed awning. A glass screen stood between the two railway lines (and also apparently across the platform circulating area), defining the limits of the first and third class platforms, and dividing the different classes of mourners.

The third class building was situated next to the private driveway as it joined Newnham Terrace. It is interesting that this part of the station was designed to separate the poor by providing a separate entrance. The correspondent from *The Undertakers' Journal* referred to this part of the building as 'an Annex', but referred to its accommodation 'as being of a most comfortable order. Their platform is absolutely private, and their feelings are studied in every way'. The ground floor of this part of the station included a staircase up to platform level, a gentlemen's toilet, and the LSWR entrance. This provided access to the railway company's arches, which lay under the Necropolis platforms, and ran

The main platform circulating area *c*.1902. This shows the generous doorway into the *Chapelle Ardente* (*left of centre*), the doorway to the main staircase, and the Ladies' waiting room. The passenger lift is to the right of the photograph.   *Reproduced by permission of Surrey History Service*

The Westminster Bridge Road station *c*.1902. *From left to right* are the first class platform and waiting rooms, the glass screen between the two lines, the third class platform, and the station caretaker's flat (with advertisement). The main building is at the back of the picture. The peculiar chimney is an air vent to the mortuaries at ground level.

By courtesy of the National Railway Museum

Part of the range of first class waiting rooms in the Westminster Bridge Road station as designed by Cyril B. Tubbs, General Manager of the LNC. A more utilitarian design than the original platform building, it incorporates courses of coloured glazed bricks. *Author's Collection*

The *Chapelle Ardente* in the Westminster Bridge Road station *c.*1902. The doorway on the extreme right led directly onto the platform (*see also page 38*).   *M. Wealthy Collection*

One of the private first class waiting rooms in the Westminster Bridge Road station *c.*1902.
                    Author's Collection

The Westminster Bridge Road station complex from the SR's main lines, June 1928. *From left to right*: the rear of the LNC's offices, the *Chapelle Ardente* (with advertisement), the first class waiting rooms (to the right of the water tower), and the first class platform (*extreme right*). The water tower forms part of the locomotive facilities known as 'the beach' (*see also page 146*). H.C. Casserley

along to Centaur Street. On the next floor was the large, communal third class waiting room. Above this, the top floor opened onto the short third class platform and circulating area, toilets, and the station caretaker's flat.

The Globe described the new private station as:

> . . . probably unique, comprising within its walls a Railway Station, a Private Chapel, Mortuary Chambers, Waiting Rooms, Offices, &c. The whole of the panelling of the various apartments for the use of Mourners together with the stairs is of English oak, while the furniture and the decorations are of special design. The Chapel is sumptuously and artistically furnished, and has an oak catafalque in the centre, and oak stalls for the Clergy and congregation.

The Westminster Bridge Road station continued to serve the LNC until World War II. During the blitz, there were several near misses on the Necropolis terminus, as Waterloo and its surroundings were badly bombed at this time. Moreover incidents elsewhere might cause the short-term cancellation of trains. For instance, due to enemy action the Necropolis train did not run between 7th September and 4th October, 1940. Mr Darwin, in his book *War on the Line*, has described an early near miss on the private station. During the night of 29th December, 1940, when the Luftwaffe attempted to fire-storm the City of London, the Necropolis train, berthed in its siding, was narrowly missed by several incendiary bombs and saved from damage by a screen of coal trucks standing on an adjacent line. In early 1941 there appear to have been no funeral train cancellations due to enemy action, and the Necropolis train that left 121 Westminster Bridge Road on Friday 11th April, 1941 was no cause for special

The immediate aftermath of the air raid, taken from Newnham Terrace. This dramatic photograph shows the destruction of the 'annex' or third class part of the station (*see also page* *147*). *Southern Railway Photographic Unit*

The remains of the Westminster Bridge Road station in 1948. The first class platform and waiting rooms form the centrepiece of the photograph. To the right is the third class platform. The main building has disappeared completely, but the office building still stands (*left of centre*), behind the water tower. *By courtesy of the National Railway Museum*

attention. Five days later, on the night of Wednesday 16th April, 1941, London was hit by the heaviest air raids yet. That terrible night became known to all Londoners as *'the* Wednesday'. During these raids some 890 tons of high explosive and more than 150,000 incendiary bombs were dropped on the capital. The bombardment lasted about 9½ hours, and damage was severe over a wide area. Eight major, 41 serious, and 22,000 smaller fires were started, resulting in 1,180 dead and 2,230 seriously injured. These were the worst casualties for any single night of the blitz.*

The notes in the SR air raid logbook tell the story of the destruction of most of the Necropolis station during that night:

11.02 pm: stock berthed in Necropolis siding damaged by fire.
12.05 am: damage to railway arch near Newnham Terrace and Carlisle Lane . . . [the] Arch is situated near Necropolis Station.
1.35 am: H[igh] E[xplosive] and incendiary bombs fell in Necropolis siding at 10.30 pm. One coach wrecked. Saloon coach and first burnt out and end of another coach burnt out.

When the Divisional Engineer made his report on the resultant destruction at 2 pm the next day (17th April), he noted that the 'Necropolis and buildings' were demolished. This included much of the station, waiting rooms, *Chapelle Ardente*, workshops, caretakers' flats, and the driveway; but the platforms and first class waiting rooms survived, along with the office building. The stock damaged in the air raid remained in the Westminster Bridge Road station awhile before removal (*see pages 146 and 147*).

There is an apparent discrepancy between the date of the air raid and the 'official' closure date of the Westminster Bridge Road station. From the evidence at the author's disposal there is no doubt that the station was largely destroyed during the night of 16th-17th April, 1941. The 'official' date of closure, usually given as 11th May, 1941 (but sometimes as 15th May), is entirely irrelevant when the air raid had effectively closed the station.

Nothing could be done until after the end of the war, when the LNC had to decide whether or not to rebuild the station and reinstate the Necropolis train. They were not keen to do so. The cost of reconstruction, despite compensation from the War Damage Commission, seemed high if used to restart the outmoded train. New stock was needed to replace that damaged or destroyed, and the cemetery branch, largely unused since 1941, required considerable attention. Hence, the Directors concluded (in September 1945) that 'past experience and present changed conditions made the running of the Necropolis private train obsolete.' The LNC therefore sought permission from the Southern Railway (hereafter 'SR') to sell the remainder of the premises in return for the surrender of the 999 year lease.

The terms of surrender of the LNC's station took some time to be drawn up, largely due to the special nature of the site. Eventually it was agreed that the railway portion (platforms, waiting rooms and the caretaker's flat) would be returned to the SR, whilst the remainder of the site (main building, driveway and office block) could be sold or let by the LNC. An agreement to this effect

* This air raid was surpassed only by the night of 10-11th May, 1941, which effectively marked the end of the London blitz.

was signed in December 1946. Although the 'Bridge Road Property Trust Company' acted as assignees of the LNC for the remaining term of the original lease, it appears the ground site was sold in 1947 to the British Humane Association for £21,000. The LNC took another lease from the SR for No. 123 Westminster Bridge Road as a local office and (from December 1947) its official registered premises. The final documents were signed and sealed in May 1947, and the headquarters of the LNC was transferred to Brookwood soon afterwards.

It is interesting to note that the SR could have made the LNC reinstate the premises to their original condition, under a clause in the lease granted for the station in 1902. But it was not to be. The decision to end the Necropolis service was realistic; it was an expense to both the LNC and the SR, with increasingly diminishing returns. The motor-hearse had triumphed.

The Present Scene

Much of the two station sites have now disappeared. That of the York Street station lies under the widened railway viaduct that was built after 1902 for the new Waterloo. The Westminster Bridge Road site is largely under new office developments; but the iron columns, which used to support the Necropolis platforms and tracks over the LSWR's access road, can still be seen off Newnham Terrace; and the office building at 121 Westminster Bridge Road is still standing, along with a portion of the driveway (now used as a car park), which once led through the station. This building has been altered to include a new mezzanine floor which obscures the top of the entrance archway. The name 'London Necropolis', which was cut into the stonework above the arch, has been covered over. Since 1983 the entire frontage has been cleaned and is now in a state similar to when it was first built, with its splendid red brickwork and terracotta decorations. On the side wall facing the railway it was possible for many years to discern *London Necropolis Company* and *Funerals Furnished* in the brickwork, but all traces have gone since this wall was renovated *c.*1990. The Boardroom was 'refurbished' in the late 1980s and all the original furnishing and fittings were destroyed. One of the chimneys from the station was apparently removed and placed on the substation adjacent to the site of the Necropolis station buildings, but is no longer there.

The two sidings into the Westminster Bridge Road station were for many years used as storage space, especially for departmental and service stock. The connections into the station site (points, signals, etc) were removed at intervals between February 1956 and February 1960. This was after some discussion by the SR and BR (SR) concerning alternative uses for the site.

Chapter Three

The Cemetery Branch

'The London Necropolis Company Ltd, proprietors of Brookwood Cemetery:
the Cemetery Beautiful.'
(LNC advertisement)

To establish its perpetual metropolitan burying ground, the LNC purchased over 2,000 acres of Surrey heathland from Lord Onslow. This vast estate stretched from the area around Woking station in the east, to what is now Brookwood village in the west. It was at this western extremity that over 400 acres, south of the LSWR's main line, was set aside as the initial site of the London Necropolis. Here the lie of the land meant the minimum of work in constructing the cemetery and its branch line. If it became necessary to extend the cemetery, the branch could easily be extended towards Hook Heath and Woking.

Early Schemes

Had Broun's scheme been implemented, there would have been no private cemetery branch. Instead, he envisaged the construction of several 'morgue chapels', which would have flanked the LSWR and provided for the deposit and storage of bodies prior to burial. These chapels would have been situated within easy access of each religious portion of his Necropolis. Connected to the 'morgue chapels' were the intended 'reception houses' for the accommodation of mourners. Broun's plan provided for platforms beside the LSWR at the very least, or perhaps a series of 'passing loops' (one for each 'morgue chapel') at most, for the setting down of corpses and mourners.

The LNC's first architect, Henry Robert Abraham, also produced plans for the arrangements at Woking that were never carried out. Abraham's project used the 'general plateau' (i.e. what is now Hook Heath) as the location for the main buildings of his London Necropolis. A report compiled in February 1853 by the LNC's first Engineer, William Moorsom, gives a good impression of the scale and scope of Abraham's scheme:

> To carry into effect the general design of your Company . . . to execute a large burial business . . . & at the same time to commence that business as early as the month of May a station will be required of such a character as may be completed in a few weeks; and the earthworks or other subsiding work, requisite for the foundations of & the approaches to that Station, and of egress from it should also be of a character sufficiently light to be accomplished within a period which shall enable us to complete the whole of the works & buildings within those few weeks.
>
> Bearing in mind that this should be done upon a spot which may now be approached by those lines of railway belonging to the Necropolis Company which are to be the sole & permanent entry (by railway) upon the property it appears that the site already

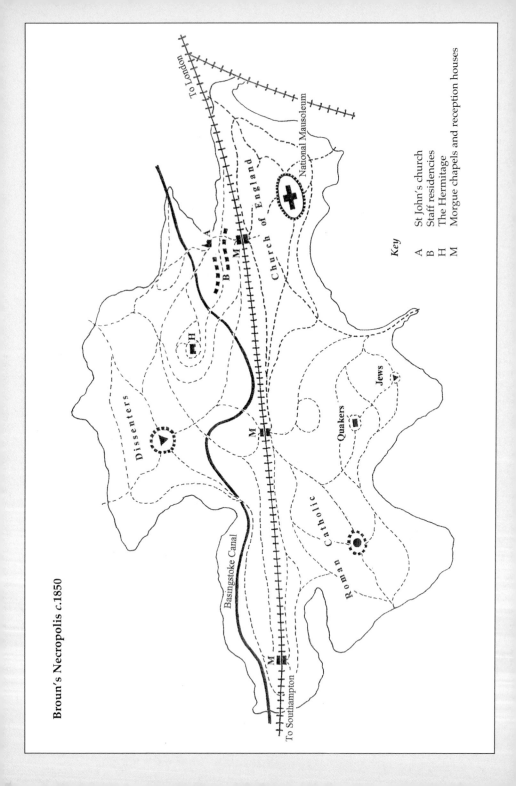

Broun's Necropolis c.1850

To London

National Mausoleum

Church of England

The Hermitage

Dissenters

Basingstoke Canal

Quakers

Jews

Roman Catholic

To Southampton

Key

A   St John's church
B   Staff residencies
H   The Hermitage
M   Morgue chapels and reception houses

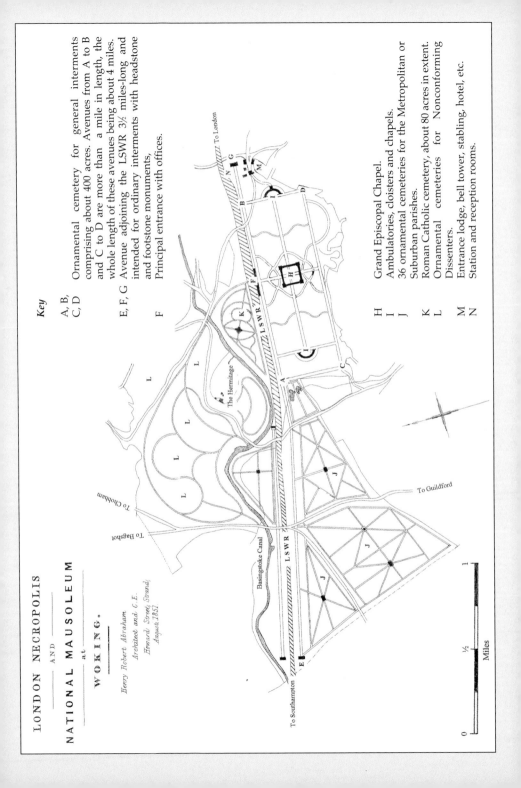

LONDON NECROPOLIS
AND
NATIONAL MAUSOLEUM
at
WOKING.

Henry Robert Abraham
Architect and C.E.
Howard Street, Strand,
August 1851

Key

A, B,
C, D   Ornamental cemetery for general interments comprising about 400 acres. Avenues from A to B and C to D are more than a mile in length, the whole length of these avenues being about 4 miles.

E, F, G   Avenue adjoining the LSWR 3½ miles-long and intended for ordinary interments with headstone and footstone monuments,

F   Principal entrance with offices.

H   Grand Episcopal Chapel.
I   Ambulatories, cloisters and chapels.
J   36 ornamental cemeteries for the Metropolitan or Suburban parishes.
K   Roman Catholic cemetery, about 80 acres in extent.
L   Ornamental cemeteries for Nonconforming Dissenters.
M   Entrance lodge, bell tower, stabling, hotel, etc.
N   Station and reception rooms.

To London

To Guildford

To Chobham

To Bagshot

Basingstoke Canal

To Southampton

The Hermitage

LSWR

Miles
0   ½   1

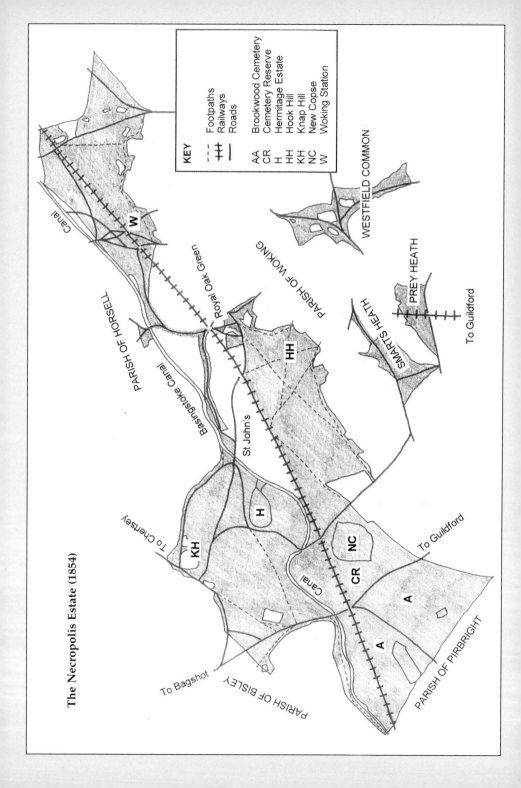

The Necropolis Estate (1854)

KEY

Footpaths
Railways
Roads

AA Brookwood Cemetery
CR Cemetery Reserve
H   Hermitage Estate
HH Hook Hill
KH Knap Hill
NC New Copse
W   Woking Station

PARISH OF HORSELL

PARISH OF WOKING

WESTFIELD COMMON

PREY HEATH

SMARTS HEATH

To Guildford

Canal

Basingstoke Canal

Royal Oak Green

St John's

To Chertsey

To Bagshot

Canal

To Guildford

PARISH OF BISLEY

PARISH OF PIRBRIGHT

W

HH

H

KH

NC

CR

A

A

selected by Mr Abraham for his Eastern Station is that which best fulfils these conditions.

By a change in the exact position of this station which Mr Abraham finds will not interfere with any of his other arrangements, the lines of rail may be so conducted to this station, & through it, with a return line, as to prevent all possibility of confusion arising to trains, if the business shall require more trains, or a more isolated arrangement of trains than Mr Abraham appears to have contemplated.

And the same line which in the first instance will probably be used only as a waiting, or a return line from the first station, will become hereafter the leading line to the second station to be erected (speaking with reference to time) on your property which second station will probably be your principal station because it will be the most central.

I should recommend that the temporary station (No. 1) be laid out by Mr Abraham with sufficient width between its platforms for two lines of rail, so that the permanent station, if erected on the same site, may have sufficient accommodation for the return as well as for the arrival of trains, and this alteration will admit of the third line of Rail outside of the building being appropriated for the use of trains proceeding to Stations west of No.1 Station in perpetuity.

[The need for flexibility in the traffic arrangements] . . . will be met by carrying the 'return line' continually onward along the side of the South Western Railway cutting & gradually rising to the general level of the plateau upon which the main buildings of your Necropolis will eventually stand, and this arrangement will enable you to execute all the business however large, which by any reasonable supposition can be brought to you for several years to come.

Reference to an 'Eastern Station' shows that Abraham intended his cemetery railway to start from the *Woking* end of the LNC's estate, in contrast to the private line as finally constructed. The description of the proposed site given to the representatives from many London parishes, who visited the location in September 1852, included reference to the entrance as follows:

. . . with the station, and the reception-rooms for arrivals and departures – where the lodge, where the church, the dissenting chapel, . . . the hotel – where were the catacombs, and the monumental plateau for the dead – where the walls, the seats, and the alcoves for the living.*

From surviving plans, it seems that Abraham intended the entrance area to include the entrance lodge, manager's house, hotel, stabling, offices, and bell tower to be grouped together off Triggs Lane, with the siding and station arrangements adjacent to the LSWR's main line nearby. However, this must have required some substantial earthworks: an embankment adjoining the main line to provide sidings for the private line(s), and terraces to offset the rising gradient towards the plateau of Hook Heath. One might argue all this was unnecessary since, if the railway entrance was located further west, off the LSWR's main line near the north-east boundary of what is now the Woking Golf Club (near the Brookwood end of the Goldsworth cutting), considerably less civil engineering work would be required as the land falls away in the direction of Brookwood and Pirbright. However, since the author has been unable to trace more detailed proposals showing the private railway network as described in Moorsom's report, it is difficult to know if this is a valid criticism of Abraham's scheme.

* *See Chapter Five* for a description of this excursion.

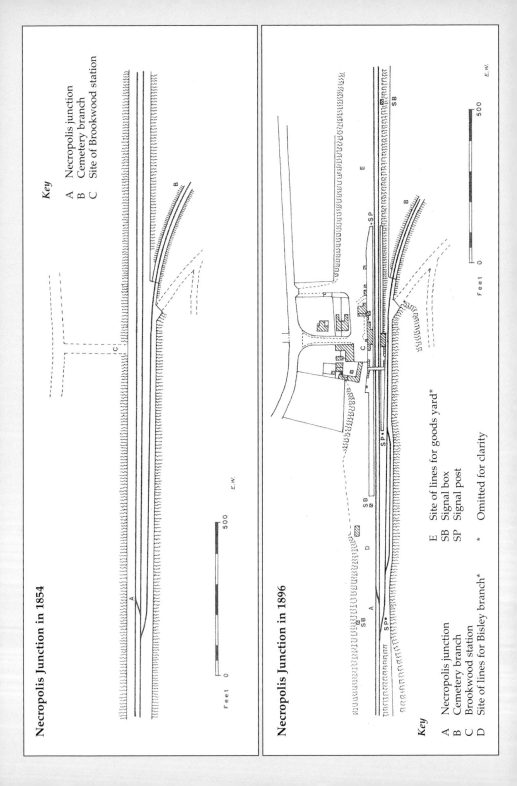

Necropolis Junction in 1854

Key

A   Necropolis junction
B   Cemetery branch
C   Site of Brookwood station

Feet 0   500

E.W.

Necropolis Junction in 1896

Key

A   Necropolis junction
B   Cemetery branch
C   Brookwood station
D   Site of lines for Bisley branch*

E   Site of lines for goods yard*
SB Signal box
SP Signal post
*   Omitted for clarity

Feet 0   500

E.W.

Necropolis Junction

Over a year later, when the LNC was once again planning its cemetery line, its new Consulting Engineer, Sir William Cubitt, recommended that the *western* end of the company's estate should become the initial site of the London Necropolis:

> I engaged my son, Mr [Joseph] Cubitt CE . . . to accompany a few of the Directors to the ground, and examine as to the most suitable portion of the property for that purpose - and he advised, that a piece of land containing about 400 acres, lying at the Western end of the estate and on the South side of and adjoining to the Railway, was the best fitted . . . inasmuch as it was capable of being easily and inexpensively connected with the Railway, and had the advantage of two public roads, branching off to Guildford and Purbright [*sic*] respectively, already passing through it, which would so much facilitate funeral operations.

Therefore the LNC constructed a single track branch reversing back into the cemetery. For the supervision of this work, in August 1854 the Directors of the LNC agreed that:

> Mr Tite should be appointed Architect of the Company for works to be erected at the junction at Woking [*sic*] on the South Western Railway Company's land, and that Mr [Joseph] Cubitt be authorized to consult with the Officers of the Company as to the arrangements to be carried out at the junction at Woking, and to report . . . as to what works are necessary to be constructed in the first instance.

Initially, Cubitt estimated the cost of the embankments for the branch at £400, but the total bill for constructing the entire branch eventually amounted to £1,419 17s. 6d. Mr Robinson was awarded the contract for the supply of rails, and work proceeded from early September to complete the branch in time for the opening of the cemetery in November.

A single trailing point from the LSWR's down line fed back into the cemetery. It appears that no run-round loop was installed when the branch was originally built, probably on the grounds of economy; this must have made operation somewhat difficult (*see Chapter Four*). A simple crossover on the main line allowed the Necropolis train to return to London. This connection, which pre-dated Brookwood station became known as 'Necropolis Junction'.

A run-round loop was incorporated into this crude system only with the construction of the first Brookwood (Necropolis) station on the main line, in June 1864. This loop stretched away beyond and behind the down platform, being further west of the station itself.

Necropolis Junction was revised again when the LSWR quadrupled its main line between Basingstoke and Woking in the years 1898 to 1902. The powers for widening the majority of this section were granted by an Act of Parliament which received the Royal Assent on 6th August, 1897. Under the terms of this Act the LNC was forced to sell a thin slice of its estate, from the cemetery to the Goldsworth cutting, to the LSWR to facilitate this project. The widening of the main line was on the south (or down) side of the LSWR. The contractor, J. Aird, built the new earthworks and the next stage was the completion of a new down

Necropolis Junction in 1915

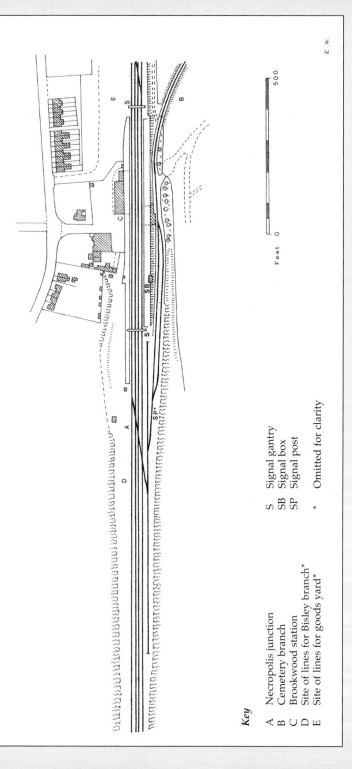

Key

A   Necropolis junction
B   Cemetery branch
C   Brookwood station
D   Site of lines for Bisley branch*
E   Site of lines for goods yard*

S   Signal gantry
SB Signal box
SP Signal post

*   Omitted for clarity

Feet   0   500

E. W.

Part of the connections with the main line, showing one end of the run-round loop, Brookwood station, September 1948. *Maurice C. Lawson*

The cemetery end of the run-round loop, June 1938. Brookwood station is on the left and the cemetery gates are on the right. Note the white painted wooden gates (*centre*) marking the boundary between the railway and the cemetery. *S. Oborne, per A.A. Jackson*

The track-bed of the cemetery railway, looking back towards Brookwood station and the site of the run-round loop. This picture was taken in the early 1960s.   *T. Coleman*

Track-bed of the cemetery railway as it curves away from Brookwood station towards North station.   *T. Coleman*

local line, followed by the rearrangement of tracks and appropriate resignalling. Ultimately a new down through line was provided, with the conversion of the original down line as the new up through line. The extension reached Brookwood East on 18th January, 1903, and through Brookwood station to Pirbright Junction on 15th November, 1903. The new up through line was not brought into use until 18th December, 1904. This resulted in a larger junction across the two new main railway lines (part of this junction still remains between the main up and main down lines just to the west of Brookwood station), and also a new run-round loop, which was located behind the rebuilt Brookwood station.

The Cemetery Branch

The Necropolis branch was about three-quarters of a mile long. After curving away from the main line, in a south-easterly direction and on a gradually falling gradient, it ran first into the Nonconformist part of the cemetery. There were wooden gates, painted white, where the branch crossed the boundary of the cemetery behind Brookwood station (*see page 53*). These gates were of a similar design to those at the Pirbright Road (Cemetery Pales) level crossing and other boundary gates located at the various entrances into the cemetery. Straightening out, the line then crossed the Pirbright Road (Cemetery Pales) on a level crossing. It then curved again, roughly eastwards, into the Anglican section, terminating just short of the Guildford-Bagshot road (the A322). The whole course of the line was flanked by wellingtonias, and portions in both the Nonconformist and Anglican sections were on a slight embankment, edged with rhododendron or laurel bushes.

Level crossing gates for the Pirbright Road (Cemetery Pales) seem to have been provided at some stage but, like so many aspects of the Necropolis service, precise details are lacking. Presumably they dated from the opening of the branch since a boundary fence was a requirement of the 1852 Act. Their design followed the same pattern as other gates around the cemetery boundary. They appear to have been removed sometime after the cemetery railway was dismantled.

The only change to this simple system was the addition of a siding to serve the LNC's new Masonry Works, which was built between 1904 and 1905.* The estimated cost, with the LSWR providing this new line, along with a gateway to protect the entrance, was £372 (August 1904). The siding was located in the Anglican section, just south-east of the Pirbright Road level crossing, and was about 100 yards long. The new Masonry Works was constructed by Messrs Harris & Company, with the machinery for the workshops ordered from Wilcox & Sons and Henderson & Company. The yard area next to the siding was provided with a 5 ton derrick (or tripod) crane which was used to remove or load stone from railway wagons. The crane can be seen in the accompanying photograph.

A low unloading platform was built beside the Masonry Works siding. A small water tower was added sometime in 1914, at an estimated cost of £35. The

---

* Prior to this, the LNC's Masonry Works was adjacent to the Cemetery Superintendent's Office beside the road to Pirbright (Cemetery Pales). The LNC operated these premises from 1889. The Masonry Showroom, opened in May 1891 at a cost of about £70, was essentially a large greenhouse facing the cemetery railway.

The level crossing area *c.*1910. This photograph clearly shows the original layout of the cemetery entrances from the Pirbright Road (now Cemetery Pales) into the Nonconformist section. *From left to right are:* the Superintendent's cottage, the entrance for carriages and pedestrians (hidden by the screen of trees), the railway crossing gates, and the entrance to the parish burial ground of St Anne's Westminster (with cast-iron obelisks).

Reproduced by permission of Surrey History Service

The level crossing area in September 1948. By this date the area shown above had been transformed after the removal of the railway. One pair of (new?) crossing gates remain closed across the track-bed leading into the Anglican section, whilst the other pair were lost with the remodelling of the new entrance into the Nonconformist section.   *Maurice C. Lawson*

reason for this additional feature was to allow engines to refill their tanks in the cemetery, before the Necropolis train left for London. The LNC had received complaints from some passengers concerning the delay which at times took place on the return journey, when engines had to stop at Woking for water. The water tower was described as being 'of brick, with the tank protected by a small wooden erection like a hut on top'. It was situated between the Masonry Works siding and the branch line, but the author has been unable to discover its precise location. The water was obtained from a well belonging to the LNC and water was pumped into the tank by a gas engine. The point for the Masonry Works siding was operated from a ground frame controlled by an Annett's key attached to the train staff for the branch.*

In the late 1930s the chairs on the cemetery branch were noted as mostly ex-LSWR and dated 1882. Some portions comprised undated ex-GWR chairs. The sandy, gravelly soil of the cemetery proved a poor foundation for the branch. Repairs were constant, especially to the sleepers. This may have been aggravated by the custom of ballasting over the sleepers, which gave the line the appearance of a tramway. The Minute Books of the LNC's Board of Directors are scattered with references to the replacement of rotten sleepers, and the purchase of second-hand rails to repair the track. For instance, in October 1877, 100 oak sleepers were purchased from Messrs Davis & Co. at 4s. each, 100 sleepers were acquired from the LSWR in February 1885, and a further 50 sleepers were obtained for 1s. each in May 1888. In October 1884 Mr Jacomb offered to exchange old rails on the cemetery line, whilst in November 1890 Mr Barratt, the Cemetery Superintendent,† was requested 'to get 2nd hand [rails] from the SWRly if possible' to repair the railway.

The SR's concern over the condition of the branch after World War II helped tip the balance against the restoration of the Necropolis train. Under the proposed postwar reorganisation of the LNC's business, the old track bed was to be converted into a 'main avenue' running from Brookwood station through to South station. This, and most of the other suggested changes proposed by the Directors of the LNC in September 1945, never materialised.

The track remained in the cemetery until c.1947, although the author has been unable to trace the exact date of removal. Maurice Lawson's sequence of photographs along the course of the line and taken in September 1948, prove that the railway had certainly been removed by this date. Ebenezer Mears were the contractors used to dismantle the railway, and it is interesting to note that some of the materials were re-used by the LNC elsewhere in the cemetery.#

Following the removal of the Cemetery branch, buffer stops were fitted to the ends of the truncated run-round loop and headshunt, thus providing useful siding accommodation at Brookwood station. These sidings lasted until 30th November, 1964 when they were finally taken out of use.

* See Chapter Four for further details of operating the branch.

† George Barratt (c.1852-1927), Cemetery Superintendent between 1886-1927. He joined the LNC in 1864 and worked in the cemetery for the rest of his life. He is buried in plot 100 in the cemetery.

Information kindly supplied by Mr Edward Evans, whose father was employed by Ebenezer Mears. As a boy, Mr Evans can remember being taken to watch some of this work taking place. The bridge over the drainage channel in the Glades of Remembrance was built from sleepers and rails salvaged from the cemetery railway.

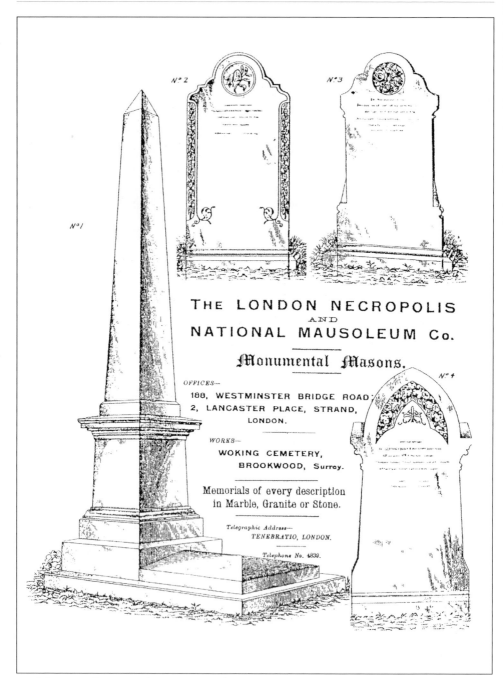

'Monumental masonry' from a LNC brochure of 1899.   *Author's Collection*

The Masonry Works siding, looking towards the main line, *c.*1910. Note the two wagons near the end of the siding and the derrick crane. The connection to the branch was to the right of the picture. *Reproduced by permission of Surrey History Service*

The broad sweep of the cemetery railway through the Anglican section *c.*1910. The photograph is taken from St Andrew's Avenue looking back towards Cemetery Pales. Note how the railway is camouflaged by the low laurel hedge (*see also page 94*). *Reproduced by permission of Surrey History Service*

An early engraving showing North station and a funeral train in 1858. Note that the engine is at the head of the train, apparently with the hearse carriage behind the tender. It is not clear how the engine is so placed since there were no run-round facilities at this time; nor is there any evidence of the use of horses to draw the train through the cemetery. A funeral party appears to be leaving the train and entering the large communal waiting room in the station. To the right is the parsonage house, although the Anglican chapel (*right*) is poorly placed in this illustration. A funeral is taking place in the recently opened Actors' Acre (*centre left*, with the single obelisk), whilst to the right is the Swedish burial ground with its twin obelisks. *Author's Collection*

View into the cemetery sometime in the 1890s. The photographer is standing near the site of the run-round loop and is looking towards North station and the Nonconformist chapel, both of which can be seen through the trees. *Author's Collection*

The Cemetery Stations

Two similar stations were provided, to serve each part of the cemetery grounds. That in the Nonconformist section, nearest the LSWR's main line, was called 'North station', whilst that in the Anglican portion was called 'South station'. After the track was removed, but whilst the stations were still open to provide refreshments for visitors to the cemetery, they were referred to as the North or South 'Bar'. However it is likely the stations were more usually referred to as 'bars' years before the removal of the railway. The most likely explanation for the station names is that they reflect the division of graves in a traditional churchyard. The south or sunny side is generally considered to be the pleasanter area in a churchyard, and was usually appropriated for those being buried according to the rites of the Church of England; by contrast, the north side was less fashionable, and was used for the burial of those who were unbaptised, or who did not wish to have the burial service of the Established Church read over them.

Both stations were designed by the LNC's Architect, Sydney Smirke. On the advice of Sir William Cubitt, they were built in a temporary manner so that the LNC could gain the most experience of its exact requirements at the least cost; yet these stations were never replaced, and both stood for over a century! The original plans of these stations were presented to the Board of Directors by Smirke in March 1854. Tenders for the construction of the two stations, along with the adjacent chapels, were then invited. The tenders were presented to the Board on 12th April when that of Messrs Lucas 'for the sum of £6,040' was accepted on condition 'that the said erections shall be completed in all respects within 3 months from 19th April, 1854'.

The stations were described in 1854 by a reporter from the *Surrey Standard*:

> The stations are constructed with peculiar neatness, and are situated at a very convenient distance from the chapels. They comprise first class and general reception rooms, apartments for the officials, and first and second class refreshment rooms. The latter have semi-circular counters formed of marble. Attached to each station is a courtyard of small dimensions for the conveniences of the *attachès* of the company. The south, or Church of England station, is situated about half a mile from the South-Western main line.

Each station consisted of a single-storeyed range of buildings clustered around a square courtyard, with the side nearest the railway left open. From this end two wings extended, parallel to the platform edge. A large roof overhang on the platform side was supported by curved brackets made from lengths of rail, which made a cheap awning. The walls were of battened wood construction. Brick was hardly used, save for the foundations, platform faces, and chimney stacks. All the wood was painted white, with the drainpipes and guttering green; both stations were originally painted drab and white. The platforms incorporated one curious feature. There was a dip, to the depth of one brick course and the width of the courtyard, along the platform face. Each dip was carefully constructed since the blue bricks which formed the platform edges were normally cut square, but those used for edging the 'dip' had a rounded

North station as approached from the run-round loop, *c.*1900. The level crossing gates for the Pirbright Road (now Cemetery Pales) can be clearly seen in the distance.

Author's Collection

North station, looking towards the run-round loop, September 1948. Note the offset platform steps at this end of the platform.
Maurice C. Lawson

edge. These 'dips' were, presumably, to facilitate the unloading of coffins from the bottom 'shelf' of the hearse carriages. Both stations contained a series of mourners' waiting rooms, toilets, chaplain's rooms, living quarters for the station caretaker, and a refreshment room - complete with bar (*see plan on page 68*). Although of similar design and construction, it is possible to describe the differences between the two stations, and to list some of the occupants of each.

North Station

As originally built, there were no cellars to either station. In April 1855 William Austin, Deputy Chairman of the LNC,* suggested that these might usefully be added. James Bailey, then Superintendent at North station, was directed to construct the cellars at his station (May 1855) and, once completed, the same was done at South station. About the same time, the 'large coffin reception rooms' at each station were converted into 'Pauper waiting rooms'. These were the large rooms on the left-hand side of each station courtyard. The refreshment room, which was at the back of the courtyard, never had windows looking out towards the railway, only those facing the cemetery. The platform of North station was about 210 ft long and was unusual in having steps at each end, rather than a conventional platform ramp. Unlike the platform at South station it was never rebuilt or extended.

As noted above, in 1854 the station was occupied by the Superintendent for the Nonconformist section, James Bailey, who had accommodation adjacent to the refreshment rooms. However, by 1861 he had become the sole Cemetery Superintendent and it is assumed he was given accommodation in one of the cottages elsewhere within the cemetery grounds. Thereafter the station was used as living quarters for one of the cemetery porters, Richard Lee, who lived there with his mother Ann (who died in 1865). By 1871, Richard Lee was living there with his wife Charlotte. Ten years later, the records show that the station was occupied by Robert and Caroline Spooner and their son Robert. The Spooners remained in the station until *c*.1892 when they moved to South station following the dismissal of Walter Parker. In 1901 the station was occupied by Alfred Gillard, his wife Alice, and their son Alfred. The subsequent occupants of the station are not known until Mr and Mrs Stonard, who ran the refreshment room between 1928-41. Gwen Spencer, their daughter, remembers:

> In the early days we has no running hot water, although there was a big coal fire range to cook on. My mother catered for funeral parties, sometimes up to and over 100 people, with teas, coffee, sandwiches and cakes, which were all homemade. The ham was home cooked, with whole gammons cooked in a large iron pot for several hours. The charge was 2*d*. per sandwich and the little fairy cakes were 1*d*. each.
>
> As well as catering for mourners, who mostly came down from London by train, we also had local people who walked through the cemetery calling in for afternoon tea. Of course the bar was an added attraction, as it had a full licence and kept to pub opening hours, much to the delight of the locals.

* William Austin (1820-1909) was associated with the LNC from 1851, investing £20,000 in the scheme. He became a Director of the LNC, and was Deputy Chairman (1853-1870), and Chairman (1870-1902). He was also involved with the promotion of the Metropolitan and Metropolitan District Railways.

Part of North station, August 1948. Note that the track has already been removed. The small window (*left of centre*) denotes the Ladies' Room.   *R.F. Roberts*

The cemetery side of North station in the early 1930s. The lady in the bath chair is Mrs Spencer's grandmother.   *Courtesy of Mrs G. Spencer*

The wedding reception of Ada Morris and Richard Hoggins, North station, 1920. The group photograph was taken just outside the refreshment room, where the reception took place. Note there are no windows facing onto the courtyard from the refreshment room.

Courtesy of Madge Spiers

The site of North station in 1982. *Author's collection*

The track-bed of the cemetery railway curving towards the Anglican chapels and South station, September 1948. *Maurice C. Lawson*

The level crossing at St Andrew's Avenue, close to the Anglican chapels, May 1930. The notice warns motorists 'Special caution: level crossing'. The Keith family mausoleum faces the railway. *H.C. Casserley*

Across the back of North station were our living quarters with the bar in the middle. We had to go through the bar to the bedrooms. Down the sides were four waiting rooms with toilets between, men one side, women the other. We had to use these toilets and it wasn't very pleasant having to go out in the cold and rain, but in those days millions of people had to do the same.

Behind North station on top of the hill was the chapel, which my father used to clean. Every day at 8 am and again at 5 pm he would ring the bell for the staff to start and finish work. As well as looking after North station, my father was part of the undertaking service and towards the end of the 1930s the men were issued with a top hat and tails uniform, complete with wing collars on their shirts.

There is another short gap in our knowledge of the occupants of North station until Mr and Mrs Dendy, who ran the refreshment rooms from 1948-56, when they retired. By this time the railway track had been removed, but the station was otherwise unaltered, except being renamed the 'North Bar'. Their son remembers:

There was no electric light or gas at the North Bar. Lighting was by oil lamps and the cooking was done on a range - my mother loved cooking with it…On average my mother catered for about three funeral parties a week, with sometimes as many as sixty people. At this time the cemetery chapels were in constant use (depending on the religion) and I believe the hand biers were still being used at funerals. My father would prepare the chapels for the services required. The refreshment bar was a very civilised place for mourners to adjourn to for a welcome drink and something to eat before their return journey. The undertaker made arrangements with the Necropolis Company so that the cost of refreshments was included on the bill for the funeral.

I was married from [the North Bar] in 1950 [and] we stayed there for about six months before getting our own house. We occupied a large room at one end of the Bar. I used to wake up some nights with my hair standing on end, and the feeling that someone was standing beside me. It was uncanny. At the time I never told my wife, but one day she met me from work looking somewhat upset. She told me she was working in the room when it felt as if someone was standing beside her. She just dropped her tools and ran. She also told me that she had sometimes woken at night and felt there was someone there. We discovered that our room had been used as a temporary mortuary for American soldiers who were removed from the military cemetery and being sent back to America.*

After the Dendys retired in 1956, the station remained empty until it was demolished sometime in the 1960s due to dry rot.

South Station

Another difference between the two cemetery stations was the shed for hand biers, used to transport coffins to graves at some distance from the station. The shed was erected behind the chaplain's rooms and the door into this shed may be seen on page 70. A further alteration was a proposed 'covered passageway' between South station and the chapel, but this was never constructed. South station also had a conventional ramp, rather than steps, at the chapel end of the platform. The platform at South station appears to have been lengthened,

---

* Mr. Dendy's recollection of the use of North station as a temporary mortuary is quite correct. Between April 1942 and August 1944, over 3,600 American servicemen were buried in several plots in the military cemetery. These bodies were exhumed during the period January-May 1948, under the authority of the Office of Quartermaster General, Washington, and by the American authorities.

South Station

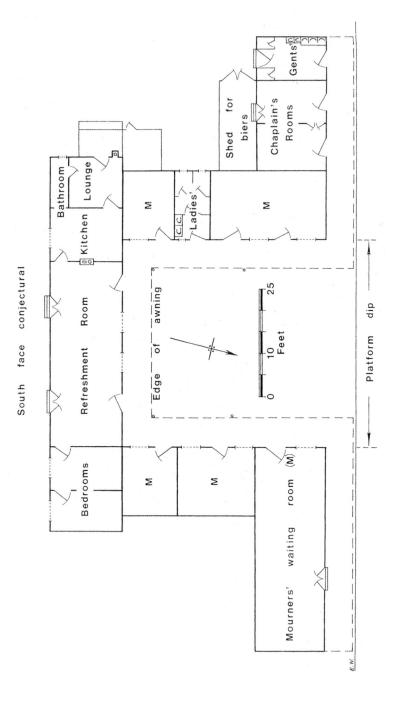

probably to assist with the unloading of materials and equipment requested from London for use in the cemetery. The date of the extension or rebuilding of part of the platform is not known. The extension may have replaced the station ramp (or steps) originally provided at the Woking end of the platform. The original length of the platform appears to have been about 128 ft, as shown by the blue bricks forming the platform edge. The reason for the platform to be about 80 ft shorter than the one at North station is not known, although it is possible the extension resulted in some repair or rebuilding of the far end of the platform. The platform extension appears to have more than doubled its length to over 256 ft, and may be clearly identified by the conventional red bricks used for the platform edge which distinguishes it from the original blue brick edging. The precise length of this platform cannot be exactly determined since it continues into the general land level just short of the boundary wall with the A322. The extension beyond the station building would have allowed the unloading of equipment to be done discreetly.

In 1854 South station was occupied by the Superintendent for the Anglican section, George Bupell, who had accommodation adjacent to the refreshment rooms. Later the station was used as living quarters for one of the cemetery porters, Stephen Bassett and his wife Catherine. After she was widowed in 1880, Catherine remained in the station with her niece Annah Meetens until her death the following year.*

Subsequently Walter Parker and his wife Mary lived here, but Parker was dismissed in October 1892. The precise circumstances of his dismissal are not clear, but it is known that two years previously Parker was reprimanded by the LNC's Secretary following a complaint by a Mr Henwood for Parker's refusal to serve him with refreshments. It is possible that a similar incident occurred resulting in his dismissal. Then Robert Spooner moved here from North station, and quite probably remained here until his retirement.†

In 1901 the station was occupied by James Wells and his wife Elizabeth. The subsequent occupants are not known, although Mr and Mrs Wilkins lived there in the 1930s. After the cemetery railway was closed, the refreshment rooms remained open as the 'South Bar', providing food and drinks for funeral parties. At this time the refreshment room was run by Mrs Opey (or Opie), who retired in 1960 and was replaced by Mr and Mrs Ladd. They are the last known occupants of these premises. After they retired in the late 1960s, the building was used as a store until it was burned down in September 1972, in what was almost certainly an act of vandalism. About half the station was destroyed. There were some attempts to preserve the buildings as an unique example of Victorian railway architecture, but the site was cleared shortly after the fire.

Neither station had a piped water supply until 1906. South station had the luxury of a hot water heating supply when the Anglican chapels were converted to Messrs Werner Pfleiderer & Perkins' system in early 1909. During the lifetime of the railway service there was no electric light or gas supply to North station (certainly) or South station (probably); lighting was by oil lamps, and cooking was done on a coal range.

---

* Stephen (*c.*1820-1880) and Catherine Bassett (*c.*1816-1881) are buried in plot 82 in the cemetery.

† Robert Spooner (*c.*1829-1914), his wife Caroline (*c.*1831-1893), and their son Robert (died 1913) are buried together in plot 119 in the cemetery.

South station and the original Anglican chapel looking towards the buffer stop, sometime in the 1930s. *Lens of Sutton Collection*

South station, looking towards the buffer stop, April 1970. The shed for biers, unique to this station, is on the right. The three doors on the nearest wing are (*from left to right*) the chaplain's rooms (*two doors*) and the gentlemen's toilet. *G.R. Weddell*

Left: The courtyard of South station, 1948. Note the absence of windows in the refreshment room at the rear.
Maurice C. Lawson

Below: The courtyard of South station, 1972. There are now windows in the refreshment room. The doors on the left led into mourners' waiting rooms.
G.R. Weddell

Right: The cemetery side of South station, April 1972. The brick-built extension contained the bathroom, kitchen and lounge for the station caretaker. Beyond is the refreshment room (with two separate entrances), whilst the far end of the building contained further living accommodation for the caretaker.
David Fairhurst

South station, looking back towards the main line, c.1904. Note the lengths of rail supporting the roof overhang. Part of Smirke's Anglican chapel peeps over the roof line. The building in the middle distance is the Keith mausoleum.   *M. Wealthy Collection*

A similar view of South station, April 1970.   *G.R. Weddell*

The site of South station in August 1976. *Author*

The aftermath of the fire at South station, 22nd September, 1972. Nearly half the station survived; nevertheless it was demolished soon afterwards.

By permission of the Surrey Advertiser

Some visitors may have been surprised by the existence of licensed premises in the stations, but few untoward incidents occurred. In fact, after a driver was dismissed having been found drunk in charge of the Necropolis train in January 1867, the LNC suggested that they provide a lunch of one pint of beer together with bread and cheese, and this custom appears to have persisted until the last train ran into the cemetery. For instance, driver Bill Mullins remembered that in the 1920s the train crew were allowed goods to the value of 4d. each from the refreshment room. Visitors to the station bars remember that there were notices displayed stating 'Spirits served here'!! Like North station, originally the refreshment room had no windows to the courtyard, a fact proven by one of Maurice Lawson's photographs of the station and dated September 1948. However, later photographs show two windows facing onto the courtyard. The date of this alteration is not known, but it may have taken place sometime in the 1950s.

Although cheaply built, the stations provided suitable accommodation for funeral parties. A contributor to *The Railway Magazine* in 1904 somewhat romantically described one of them as follows:

Possibly this is the most peaceful railway station in the three corners of the kingdom - this station of the dead. Here even the quiet subdued puffing of the engine seems almost sympathetic with the sorrow of its living freight. But this is a sad station, the saddest in our islands. For every time it is used means an occasion of grief and pain to those who tread its platforms. It has its reminders to thoughtful minds, this station in a cemetery; it suggests its own comparisons. One is forcibly reminded of the last great station on the railroad of life; of the final platform; of the completion of this world's journey. And thus this cemetery station preaches sermons more effective than those of most parsons who stand in the pulpits of our land.

Whilst as early as 1854, *Punch* made the comment:

The London Necropolis Company advertises First and Second Class graves, and First, Second, and Third Class Funerals. This sort of nomenclature suggests the remark that Life is a railway, of which the terminus is at the Cemetery.

Both cemetery stations were destined to last longer than the London terminus. They became fairly well known, and were visited by many railway enthusiasts, North Bar surviving until sometime in the early 1960s, and the South Bar until 22nd September, 1972. It remains a tragedy that despite local efforts to restore the relatively undamaged part of South station as a peculiarly interesting example of Victorian architecture, the rest of the station was demolished soon afterwards; it was then nearly 120 years old.

Brookwood (Necropolis) Station

When the London Necropolis opened in November 1854, it was not served by a station on the LSWR's main line save that at Woking, which was some four miles distant. Access to the cemetery, by relatives and friends of the deceased, visitors, or shareholders of the LNC, was therefore largely restricted to the daily Necropolis train, which might be inconvenient.

Despite verbal promises for a station adjacent to the cemetery, made by the LSWR prior to the passage of LNC's Act, nothing happened until 1863. In that year, constructive negotiations took place between the LNC and the LSWR upon this subject, the latter company attracted no doubt by the possibilities of new and potential traffic to be drawn from visitors to the Necropolis, and also the Officers of the nearby convict prison, visitors to the planned County Lunatic Asylum (which was to be situated near Brookwood), and the villagers of Brookwood.

The result of these negotiations was that the LSWR agreed to construct the station, goods yard and a new siding (including a run-round loop) into the cemetery, if the LNC would supply all the necessary land for all this, build a station master's house, and the approach roads to the station. However, the LSWR's solicitors stated (in 1890) that Brookwood station was erected at the 'request and cost' of the LNC, and upon land owned by the cemetery company. The station was 'practically handed over' to the LSWR on condition 'to have and work the station'. It appears that no conveyance or other agreement was formally drawn up concerning this. The station - called Brookwood (Necropolis) - was opened on 1st June, 1864.

Many travellers on the LSWR must have noticed the vast expanse of Brookwood Cemetery, then the largest in the world. The railway company referred to it in their illustrated guides. The following description, so typical of the view from the LSWR's main line, is taken from the 1915 edition:

> BROOKWOOD station [adjoins] the London Necropolis Cemetery [sic] at Woking, ... spreading over the adjoining common, and forming a beautiful resting-place amidst the purple heather and evergreen pines for many thousands that once mingled in the million-peopled city. It is profusely planted with ornamental shrubs and trees, amidst which may be seen picturesque ivy-clad chapels and mausoleums.

The station yard was enlarged in the early 1880s, resulting in difficulties with the LNC. The planned rebuilding included an extension to the goods yard, which the LNC petitioned against. The decision went to arbitration after the LNC refused an offer of £385 for just over 2 acres of land on the Brookwood side of the railway embankment. The award was made in favour of the LSWR (February 1882), with the land being conveyed later that year.

In 1890 the station building was extended at a cost of £4,400. Parts of this may be seen today. For instance, above the entrance hall from Brookwood is a gable end wall which displays the initials 'L&SWR' and the date 'A.D. 1890'. The LSWR had wished to provide a subway connecting both platforms, but were unable to do so as the LNC refused to sell or lease additional land to the railway company on the down (i.e. cemetery) side of the railway embankment. A footbridge was provided instead.

More drastic rebuilding took place in 1903, due to the quadrupling of the main lines (*see above*). The old down platform was demolished to provide the necessary room for the two new tracks. A new 576 ft platform with waiting rooms was constructed on the down (cemetery) side, serving the new down local line. Prior to the completion of the new down through line, this platform was connected by a subway to the new buildings on the up platform. The old

Brookwood station.

Brian Parsons' Collection

Brookwood station *c.*1905.

Author's Collection

down platform and footbridge were then removed, allowing the new down through line to be constructed. In addition, the buildings on the up side were also extended. Largely the station has remained in this form.

Signalling Arrangements

The first signal box at Brookwood station was opened *c*.1870 of unknown type. It was located just to the west of the down platform (according to G.A. Pryer)* or just to the west of the up platform (according to the 1896 25 in. Ordnance Survey), and comprised a Stevens' frame with 10 levers. The cemetery branch appears to have been controlled by a ground frame with nine levers. This was located adjacent to Necropolis Junction and its nine levers operated the ground signals controlling access to the Necropolis siding, the home signal controlling access back onto the down line, and the crossover that allowed the Necropolis train to return to London on the up line.

Although not mentioned by Pryer, at some stage a further signal box was provided on the down side embankment and well to the east of Brookwood station itself. This was located approximately opposite plot 102 in the cemetery. It is shown in the 1896 25 in. Ordnance Survey and is mentioned further in the cemetery grave location registers, where 'near signal box' refers to graves located in plots 101, 102 and 104. It is not known when this box was dismantled, but it is most likely to have been removed consequent to the quadrupling of the main line described above.

The original signal box was closed in December 1903 and replaced by two temporary boxes used in connection with the quadrupling stageworks. These in turn were dismantled and replaced by a new LSWR type '4' box which opened in 1905 as part of the low pressure pneumatic signalling scheme. This box was located on the down platform of Brookwood station and windows at the rear allowed excellent observation of the movement of the Necropolis train as it entered or left the cemetery. The box was converted to electro-pneumatic operation in June 1931. The box finally closed on 5th June, 1966, after the remnants of the Necropolis siding had been taken out of use, and control was transferred to Woking box.

The Present Scene

The course of the cemetery branch is still relatively easy to follow. By default much of it has become another main avenue in the cemetery, but on a more modest scale than that proposed by the LNC in September 1945.

The location of the principal features of the branch - run-round loop, stations, level crossing and sidings - are easily traced. Behind Brookwood station the site of the loop is discernible by the relative absence of vegetation. This area has recently been extensively landscaped and planted by the station master, who also arranged for a short section of railway track to be located adjacent to the

---

* G.A. Pryer *Signal Box Diagrams of the Great Western & Southern Railways: Volume 17: SR Lines: North-East Hampshire* (G.A. Pryer, n.d.), p.32.

cemetery entrance/exit. Further along the route, the site of the level crossing is now a slight bump along Cemetery Pales, whilst the Masonry Works was leased to Messrs Clements sometime after the last war, who continued operating the works until the early 1980s. The area then became one of several sold off under the terms of the 1975 Brookwood Cemetery Act. The works were sold to a firm of architectural consultants who sympathetically adapted the old workshops into office accommodation, now known as 'Stonemasons' Court'. The rest of the yard has been made into a car park, but it is still possible to see the two stone-capped brick pillars in the undergrowth which was once the railway entrance into the site.

One railway chair remains *in situ* where the line crossed Long Avenue, immediately before the platform steps of North station. Both station platforms remain as a reminder of these two unusual stations. That of North station is now fenced off, as it forms part of a Muslim burial ground reserved for the Najmee-Baag (for Dawoodi Bohras); however, access to the site of the station is usually possible through a side gate. The site of South station, including the platform and the two Anglican chapels, is now owned by the St Edward Brotherhood. This Orthodox monastic community conducts daily services in their Church, maintains the shrine of St Edward the Martyr (a Saxon king, *c*.959-978/9) and an Orthodox Christian Cemetery (the old plot 39). Both chapels have been repaired, restored and sympathetically adapted to their new purposes: the large chapel, built 1908-09, is now the Church of St Edward the Martyr; whilst Smirke's chapel of 1854 has been converted for parochial purposes and living quarters for members of the Brotherhood. The St Edward Brotherhood is currently raising money for a larger house for members of their community. Planning permission has been granted by Woking Borough Council for this to be located on the site of the courtyard of South station. The planning consent requires the Brotherhood to mark out permanently the plan of South station, to restore the platform, to provide interpretation boards for visitors, and to create a small museum that will explain the history of the site and provide further information about the Brotherhood. For further information about the St Edward Brotherhood, visit their website at www.saintedwardbrotherhood.org

Chapter Four

Operation: The Normal Necropolis Service

'Everything worked smoothly and in perfect decorum.'
(The Era)

The Arrangements at the London Terminus

Early Proposals (1849-53)

The LNC's mode of operation revolutionised funeral practices, not least by its use of the LSWR. Indeed, the employment of the railway was a distinguishing feature of the LNC's business. This reform was considered necessary to mitigate the evils of metropolitan burial. Under Broun's scheme, coffins collected from all over London would have been placed in 'reception chambers' (or coffin depositories) in the arches of the LSWR's viaduct outside Waterloo. They would then have been conveyed, by a train of special hearse vans, to the 'morgue chapels' alongside the LSWR between Woking and Brookwood, one chapel for each religious portion of Broun's Necropolis. These coffin trains would have travelled to Woking between 10 and 12 pm or 5 to 7 am, under the supervision of attendants from the LNC. At each 'morgue chapel' the relevant coffins would have been removed from the vans, placed in the chapel, and left until the day of the funeral. Sanitation made the prompt removal of corpses from London essential, although every arrangement would have been made to make this acceptable to public feeling. Hence the dead and living would not have travelled by the same train. Mourners would have journeyed separately, by day trains composed of carriages used exclusively for this purpose, on the day fixed for the funeral. As Broun explained in 1851:

> It does not form portion of my plan that the dead and living should be conveyed by the same train. Two or three hundred mourners in the wake of fifty or sixty corpses, would not by any means be agreeable. A large Hearse-van ... will go down to the NECROPOLIS [overnight] ... Chief mourners and their immediate relatives will proceed by day trains, and in carriages set apart for their private use. The separation which this mode implies, will perhaps occasion at first some dissatisfaction.

This proposal may have gone further than 'some dissatisfaction'. In the following year, *Herepath's Journal* discussed some of the issues concerning the proposed funeral trains:

> How are we to work the dead traffic, either independent of the live or mixed with them, and either with or without the relations of the dead?
> Relations as we know will not send corpses unaccompanied. Hence the dead cannot go at night; if by day they must either go all by an early morning train or by several trains during the day. If by an early train, then mourners will often have to wait six or eight hours for the funeral, for if numbers be great, funerals cannot all be performed

LONDON NECROPOLIS COMPANY, FUNERAL FURNISHERS,

REVISED SCALE OF CHARGES

FOR FUNERALS WITHIN THE METROPOLITAN RADIUS TO NECROPOLIS, BROOKWOOD, OR ANY OF THE METROPOLITAN CEMETERIES.

"Earth to Earth" Coffins supplied in any Class, except 10 and 11, without additional charge.

CLASS		£	s.	d.
1.	Open Car, or Glass Hearse and Pair, Three Broughams and Pairs, Elm Shell lined Swansdown, Lead Coffin, Oak Case, French Polished, Brass Fittings, Engraved Plate of Inscription, Memorial Service Books, Superintendent and Assistants, from	35	0	0
2.	Similar, without Lead Coffin	25	0	0
3.	Open Car, or Glass Hearse and Pair, Two Broughams and Pairs, Elm Shell lined Swansdown, Oak Case, French Polished, Brass Fittings, Engraved Plate of Inscription, Memorial Service Books, Superintendent and Assistants...	21	0	0
4.	Open Car, or Glass Hearse and Pair, Two Broughams and Pairs, Oak Coffin, French Polished, Brass Fittings, Engraved Plate of Inscription, lined Swansdown, Memorial Service Books, Superintendent and Assistants	15	15	0
5.	Open Car, or Glass Hearse and Pair, One Brougham and Pair, Elm Shell, lined Swansdown, Elm Case, Brass Fittings, Plate of Inscription, Superintendent and Assistants	15	0	0
6.	Similar, without Elm Shell	12	12	0
7.	Glass Hearse and Pair, Coach and Pair, Elm Coffin, French Polished, Brass Fittings, lined, &c., Engraved Name Plate, Superintendent and Assistants	9	9	0
8.	Similar, with less expensive Coffin	7	7	0
9.	Glass Hearse and Pair, Coach and Pair, Elm Coffin, Polished, Brassed Fittings, lined, &c., Name Plate, Superintendent and Assistants	5	15	0
10.	Hearse and Pair, Coach and Pair, Elm Coffin, Black Fittings, lined, &c., Name Plate, and Attendants	4	0	0
11.	Pair Horse Carriage to convey Body and Mourners, Smooth Elm Coffin with appropriate Fittings, Attendants, &c.	3	3	0

CREMATION, Inclusive Charge from £13 13s. See page 10.

A Telegram at any hour to "TENEBRATIO, LONDON," secures the immediate attendance of a Trained Funeral Director, who will carry out all arrangements connected with Funerals and Cremations.

together; hence we shall have to put on several funeral trains, say at 9, 12 and 2. How will you work these trains along with ordinary traffic? How will you load them with dead and live mixed? How will you separate mourners with their tickets from others?

Therefore these radical suggestions were moderated by the LNC. Probably the company feared Broun's plan went too far in reforming traditional funeral practices, and that the separation of the dead from the living might prove so unpopular as to impair its trade. *The Spectator* alluded to some of these issues in its account of the opening of the cemetery in November 1854:

> The new enterprise will introduce more than one change in our [burial] customs. . . . Hitherto we have but slowly departed from the arrangement by which our forefathers were lodged in the church of our own native town. Generations have been born, have lived, and have been buried upon the same spot. Henceforward the homes of the living are to be separate from the broad lands allotted to the dead. . . . The journey, though not more tedious, expensive, or troublesome, is to be longer in distance. The novelty of the railway train is to have the newer novelty of the funeral train.

The LNC's Railway Funerals

In its early days, the LNC used London undertakers to assist with the funeral arrangements. In November 1854 the firms of Barnard, Bedford and Dottridge were used to facilitate the company's business. However, in due course, the LNC expanded its activities and eventually operated its own undertaking service, including coffin making, statuary and masonry work, floral tributes, etc.

Under the LNC's scheme of undertaking, the arrangements for a funeral were not that different from any other arranged in London, except that a railway journey rather than the traditional hearse and carriage procession transported the coffins and mourners to Brookwood Cemetery. After death, the corpse was usually left at home until the funeral arrangements were concluded. If required, invitations to attend funerals could be sent out from the LNC's offices. These letters eventually included details of the waiting room(s) allocated to the funeral party, the departure time of the train, and the expected time of arrival back in London (*see page 90*). Then the customary hearse and carriage procession took place on the appointed day, from the deceased person's house to the local parish church (if the funeral service was to take place in London) and then proceeded to the LNC's private station; otherwise the procession went directly to the LNC's private station (assuming that the main part of the funeral service was to take place in the station or at Brookwood). Upon arrival, the mourners were led to a private waiting room during the brief interval wherein the final preparations were made for the departure to Brookwood. Separate waiting rooms were provided for those attending a better class funeral (available in first or second class),* whilst those accompanying the cheapest (third or pauper

---

* The distinction between the three main classes of funeral was equivalent to the class of grave space purchased. Therefore a 3rd class funeral resulted in a '3rd class' grave, or one allocated to those buried at parish expense and located in a designated area of the cemetery. For obvious reasons these graves were rarely purchased by the family (so that a permanent memorial could be erected), but it should be noted that the LNC's Act forbad more than one body in any grave (except next of kin). A '2nd class' grave could be selected with some choice of location, but the standard fee of £1 excluded the right to erect a

REVISED SCALE OF CHARGES

FOR REFORMED FUNERALS WITHIN THE METROPOLITAN RADIUS.

Under the system of Funeral reform inaugurated by the London Necropolis Company the procession may be entirely dispensed with, and the mourners, instead of meeting at the residence of the deceased, assemble at the Company's Private Station in the Westminster Bridge Road, where separate waiting-rooms are reserved for each Funeral.

CLASS		£	s.	d.
A.	Elm Shell, lined Swansdown, Lead Coffin, Oak Case, French Polished, Brass Fittings, Engraved Plate of Inscription, Hearse and Pair, Superintendent and Assistants, from	25	0	0
B.	Similar, without Lead Coffin	15	15	0
C.	Elm Shell, lined Swansdown, Oak Case, French Polished, Brass Fittings, Engraved Plate of Inscription, Hearse and Pair, Superintendent and Assistants	12	12	0
D.	Oak Coffin, French Polished, Brass Fittings, lined Swansdown, Engraved Plate of Inscription, Hearse and Pair, Superintendent and Assistants	10	10	0
E.	Similar, with less expensive Fittings	8	8	0
F.	Elm Shell, lined Swansdown, Elm Case, Brass Fittings, Plate of Inscription, Hearse and Pair, Superintendent and Assistants	8	8	0
G.	Elm Coffin, French Polished, Brass Furniture, lined, &c., Engraved Plate of Inscription, Hearse and Pair, Superintendent and Assistants	6	6	0
H.	Similar, with less expensive Fittings	4	4	0
I.	Elm Coffin, Polished, lined, &c., Brassed Fittings, Hearse and Attendants	3	10	0
J.	Elm Coffin, Black Fittings, Two Rows of Nails, Name Plate, Hearse and Attendants ...	2	15	0

CREMATION, Inclusive Charge, from £13 13 0. *See Page* 10.

Funerals to any part of the WORLD at Moderate Inclusive Charges.

A Telegram at any hour to "TENEBRATIO, LONDON," *secures the immediate attendance of an Efficient Representative, who will carry out all arrangements connected with Funerals and Interments.*

class) funerals were escorted to one large communal waiting room. The separation of mourners from the corpse therefore still existed, but in a less extreme and more limited form. Meanwhile the coffin was unloaded from the hearse in the LNC's driveway and sent up to platform level by lift. Then, one party at a time was summoned from their waiting room and escorted to a compartment in the train. Small cards, with the name of each funeral party, were placed on the relevant waiting room doors, and on the corresponding compartment doors of the passenger and hearse carriages, to prevent any embarrassing errors. Relatives and friends attending an expensive funeral could also, if they wished, watch the coffin being placed in the hearse van (*see page 88*). This process continued until all funeral parties were in the train, although mourners attending third class funerals would be escorted to the train as a group, and would not be allowed to see the coffins being loaded.

Alternatively the LNC's 'reformed funeral' could be adopted. This followed Broun's scheme more closely, as the corpse was brought to the company's private station and was placed either in one of the private mortuaries, in the communal mortuary (used for the cheaper funerals) or - in the case of the Westminster Bridge Road station - in the splendid *Chapelle Ardente*, the private chapel of rest at platform level (*see page 40*). Whatever the option, there the coffin remained until the day of the funeral, when the mourners would arrange to meet at the LNC's station and the procedure would revert to that described above. This arrangement was usually adopted by those Guardians of the Poor of the metropolitan parishes which had contracted with the LNC for the burial of paupers under their jurisdiction. However, this arrangement also appealed to those who preferred to meet at the Necropolis station and avoid the conventional funeral procession through crowded streets. It also proved invaluable to those friends or family who might be unable to accompany the body to Brookwood for the final rites, in which case the first part of the funeral service would take place in the *Chapelle Ardente* within the station precincts.

Further details about the arrangements for pauper funerals in the Borough of Southwark have been located. It seems likely that similar provisions were made for other metropolitan parishes who had contracts with the LNC for the burial of the poor. Paupers dying in the Borough of Southwark, either in a workhouse or in hospital, were buried at 'parish' expense unless the body was claimed by relatives (if this happened, the cost of the funeral was met by the family rather than the parish or Borough, and was classed as a 'private' burial). If the deceased was to be buried by the Borough, a travel 'warrant' was issued by the Town Clerk which authorised up to two third class mourner tickets to be granted to the immediate relatives, who could accompany the body to Brookwood. All this was charged at the appropriate rate by the LNC to the Borough. Additional mourners might also travel to the cemetery, but the family would have to pay these extra fares. Under the terms of the original contract

permanent memorial (which was 10s. extra). If no permanent memorial was placed, the company reserved the right to re-use the grave space at some future date. A '1st class' or 'private' grave could be located virtually anywhere in the cemetery, although 'special' positions (designated by the LNC) were charged extra. A permanent memorial was expected to be placed over '1st class' graves in due course. Prices ranged from £2 10s. 0d. for a standard 9 ft by 4 ft plot, to £5 5s. 0d. and upwards for a similar grave in a 'special' position. Further information about these prices may be gleaned from the pages of a LNC brochure reproduced elsewhere in this book.

THE LONDON NECROPOLIS, BROOKWOOD CEMETERY, WOKING.

INCORPORATED BY SPECIAL ACT OF PARLIAMENT, 1852.

Telegrams: Tenebratio, London.   Telephone 839 Hop.

CHARGES AND FEES.

PRIVATE GRAVES.

* Private Grave in Perpetuity, 9 feet by 4 feet, including Conveyance of Body from the "Necropolis" Private Station, Westminster Bridge Road, Funeral Service and Interment ... ... £2 10 0   Subsequent Interments £2 2 0
* Ditto, Children, Do. Do. ... 1 10 0
* Special Positions ... ... from £5 5 0 to 52 10 0 do. do. ... 4 4 0

SECOND-CLASS GRAVE.

Grave space, including Conveyance of Body rom the "Necropolis" Private Station, Westminster Bridge Road, Funeral Service and Interment ... ... £1 15 0   Subsequent Interments Do. ... £1 0 0

Children under 10 years of age ... Privilege of placing Head and Foot Stones Do. ... 10/- extra. ... 0 15 0

In case of the Erection of a Monument or Enclosure of an Allotment, a margin of not less than 9 inches must be left on every side, thus only 7 feet 6 inches by 2 feet 6 inches may be enclosed of an ordinary grave space 9 feet by 4 feet.

The Cemetery is accessible in forty minutes by Special Train from the Westminster Bridge Road Station, or by the South-Western Railway to Brookwood, which station is at the Entrance to THE NECROPOLIS.

PRIVATE VAULTS.

	Area of Ground.	Purchase of Ground.		Brick Work, with York Landing.	Fees on Subsequent Interments.
		Special Positions.	Other Parts.		
		Per Foot.	£ s. d.	£ s. d.	£ s. d.
* Private Vault for Two Coffins ...	9 ft. × 6 ft.	5/- to 25/-	10 10 0	17 0 0	7 7 0
* Private Vault for Six Coffins ...	9 ft. × 9 ft.	5/- to 25/-	15 15 0	30 0 0	7 7 0
* Private Vault for Twelve Coffins ...	9 ft. × 9 ft.	5/- to 25/-	15 15 0	40 0 0	7 7 0

BRICK GRAVES.

	Area of Ground.	Purchase of Ground.		Brick Work, including Stone.	Fees on Subsequent Interments.
		Special Positions.	Other Parts.		
		Per Foot.	£ s. d.	£ s. d.	£ s. d.
* Single Grave for One Coffin ...	9 ft. × 5 ft.	5/- to 25/-	7 7 0	5 5 0	4 4 0
* Single Grave for Two Coffins ...	9 ft. × 5 ft.	5/- to 25/-	7 7 0	5 10 0	4 4 0
* Single Grave for Four Coffins ...	9 ft. × 5 ft.	5/- to 25/-	7 7 0	13 0 0	4 4 0
* Single Grave for Six Coffins ...	9 ft. × 5 ft.	5/- to 25/-	7 7 0	15 15 0	4 4 0
* Double Grave for Two Coffins ...	9 ft. × 7 ft.	5/- to 25/-	12 12 0	7 7 0	4 4 0
* Double Grave for Four Coffins ...	9 ft. × 7 ft.	5/- to 25/-	12 12 0	10 10 0	4 4 0
* Double Grave for Six Coffins ...	9 ft. × 7 ft.	5/- to 25/-	12 12 0	15 5 0	4 4 0

EXTRA DEPTH OF GRAVES.

From 6 to 10 feet ...	£0 1 6 per foot.		From 14 to 17 feet ...	£0 3 0 per foot.
10 ,, 14 ,, ...	0 2 6 ,,		17 ,, 20 ,, ...	0 5 0 ,,

RETURN FARES TO BROOKWOOD (*per Necropolis Private Train*).

First-Class, Return ... 6 -   Second Class, Return ... 3 6   Third-Class, Return ... 2/-

ADDITIONAL CHARGES.

Consecration Fee ...	£0 6 2	Entry of Grant (Stamp Duty *Ad Val.*) ...	£0 2 6
Turfing Grave, 9 ft. × 4 ft. ...	0 2 6	Use of Shelter ...	0 10 0
Keeping Turf cut and in good order, 9ft. × 4ft., per annum	0 10 6	Use of Tent for 25 persons ...	0 2 6
Ditto ditto and maintenance in perpetuity ...	10 10 0	Certificate of Burial ...	0 2 0
Planting Grave with Spring Flowers ...	0 10 6	Comparing and searching Register, one year ...	0 1 0
Planting, Turfing and Maintenance in perpetuity 9ft. × 4ft.	21 0 0	Ditto, every additional year ...	0 0 6
Lining Grave with evergreens ...	1 1 0	Removing and Replacing Monuments and Grave }	According to
Lining Grave with evergreens and flowers ...	1 2 0	Stones ... ... }	Assisted Charge.

* *Over which a Monument or Grave Stone, 1) a design to be approved by the Company, must be erected within 12 months.*

OFFICES.—188, WESTMINSTER BRIDGE ROAD, S.E. ; 2, LANCASTER PLACE, STRAND.

Page from a LNC brochure of 1899.

Author's Collection

THE LONDON NECROPOLIS,

CHORAL SERVICES

Choral Services arranged as desired, from 8 guineas.
Special Choirs of trained voices.

ORGAN

An Organ is provided in the Church for Choral Services.
Charge for Organist and Organ, £2 2s.
Use of Organ only, £1 1s.

EMBALMING

Modern Embalming, either temporary or permanent,
by Certified Specialists. Inclusive Fees from 15 Guineas.

RAILWAY FARES (per Necropolis Train).
1st Class Return, 6s.; 3rd Class Return, 2s.

LUNCHEON AT BROOKWOOD.

Light Luncheon can be provided if one day's notice
is given at the Chief Office.

London, Woking, and Brookwood.

THE LONDON NECROPOLIS,

ADDITIONAL CHARGES AT
CEMETERY

	£	s.	d.
Consecration Fee	0	6	2
Turfing Grave, 9-ft. by 4-ft. . from	0	7	6
Keeping Grass cut and in good order, per annum	1	1	0
Keeping Turf cut and maintenance in perpetuity . . . from	26	5	0
Planting Grave with summer flowers . from	1	1	0
Planting Grave with Bulbs for Spring Flowering . . . from	1	1	0
Planting, Turfing and maintenance in perpetuity, 9-ft. by 4-ft. . . from	52	10	0
Lining Grave with Evergreens	2	2	0
Lining Graves with Evergreens and Flowers	4	4	0
Entry of Grant (Stamp Duty, ad. val.) .	0	5	0
Certificate of Burial . . .	0	3	7
Comparing and searching Register, per year .	0	2	6
Clergy Fee	0	10	6
Removing and Replacing Monuments and Grave Stones			

According to Assessed Charge

London, Woking, and Brookwood.

with the parish of St Saviour's, Southwark (1854), a child's pauper funeral cost 10s., (including the conveyance of one mourner or attendant), an adult's 14s. (including the conveyance of up to two mourners or attendants), whilst additional mourners or attendants were charged at 2s. each. The body of the deceased would be transferred to the LNC's station before the funeral, whilst any mourners attending the funeral would meet in the third class communal waiting room prior to the departure of the train.

Also travelling in the train, at no direct cost to themselves, were the LNC's chaplains who would perform the last rites in the cemetery in place of the deceased person's own minister. The local clergyman could attend, if invited by the family, to lead the funeral service. Under the terms of the LNC's Act (1852), irrespective of which minister performed the funeral service, a fee of 6s. 2d. was payable to the incumbent of the parish from which the body was removed (assuming it was buried in the consecrated section) except if the body was buried at the expense of the parish, in which case the fee was reduced to 1s.

The Necropolis train was originally divided into classes *and* religions; moreover these divisions applied not only to the living travelling in the train, but also the dead. The passenger carriages were divided into different classes in the usual way, with each funeral party having a separate compartment. In the case of a large, wealthy family, a saloon coach might be specially inserted in the train (*see page 92*). To ensure sufficient accommodation on the train, the LNC required notice of the number of coffins and mourners by noon on the day before the funeral. This allowed the LNC time to arrange with the LSWR for sufficient stock to be marshalled. An early LNC brochure stated that:

Orders for Funerals are received at the Offices of the Company, No. 2, Lancaster Place, Strand, and notice must be given before 2 o'clock, P.M. of Burials intended for the following day. Funerals must arrive at the London Terminus in the case of the First Class 10 minutes, those of the Second Class 20 minutes, and those of the Third Class 30 minutes at least before the time of starting of the Train.

This arrangement was designed to avoid unseemly congestion within the station, but it is not known how long these timings for funerals was adhered to. It was the responsibility of the LNC's station caretaker to make these arrangements with the LSWR (and later the SR). It was his duty to inform the railway company if no train was needed, otherwise the Necropolis train would run regardless of passengers! Mistakes did happen, but only very rarely!*

The hearse vans were similarly divided into 'compartments' for the different classes of coffins. The main distinction between first, second, and third class coffin accommodation was apparently the quantity of ornamentation on the 'compartment' doors, although this does not seem to be very clear in surviving photographs of the hearse vans.

Then there was the division caused by religion. It seems that the train was originally formed in two distinct portions - Anglican and Nonconformist - each with its own passenger and coffin accommodation. The hearse vans were usually arranged at the rear of the relevant portion of the train for the outward journey - another departure from traditional funeral custom. This formation

---

* The author is aware of one occasion when the Necropolis train was dispatched to Brookwood with nobody on board except the train crew.

was not invariably used. Often, and especially during the latter years of the service, the hearse vans were arranged at the front of the train, behind the locomotive (*see page 92, lower*).

It is impossible now to ascertain exactly how the train was marshalled at the LNC's terminus. Probably, in the original York Street station (1854-1877), once the requirements for the following day's funeral were known, the train was formed accordingly by shunting between the two private sidings, forming a 'set' tailored to the needs of the hour. Exactly when this was done it is impossible to say. Any surplus stock would have been berthed in the spare siding. In the constricted York Street station of 1878-1902, the position is even more ambiguous. There was no spare siding for the surplus stock, whilst the necessary shunting movements would have been more difficult, owing to the volume of normal passenger traffic on the LSWR, unless they were performed in the evening or early morning, prior to the departure of the train. The Westminster Bridge Road station (1902-1941) allowed more flexible arrangements to be made, using the LNC's two fairly long sidings. Possibly, the shorter third class platform was used exclusively to place coffins in the hearse vans. However, this would have required the passenger sections of the train to be formed in two separate and uncoupled parts, both in the longer first class platform, and involving several shunting movements to position the correct vans at the rear of the relevant passenger portions of the train. All this would have to be done just prior to departure, and with the mourners and coffins already in the various parts of the train. Alternatively the shorter platform may have been used solely for Nonconformists (or the shorter part of the train, be it Anglican or Nonconformist), so that the two halves of the train were already marshalled up, and only required joining before departure. It is also possible the third class platform was reserved solely for use on 'parish days', when only pauper funerals were catered for. However, none of this exudes the sense of smoothness, of 'decency and decorum, the freedom from noise, anxiety, and bustle' which the LNC always emphasised of its arrangements. For instance one brochure stated 'the funeral trains draw up alongside the [first class] Waiting Rooms and Mourners pass straight into the reserved carriages.' It seems more likely that the stock not required was left in the shorter platform, whilst the ready-made Necropolis train stood in the longer platform, as in the original York Street station. Thus, once the mourners and coffins were safely aboard and the engine coupled, the train could depart without further ado.

The Journey to and from Brookwood

In its earliest years, the Necropolis train left London for Brookwood at 11.35 am on weekdays, and at 11.20 am on Sundays. Necropolis Junction was reached at 12.25 pm and 12.20 pm respectively. These times varied by no more than 20 minutes throughout the entire duration of the Necropolis service. Strangely, the LNC's brochures invariably quote the journey time as 40 minutes, but the Working Timetables do not support this claim until the 1920s (*see Appendix One*). Indeed, although a draft agreement between the LNC and LSWR (dated

A coffin being loaded into hearse van No. 378(?) at the Westminster Bridge Road station, *c.*1905. The van is in the 1st class platform and is at the rear of the train. The funeral party has probably just emerged from one of the private waiting rooms on the left and are watching the coffin being loaded into the hearse van. Note the 'shelves' in the coffin compartment and the card holder in the waist panelling of the van door on the right. *M. Wealthy Collection*

The Necropolis train waiting to leave the Westminster Bridge Road station on a damp morning in mid-1938, with an unidentified 'M7' 0-4-4T. *Lens of Sutton Collection*

1854) required that journey times be no greater than 50 minutes, even this was not always attained before World War I. From the 1920s, the journey was reduced to about 40 minutes generally, both outward and return, possibly to try and attract more custom. Nevertheless, the LNC emphasised the easy journey to Brookwood from London by train:

> . . . it is only popular delusion that imagines the journey to Woking to be objectionable on the score of its length. The whole distance is traversed in forty minutes, [*sic*] a less time, indeed, than a mourning coach takes to crawl to Highgate or Kensal Green.

But *The Undertakers' Journal* noted (in 1898):

> Throughout every day in the year the bodies are arriving at the station mortuary, until when the . . . coffin express is ready to start there are from thirty to seventy corpses booked as passengers, for whom the railway journey with its fields and flowers and hedges *en route* presents no attractions - passengers who are never likely to grumble at the speed of the train. . . . which might easily give points to the South-Eastern express.

A remarkable and fascinating insight into the operation of the funeral trains is given in the diary of Hirohachi, the leader of the Japanese Imperial Troupe. His party of 17 performers left Japan in December 1866 and toured North America and Europe between 1867 and 1869. One member of the troupe, Kikujiro Matsui, died of consumption on 3rd April, 1868, shortly after his arrival in London from France. Arrangements were made to have his body buried at Brookwood. Hirohachi's diary continues:

April 4, 1868
    This morning, it snowed heavily. We held the funeral around noon. There is the cemetery, some 50km from London, which can accommodate the whole of London. Both the dead and attendants reach the cemetery by steam locomotive. The coffin was superbly prepared. In Japan, such a beautiful funeral would not be possible for those who belong to the trading class and farmers to perform.
    The dead are carried in a different carriage. In the cemetery we erected a large stone, in which we have carved the name [of Kikujiro] and ours. There are two other Japanese graves, which we visited and offered flowers and incense.

July 20, 1868
    Today, the headstone of Kikujiro was erected and we performed the ceremony of commemoration. We went to the cemetery and paid our respects and bid farewell for two consecutive days. Today was the last performance here [in London] and we had the celebration [after the final curtain].

July 21, 1868
    Today, we packed up. We also went to the grave. We then rested.*

---

* I am greatly indebted to Minister Haruhisa Takeuchi for supplying this extract and translation. This arose from a visit to the cemetery in February 2004 when the Minister, accompanied by several colleagues and friends, visited the Japanese graves in Brookwood Cemetery. These include the earliest known grave of a Japanese traveller to England, that of the student Yamazaki Kosaburo (*c.*1844-1866). Since Hirohachi's diary identifies *two* existing Japanese graves (Yamazaki's being one of them), research continues to identify the second.

The London Necropolis & National Mausoleum Company.

OFFICES — 188, WESTMINSTER BRIDGE ROAD.
2, LANCASTER PLACE, STRAND.
PRIVATE STATION — 188, WESTMINSTER BRIDGE ROAD.

REGISTERED TELEGRAPHIC ADDRESS.
"TENEBRATIO, LONDON"
TELEPHONE No. 1639 HOP.

188, Westminster Bridge Road,

LONDON _____ 189

Dear Sir,

I am desired to request your attendance at the Funeral of the late _____ which will take place on _____ day next, the _____ at the London Necropolis, Brookwood, Woking.

Friends will assemble at the Necropolis Station, Westminster Bridge Road, about 11.30 a.m., where Waiting Room, No. _____ will be reserved.

The Special Train leaves at 11.45 a.m., and is due on its return journey at 3.50 p.m.

I am,

Yours truly,

Cyril. B. Tubbs.
Gen¹ Manager.

R.S.V.P.

Another funeral invitation of the late 1890s.
Author's Collection

The London Necropolis Company,

188, WESTMINSTER BRIDGE ROAD,
AND
2, LANCASTER PLACE, STRAND.

10 November 1891

Dear Sir,

The favor of your Company is requested to attend the Funeral of the late George H. Haydon which will take place on Thurs day next the 12th Inst. at the London Necropolis Cemetery at Brookwood.

The special train leaves Westminster Bridge Road Necropolis private Station at 11.45 a.m., and is due to arrive at Waterloo Station on its return journey at 3.50 p.m.

I am,

Your obedient Servant,

J. LARKMAN,
Secretary.

The favor of an answer will oblige.

Invitation to attend the funeral of George Haydon, November 1891.
Author's Collection

The Necropolis train originally ran non-stop from London to Brookwood. Between 1890 and 1910 the LSWR agreed to allow stops at Clapham Junction and Vauxhall, for the convenience of mourners attending funerals arranged with the Wandsworth & Clapham Union and who did not wish to return to Waterloo. These stops varied from time to time, but were never re-introduced after World War I. Some optional stops were also included for the pre-1914 period, at Woking or Walton-upon-Thames, for the engine to take water if required.

A draft agreement between the LNC and LSWR (dated 1854) provided for at least two trains from the LNC's terminus to the cemetery and back, the first leaving at 9 am (or between 8 am and noon) and the second at 11 am (or between 8 am and 2 pm). Both were to have left the cemetery 30 minutes after the completion of the funeral ceremonies. A third train was to have run if the volume of monthly burials exceeded a certain previously agreed level; but this intensive service never materialised. Probably, both companies agreed to a single daily train at first, and to include further trains only if the pressure of burials in the London Necropolis warranted them. But the LNC only ever succeeded in drawing off a tiny proportion of the total metropolitan burials. For instance, during the first 20 years of the service operating (1854-1874), the total number of burials in the cemetery never exceeded 4,100 in any one year, and only averaged 3,200 per annum, in years when the average number of annual deaths in London was over 50,000. Moreover this average declined further over time. By November 1954, the centenary of the cemetery, total burials amounted to 216,390, with an overall average of 2,163 burials a year. Hence, the extra trains were never required, and it seems likely that the train often had spare capacity, especially since only two hearse vans were ever used after 1899.

From November 1854 to October 1900 the Necropolis train apparently ran daily, as shown in the working timetables. In fact it appears to have operated on an 'as required' basis throughout its operational life. For instance, in the first month of operation (November 1854), the Necropolis train did not run on 14th and 26th, since there were no funerals taking place. The 'regular' Tuesday and Friday trains, which remained right up to the very last train in 1941, appear to have established themselves early on. These trains were principally for the London parishes and pauper burials, although other funeral parties might also be carried at the same time (or arranged on alternative days if the families preferred). Cyril Tubbs, the LNC's General Manager, noted in 1889 that 'our regular trains start at 11.50 every Tuesday and Friday & generally at least two other days in the week, & on Sundays at 11.30'.

After 1st October, 1900, the Sunday Necropolis train ceased to run. Despite the Victorian obsession with 'church hours', within which the Necropolis train always ran, for many years Brookwood was one of very few cemeteries to offer burials on Sundays. Traditionally, Sunday was a day for working class funerals since the poor needed time to find the money for undertakers, mourning clothes, and the funeral tea. Moreover, on Sundays, friends and relatives could attend the funeral as they would be free from work. The availability of Sunday funerals was a key factor in the choice of Brookwood Cemetery as the site of the

The Necropolis train *en route* to Brookwood, passing Wimbledon, on 25th June, 1902. Note the two distinct religious portions to the train, each with its own hearse van (these are the third and last vehicles); the six-wheeled arc roofed coaches (30 ft braked third, 34 ft composite, 30ft brake third, 30ft second or third); and the four-wheeled 24 ft 'Windsor' semi-saloon (the fourth vehicle).   *Lens of Sutton Collection*

'M7' 0-4-4T No. 321 hauling the Necropolis train near Wimbledon, *c.*1934. On this occasion both hearse vans are at the front of the train, and Set 100 consists of only three bogie carriages.
                                                                                        The late J.M. Craig, per R.C. Riley

'Actors' Acre' (plot 118), since no theatrical performances took place on Sundays.*

About the same time the weekday service was also changed. In the period October 1902-May 1903, the train was advertised as running 'each Wednesday and *nearly* every other day'. Thereafter, the Necropolis train usually ran on 'Wednesdays, Saturdays, and *nearly* every other day'. From sometime in 1928, this was further reduced to Tuesdays and Fridays, the previously noted 'regular' trains. In all cases the train ran more often if required. So the Necropolis train continued to operate until the air raid in April 1941. After World War II, an Officer of the SR remembered that the train ran 'once a week at most', but this was a simplification of the facts. The working arrangements did not specify particular days for running the Necropolis train in order to accommodate any short-term increase in traffic that might arise. For instance, the final LNC ticket book records the following additional trains during the period January 1938 to Easter 1940:

> Saturday 9th April, 1938; Thursday 14th April, 1938 (just before Easter); Saturday 16th April, 1938; Monday 25th July, 1938 (a special train for the funeral of Sir Nowroji Saklatvala, Chairman of Tata & Sons Ltd, which conveyed 155 mourners, all travelling first class); Thursday 19th January, 1939 (a special train for the funeral of Sir Henry Mordaunt, when 16 mourners travelled first class); Saturday 4th March, 1939 (another special train for the funeral of Effie Carr, when 15 mourners travelled third class); Thursday 6th April, 1939 (avoiding Good Friday); Saturday 8th April, 1939 (Easter Saturday); Monday 9th October, 1939 (a special train for the funeral of Farijee Cowasjee, when 50 mourners travelled third class); Wednesday 6th November, 1939 (another special for the funeral of Frank Haydon, when 14 mourners travelled third class); Monday 29th January, 1940 (a special train for the funeral of Emma Austen-Leigh, with eight mourners travelling 1st class); and trains running again on Tuesday, Thursday and Saturday for Easter 1940.

There could also be short-term reductions in traffic in winter. For instance the funeral trains were cancelled due to snow on Wednesday 28th December, 1938 ('no funerals, no passengers - train cancelled 11.40 am'); Friday 2nd February, 1940 ('no funerals and snow at Brookwood'); and on Tuesday 26th March, 1940 ('weather bad - no passengers').

Using the surviving LNC ticket book, which covers the period 1937-1941, it is interesting to discover that the highest number of mourners carried was 155 on the special funeral train for Sir Nowroji Saklatvala that ran on 25th July, 1938. All the mourners travelled first class at a total cost of £46 10s. 0d. The next highest figure was the train that ran on 13th September, 1938 for delegates attending the International Congress of the World Union of Freethinkers to visit the grave of Charles Bradlaugh. A total of 142 mourners travelled to Brookwood at a cost of £14 8s. 0d., all but one travelling third class.† The highest number of coffins carried during this period was a total of 24 (three seconds and 21 thirds), carried on 23rd November, 1937 at a total cost of £3 7s. 6d.

---

* Members of the theatrical profession found it distressing to attend a funeral during the week and then have to play in the theatre the same evening. The 'Actors' Acre' was inaugurated on 9th June, 1858.

† On arrival at Bradlaugh's grave, the delegates were embarrassed to discover the bust of Charles Bradlaugh had been stolen. *See Chapter Five* for more information on Charles Bradlaugh.

The Necropolis train proceeding through the Anglican section of Brookwood Cemetery in mid-1938. Here the line was on a slight embankment, edged with laurel (*see also page 59*).

Lens of Sutton Collection

'M7' 0-4-4T No. 127 running round the second Set 100 (with birdcage lookouts), *c*.1939. The set is incorrectly numbered in the painting.

From a painting by M. Jeffries, reproduced by permission of Mrs F. Rowley

For the same period, the lowest number of mourners carried was four, on 10th January, 1941. They all travelled third class, for the combined total cost of just 9s. 8d., along with six coffins (one first and five second class), for a combined total fare of £3 1s. 6d. However, on 7th July, 1939, the Necropolis train ran with 20 third class mourners and one first class coffin for a combined total fare of just £3. The least number of coffins carried would be one, typically for a special train or a quality funeral. However the train would never run with just a single third class (pauper) coffin, nor apparently with a single second class coffin. In these cases the coffins would travel by the next available service. Occasionally the train ran just for mourners, such as 11th October, 1938, when 41 mourners (two first, 39 third) travelled for a combined fare of £4 10s. 0d.

During World War II, once the blitz began, there were more substantive reasons for short-term cancellations. Due to enemy action, the Necropolis train was unable to operate during the period 7th September to 4th October, 1940, whilst the train scheduled to run on 11th October, 1940 was cancelled. The service was unable to resume until Tuesday 24th December, 1940. It is difficult to ascertain the very last burial by the Necropolis train, partly because some coffins were sent down to the cemetery prior to the funeral. For instance, amongst the special trains previously described, those for Effie Carr, Frank Haydon and Emma Austin-Leigh all carried additional coffins. From the cemetery's location register, which records the funerals on each day, it appears the very last railway funeral was that of Edward Irish, a Chelsea Pensioner, whose final journey took place on 11th April, 1941, burial number 203,041.* Even so, this final funeral train carried an additional coffin that is now impossible to identify against a subsequent burial in the cemetery.

Almost immediately after the destruction of the private station in April 1941, the SR offered the LNC temporary and interim facilities at Waterloo so that the service could continue as required from time to time, despite the fact that the train continued to appear in the Working Timetables until at least May 1945 with the note 'suspended'. Mr Miller, the LNC's Secretary,† met with Mr Greenfield, station master at Waterloo, in early May 1941 to discuss this. The matter was referred to Mr Sharpe, of the London West Divisional Superintendent's Office at Woking who confirmed on 5th June, 1941 that:

> … arrangements can be made to accommodate your train in No. 11 or 12 platform roads at Waterloo and the coffins could be loaded from the roadway into the vans [sic],# practically out of sight of the public. In addition, if it be considered necessary, a portable booking office could be allocated to your Company for the purpose of the sale of tickets. It is our desire to assist your Company in every way possible.

---

* According to the Hospital's records, Edward Irish was born c.1868 and was a member of the Bedfordshire Regiment. I am very grateful to Mr Jon Nuttall of the Royal Hospital Chelsea for confirming these details.

† Charles G. Miller (c.1891-1961). Director of the LNC. Miller was Secretary (1937-1943), and succeeded John B. Walker as Managing Director in 1943. He retained this position until the LNC ceased to exist as an independent company in 1959-60. He is buried in plot 119 in the cemetery.

Yet hearse van No. 1425 was destroyed in the air raid.

The Necropolis train approaching North station on its return working to London, *c.1907*. The train is drawn by an unidentified 'M7' 0-4-4T. The two hearse vans appear to be leading the train formation. Note the dip in the platform edge, the potted plants around the station courtyard, and the hanging flower baskets   *Kingsway Series postcard*

The Necropolis train at South station, 30th May, 1930. The engine is 'M7' 0-4-4T No. 244. The next vehicle appears to be one of the hearse vans. The building on the right is Smirke's Anglican chapel.   *H.C. Casserley*

In his reply, Mr Miller much appreciated this offer and confirmed the LNC wished,

> ... to avail ourselves of these facilities, as and when the need arises' with 48 hours notice to be sent to Waterloo whenever a train was required. However he noted that 'owing to evacuation a very large proportion of grave-owners have left London, consequently bodies for burial at Brookwood come direct by rail or road from other parts of the country.

Mr Miller also enquired if 'facility could be granted' to the LNC to continue issuing tickets from their offices so that mourners and visitors could travel from Waterloo to Brookwood at the same rates as the existing arrangements. He referred to the frequent enquiries about the cheap tickets since 'many people would visit the Cemetery who otherwise could not make the journey ... strict instructions would be given for these tickets to be issued to mourners attending funerals or to those actually visiting graves within the Cemetery only.' Some examples of comments received by the LNC from grave owners during the latter part of 1941 are:

> The ordinary fare, I am afraid, will preclude my frequent visits, and I wondered if you may have entered into any arrangement with the SR for special tickets to be issued.

> I was greatly distressed last week, in going for the 11.40 Necropolis train to find that it no longer existed & that I should have to go by the ordinary train & walk from Brookwood Station. Kindly let me know if you are considering issuing any special tickets to the special stations at all. I am a constant visitor to my husband's grave & ... I am unable to walk the distance from the ordinary station & so it makes a visit much valued almost an impossibility.

> Can you tell me if there is any way of getting to Brookwood cemetery by a Cheap Train for Visitors, as usual, when there is a funeral going, if so what is the fare and time of train?

The request for cheap mourner tickets for use on ordinary trains was declined, but the SR did offer to accommodate funerals from platform 11 or 12 of Waterloo station. Although practically all the LNC's metropolitan business was sent by road after 16th April, 1941, it does seem likely that funeral trains were operated by this facility from time to time. Any evidence of this would be welcomed by the author. It is not clear what stock would have been used during this period, although it should be remembered that one of the hearse vans (No. 1426) survived the bombing, whilst at least part of the old train formation appears to have escaped destruction (*see page 146*). The usual Necropolis tickets would presumably have been issued for coffins and mourners when the train ran under these circumstances. Indeed, under a further letter dated 16th June, 1941, Mr Perts, the SR Commercial Superintendent at Waterloo, stated that he had asked the SR Audit Accountant to replace, as soon as possible, 'the desired ticket stocks, to admit of a continuance of issue either from [the LNC] Headquarters or, if required, the portable Booking Office at Waterloo Station.' This mode of operation remained open to the LNC until the company formally told the SR (in mid-1946) that the Necropolis terminus would no longer be used.

The Necropolis Train leaves the Company's Private Station 121 Westminster Bridge Road at 11.40 a.m. and arrives at Brookwood Cemetery at 12.30 p.m. Departs from the Cemetery at 2.20 p.m. and arrives at Necropolis Station on return journey at 3.15 p.m.

Card sent to mourners attending funeral at Brookwood per the Necropolis train. The times stated do not fall easily into any of the timetables reproduced in *Appendix One*.   *Author's Collection*

In Memory of

WHO WAS INTERRED AT

THE LONDON NECROPOLIS,

BROOKWOOD, WOKING,

On........day the..........day of....................189

Aged........Years.

GRAVE No. ....

Offices :—188, Westminster Bridge Road, S.E.;
2, Lancaster Place, Strand, W.C.;
6, Munster Parade, Fulham Road, S.W.

London Necropolis memorial card, 1890s.   *Author's Collection*

The London Necropolis.

THE LATE

London Necropolis memorial card, 1920s.   *Author's Collection*

In a memorandum dated 13th May, 1946 the SR noted that although the Necropolis terminus would never again be used for its intended purpose, and as road transport would be used increasingly to cater for the LNC's business, there would be 'no difficulty' in conveying by ordinary train services any funeral traffic which might be handed to the SR by the LNC. This was subject only to the proviso that should such traffic attain 'any volume' it might become necessary to limit the number of funeral parties conveyed by any particular train. No initial problems were foreseen regarding the special fares and rates applicable to the LNC's traffic, as the rates could be reviewed later in the light of the traffic then being handled. Although it is not clear how the service was operated under these circumstances, John Schlesinger's documentary film *Terminus* (1961) does include a scene where a coffin is loaded into the luggage space of a brake end coach and this suggests the likely method of operation.*

Probably the coffin was brought from the deceased person's house, or from the LNC's premises, to Waterloo platform 11 or 12 at the appropriate time, and loaded onto the train. It seems most unlikely that the surviving hearse van, No. 1426, would have been specially used. The mourners would be provided with reserved compartments in the same train. Arrived at Brookwood station, the coffin and the mourners would join a motor hearse and limousine procession at the entrance to the cemetery and would proceed to the appropriate chapel or to the graveside.

Alternatively, the coffin could have been sent down to Brookwood by train a few days before the funeral itself and stored in the large mourners' waiting room at the appropriate cemetery station. The mourners and friends would then have assembled in the cemetery for the funeral service. Local recollection suggests that on occasion coffins and mourners were sent down to Brookwood by ordinary trains until the mid-1950s. Clearly the SR (and BR) remained interested in any funeral traffic from the LNC even without the Necropolis train. This attitude was reminiscent of the LSWR's in 1852 when the working arrangements between the two companies were explained before a Parliamentary Committee. The Secretary of the LSWR Company stated that the arrangements would continue forever 'because it is obviously in our interest to carry these bodies as long as they are brought to us.'

The Arrangements at the Cemetery

Originally, on arrival at Necropolis Junction, the engine was uncoupled, and the train pulled along the cemetery branch by black horses, probably complete with black ostrich plumes and suitably dressed outriders. In 1855, Richard Churchill, Secretary of the LNC, described the method of operation within the cemetery as follows:

That the Funeral Trains enter the Cemetery by a siding from the Main Line of the South Western Railway. . . . That on leave of the Main Line the Funeral Train is drawn by black horses.

---

* Whether the train was *en route* to Brookwood is not clear from the film.

Advertisement for burials in the Actors' Acre. *Author's Collection*

Above & right: Advertisement for burials in the Foresters' and Oddfellows' burial ground, and notice of the inauguration of the Foresters' ground in 1863.
Author's Collection

Below: Cover of the LNC brochure dated 1899. It includes a fanciful view of the cemetery and a funeral train entering the grounds. *Author's Collection*

When a correspondent from *The Builder* visited the cemetery in 1856, he described the journey to Brookwood:

> The train proceeds along the South-Western Railway to the branch line leading into the cemetery ... We descend at the station near to the chapel in the unconsecrated ground [i.e. North station], whilst some of the coffins are removed; and the train ... is drawn on by horses to the consecrated ground some distance further.

The second reference is a little unclear. It suggests either that the engine pushed the train into the cemetery as far as North station, after which the horses were used as the motive power; or that the horses pulled the train throughout. However the method of operating the funeral trains into the cemetery is clarified by a writer in *Cassell's Illustrated Family Paper* (1856) as follows:

> The train now stops, the funeral tender [i.e. hearse van] and carriages are cast off and sweep down by their own impetus, along a line of rails, to the station-house in the unconsecrated ground. Here they pause beside the wide asphalte pavement, from which, on the same level, the pretty low verandahed station, or rather refreshment house, diverges.

This clearly describes the use of gravity to move the train from the main line to North station, after which horse power prevailed. The use of horses was essential as there was no run-round loop on the branch at that time - it was just a single line feeding back into the cemetery from the down main line. Horses may also have been used because it was not thought appropriate to have noisy steam engines progressing through the cemetery whilst funerals were taking place, and because the track may have been laid very lightly to save money. It should be remembered that the line was in an area still very rural and that horses were essential for many of the tasks in and around the cemetery, like mowing, moving stones, etc. The lack of a run-round loop in the early years of the LNC's existence means the Necropolis train was almost definitely horse-drawn out of the cemetery and onto the LSWR, as there was no other means by which the locomotive could couple onto the London end of the train. This awkward system became unnecessary once the LSWR installed a run-round loop, in connection with the construction of Brookwood (Necropolis) station in 1864.

From this date the engine could propel the train through the cemetery from Necropolis Junction, under the supervision of the guard. Upon completion of the work in the cemetery, the engine drew the train from South to North station, and then onto the loop. There, the engine was uncoupled and it ran round the train, the shunting movements being supervised by the guard of the train and a member of staff from Brookwood (Necropolis) station. On being coupled to the other end of the train, the locomotive pushed it onto the down main line (or headshunt, in the junction arrangements dating from the turn of the century), crossed over to the up line and thence returned to London.

This series of movements was not invariably followed. Some authorities disliked the idea of an engine pushing a train of occupied passenger carriages. Under these circumstances, the locomotive would have run round the train before entering the cemetery (to ensure that the train was pulled rather than pushed over the branch), again whilst the funeral services were taking place and the train was empty (so that it did not matter that the engine pushed the carriages up to the loop), and once more when the train was leaving the cemetery *en route* for London. Only this complicated series of movements would ensure that the engine did not push the train, save when empty, and was employed on occasion.

As a result of the accident in May 1938 (*see Chapter Five*) some changes were made to the working arrangements within the cemetery. Before this date the instructions given in the *Western Section Appendix to the Working Timetable* read:

> The Necropolis train, on arrival at Brookwood, is run into the siding which lies parallel with the down local line, and from this siding the train is propelled to the cemetery under the supervision of the Guard of the train. Upon completion of the work in the cemetery the train is drawn forward to the loop line situated at the back of Brookwood Station signal box. The engine is there detached, and after running round the train, propels it to the siding, from whence it is drawn to the up line. The shunting operations are supervised by a member of the Brookwood Station staff.

The mode of operation as outlined above was amended from 23rd August, 1937, because over the years a number of complaints had been received from passengers at the delay on the return journey whilst the locomotive ran round the train at Brookwood. The instructions were changed from the first sentence of the extract quoted above to read:

> . . . After the passengers have alighted the train will draw back to the water column [beside the Masonry Works siding] for the engine to take water, and at 1.00 pm leave for the loop for the engine to run round, afterwards returning to the South Station for the 2.13 pm (SX Summer, Daily Winter) or 2.17 pm (SO Summer) to Waterloo . . .

To this was added, in May 1938, the following warning:

> When the train is being propelled in either direction, the Guard must keep a good lookout and at Aldershot Road [i.e.: Cemetery Pales] Level Crossing obtain a hand-signal from the Necropolis Company's Flagman before allowing the train to pass over the crossing.*

These changes were subsequently collated in the *No. 9 Supplement to the Western Section Appendix*.

North station (for Roman Catholics, Jews, Parsees, and other Dissenters) was soon reached after leaving Necropolis Junction. The train was met by staff of the LNC who escorted the mourners to the nearby chapel. The relevant hearse vans were carefully stopped opposite the peculiar 'dip' in the platform face, which helped the attendants unload the coffins from the lowest 'shelf' in the vans. The coffins were carefully placed onto a special hand-bier, drawn by the LNC's attendants, and taken to the relevant chapel.

If there were any ministers requested by the family to officiate at the last rites, they would also alight from the train.

It was left to the family of the deceased to decide what kind of service they desired and could afford. Usually, each party had a brief service in the chapel (third class funeral services were conducted *en masse* in the appropriate chapel), after which the coffin was taken to the graveside, attended by the mourners and the chaplain or minister who would perform the last rites. Sometimes, a more elaborate and expensive private service was held in the chapel, followed by the

---

* This amendment was issued as a direct consequence of the accident of 13th May, 1938 which is described in *Chapter Five*.

graveside ceremony. In some cases, the main part of the funeral service may already have taken place in London, either in the deceased's parish church or in the *Chapelle Ardente*, so that only the brief graveside ceremony took place.

A good impression of the funeral arrangements at Brookwood can be obtained from an account of the burial of the American actress 'Bonnie Goodwin',* as described in *The Era* (1907):

> The writer was much impressed at Miss Goodwin's funeral . . . Everything worked smoothly and in perfect decorum. Particularly was this noticeable at the graveside, where, in place of the old and often rather distressing method of lowering the coffin by ropes, a device called the 'National Burial Device' was in use, and, controlled by the funeral director, acted automatically when the time for committal arrived.

One of the greatest achievements of the LNC was its treatment of paupers. Every grave space - irrespective of class or cost - was 'private' in the sense of being shared with no-one else (save next of kin). For many years, Brookwood Cemetery was the only burial ground to observe this practice. The better classes of grave plots included the right to erect a memorial, to perpetuate the memory of the recently departed. Pauper graves remained anonymous and without a name; nevertheless the deceased pauper was buried decently and with the dignity of an individual grave space 9 ft by 4 ft. *The Undertakers' Journal* (1898) noted that:

> All the third-class or parish bodies are transferred to hearses drawn by three horses, capable of accommodating a matter of six or eight coffins, and the loading having been quickly done - but in unsentimental, workmanlike fashion - the biers are soon on their way to the respective graves.

The 'Actors' Acre' at Brookwood (plot 118) was largely used for the burial of actors and actresses who died in poverty. Yet, as *The Era* reported (in 1889):

> For the sum of £2 7s. 0d. the Necropolis Company furnish a respectable funeral, with elm coffin and all the usual accessories, convey it to a really private grave in a pretty cemetery, and there inter it with every decent rite.

Yet cheaper funerals were available. For instance, the price of a '2nd class grave' in the St Saviour's Southwark ground, inclusive of conveyance to Brookwood, 'interment fees, undertaker, bearers, and use of Velvet-pall', was £1.

A few untoward incidents are recorded in the LNC's Minute Books. For instance, in January 1890, the Revd Cater, the LNC's Anglican Chaplain, refused to allow another clergyman to perform the burial service. Almost a year later, the same employee was directed by the Board not to allow 1st and 2nd class funeral services to be taken into the chapel together.

After the burial service the mourners returned to the station perhaps, as suggested by one of the LNC's brochures:

> ... instead of having his mind disquieted by the unseemly bustle which invariably occurs in the crowded metropolitan cemeteries - instead of having his eyes shocked by acts of desecration of the dead ... [he] will feel invigorated by the refreshing breezes, wafted through trees, shrubs, and flowers; while his mind, lifted out of the depression to which it has for some time been subject, by a contemplation of the broad expanse of

---

* Mrs Bonnie Lizzie Barnard Lyon (1866-1907), whose stage name was 'Bonnie Goodwin'.

the picturesque and noble site of which their departed relative or friend has become a tenant ... he will hardly fail to acknowledge that even death is not bereft of consolation.

This beautiful, tranquil site was described further in another brochure:

... though trees have been planted in profusion, no mere turfing has been allowed to blot out the rich purple of the native heather, and the gorgeous masses of rhododendrons that make such a brave show in the early summer are in perfect harmony with the surrounding scene. Here indeed it seems impossible to realise that London is within 40 minutes by train, where only the glorious stretch of the Surrey Hills lies before our eyes. There is no crowding here; in many parts one comes on a grave with almost the same surprise as if it were in some private park, and there are quiet spots, shaded by trees and undergrowth, where none have yet been buried. Truly, it is just such a spot as mourners seek to lay to rest the one most dear to them; a place beautiful, 'far from the madding crowd' ... Trees of every kind flourish here; silver birches and copper beeches add beauty with their contrasting foliage, cypress trees and shrubs galore give warm shelter when the winds are cold, and stately wellingtonias stand like giant sentries keeping vigil over the sleepers till the great awakening. In addition the visitor will not fail to note the splendid show of flowers on every side, many of the graves being a mass of glowing bloom. Indeed, there is not a more beautiful cemetery in the whole world. In this respect it is safe to say that Brookwood Cemetery is unapproached, so that the whole effect produced is veritably a 'Garden of Sleep'.

At the station the mourners were shown to their private waiting room or communal room (for the cheapest funerals). All necessary conveniences were provided at each station, including a refreshment room where light luncheons could be obtained at a moderate charge - along with a wide selection of alcoholic beverages! As the correspondent from *The Era* explained:

In a hundred other ways those who use the Brookwood Necropolis will find their convenience studied by the company. . . . [It] extends to everything that pertains to the burial of the dead, from embalming, cremation, the making of coffins, the provision of mortuary chambers and *chapelle ardente*, conveyance with hearse and carriages, to the interment and the very gravestone itself.

A similar procedure as that described above was followed when the train reached South station, in the Anglican section of the cemetery.

The Necropolis train usually left South station for the return journey to London at 2.15 pm, and left Necropolis Junction at 2.30 pm. For most of the duration of the service the return trip took up to an hour, including the additional stops in the period 1890-1910; by the 1920s the journey time had been reduced to about 40 minutes.

The LNC and Cremation*

The first crematorium in modern Britain was built by the Cremation Society at St John's, Woking, in 1879. Due to various legal issues that needed to be clarified, it was not used for human cremations until March 1885. Despite the

* Much of the information for this section is based on Brian Parsons' research, now published as *Committed to the Cleansing Flame: The Development of Cremation in Nineteenth Century England* (Spire Books, 2005). I am very grateful to him for permission to quote from his book which forms a history of the early cremation movement in modern Britain and also the first history of Woking Crematorium.

potential threat to the LNC's business, the company was well placed to benefit from the crematorium being located nearby: railway fares on the Necropolis train were cheaper, coffins were also conveyed at special rates, the LNC could offer private station facilities at each end of the journey, it could provide transport onward to Woking Crematorium from the cemetery, whilst Brookwood Cemetery afforded a convenient location for the deposit of ashes.

In fact both horse-drawn transport and the railway were used to reach Woking Crematorium. In October 1885, the cremation of Charles Carpenter involved the use of a horse-drawn hearse from London to Woking; whilst in May 1887 the cremation of Roop Sing involved the use of a horse-drawn hearse to carry his coffin from Blackheath to Waterloo, where it was transferred onto an ordinary train to Brookwood station and thence by horse-drawn hearse to the crematorium.* Several early cremations involved the use of ordinary trains from Waterloo to Woking, where a locally supplied horse-drawn hearse would convey the coffin onwards to the crematorium. The firm of John Woods, using the stables of the 'Albion Hotel' next to Woking station, was invariably used for this task.

Despite the additional charges, rail transport to Woking was much cheaper than using horses. A hearse and pair of horses might cost between £5 and £6 for the journey, whereas the usual railway charge to Woking was £1 4s. 0d., assuming it was charged at the normal rate of 1s. per mile. The Cremation Society even advertised specific scheduled services from Waterloo to Woking in order to accommodate cremations, and this example is dated 1891:

Depart Waterloo	Hour of Cremation
9.30 am	11.00 am
11.45 am	1.30 pm
2.45 pm	4.15 pm

The Cremation Society also encouraged the use of Woking-based undertakers, rather than paying the expense of bringing assistants down from London on the train. The usual charge for local labour was 2s. 6d. and, with the use of the railway, the Cremation Society calculated a cremation at Woking would cost about £15 15s. 0d.

Yet for many years to come, cremation was the exception. This was partly due to the expense involved. Cremation at Woking cost £6 plus the funeral director's fees and the costs of transportation (see above). Early cremations at Woking cost from £9 3s. 8d. to over £50, whereas a second class grave in Brookwood Cemetery, with the right to erect a permanent memorial, cost just £1 10s. 0d. (including the railway fare). The LNC was not slow to realise it could benefit from this novel method of disposal, and in December 1889, Cyril Tubbs wrote to the Cremation Society requesting an interview concerning a scheme 'for the mutual benefit of both our Companies'. As correspondence in the Cremation Society's archive shows, the Society was keen to accommodate the LNC, partly to prevent them from building their own crematorium in Brookwood Cemetery. At a subsequent meeting of the LNC's Board of Directors, Tubbs reported that 'a substantial reduction in fees' had been agreed, whereby the LNC would offer

---

* The ashes of Roop Sing were subsequently buried in Brookwood Cemetery and were the first ashes to be buried there.

LONDON NECROPOLIS COMPANY, FUNERAL FURNISHERS,

Cremation

WITHIN THE METROPOLITAN RADIUS.

To those who desire this method of disposal of the dead THE NECROPOLIS COMPANY offers special advantages, as it undertakes the complete arrangements at the Crematorium of the Cremation Society of England at St. John's, Brookwood. The mourners and coffin travel by the Private Funeral Train from the Necropolis Station, in Westminster Bridge Road, to Brookwood Cemetery, thus avoiding all unnecessary publicity and delay.

Inclusive charge varies from £13 13s. to £26 5s., the following medium class being recommended for ordinary requirements.

CLASS C - (Including Cremation Society's) - £15 15 0.
Fee of £5

Special Cremation Shell. Hearse and Pair. Bearers to remove Body to Necropolis Funeral Station. Conveyance to Brookwood per Necropolis Train leaving Private Station 11.45 a.m. Hearse, Bearers, and one Carriage from Cemetery to Crematorium, and return to Brookwood or Woking. Plain Cinerary Urn for Ashes. Attendance of a Superintendent. Chaplain's Fee for Service at Crematorium (if required), One Guinea extra.

A selection of Ornamental Urns from £2 2s. to £10 10s. on view at Westminster Office.

Grave spaces at Brookwood Cemetery for Interment of Urns containing Ashes :—

PRIVATE GRAVE, £2 10s.   2nd CLASS GRAVE, £1.
INCLUDING CHAPLAIN'S FEE.

Charges for Funerals, see pages 14 and 15;

A Telegram at any hour to "TENEBRATIO, LONDON," secures the immediate attendance of a Trained Funeral Director, who will carry out all arrangements connected with Funerals and Cremations

LNC advertisement promoting cremation within the metropolitan radius, 1899.

a complete cremation package for £12 12s. 0d. to the trade and £16 16s. 0d. to the public on the following terms:

> [The LNC] will undertake to carry out every detail in connection with cremations for [the Cremation Society] . . . if your Society will send us any orders that come direct to you & will quote us a special rate at which you will do any cremations we may send to you. I think we may considerably assist your Society to become of greater use.
>
> I need hardly point out to you the advantage it will be for mourners &c to start from our private station where each party has a separate waiting room provided for them, instead of the bustle & rush at Waterloo. Again at Brookwood after an express journey [sic] without stoppage, they would arrive at our private station & start direct from there to your Crematorium, returning either by our train or an ordinary train. . . . Our regular trains start at 11.50 every Tuesday and Friday & generally at least two other days in the week, & on Sundays at 11.30.

The Cremation Society agreed, offering the LNC a reduction of 30 per cent on their normal cremation fee.

Early Cremations at Woking 1885-1897

Year	Total Cremations	By the LNC	
		Cremations	Ashes to Brookwood
1885	3	0	0
1886	10	0	0
1887	13	1	1
1888	28	0	0
1889	46	3	0
1890	54	15	3
1891	99	27	6
1892	104	35	14
1893	101	39	9
1894	125	51	21
1895	150	63	14
1896	137	52	22
1897	173	74	32

As the table indicates, this had an immediate effect on both companies' business, particularly in the late 1890s. The additional revenue created from this business was gained without any further investment by the LNC in its infrastructure, but by better use of its existing assets. This point was reinforced by the *Undertakers' Journal* which in 1897 commented: '[the LNC] are largely indebted to those who patronise cremation for passengers for their daily train'. Even after the Cremation Society opened its crematorium at Golders Green in 1902 the relationship continued to be of mutual benefit. This must have been a consideration when the LNC opened its own columbarium (a building designed for the reception of ashes) at Brookwood in 1910. Yet the LNC never constructed its own crematorium at Brookwood, despite various attempts, which might have further increased the number of funerals it arranged and consequently the use of the Necropolis train and the cemetery.*

---

* The nearest the LNC came to opening and operating its own crematorium was in 1946 and 1956 when private Acts of Parliament were obtained to allow this. Had either Act resulted in a crematorium at Brookwood, it is very likely the post-war decline in business would have been arrested and quite possibly reversed.

Telegrams:
Tenebratio, London.

LONDON NECROPOLIS COMPANY,

Telephone 839 Hop.

IN BROOKWOOD CEMETERY repose the remains of some of the most notable personages of the last fifty years. One striking feature in the Necropolis death-roll is the number of persons who have secured for themselves world-wide fame. Many distinguished men have selected their own resting-places here. The names of renowned Actors and Artists, Doctors and Divines, Laymen and Lawyers, Servants and Statesmen, Soldiers and Sailors, are conspicuous on the tombstones in almost every avenue.

Many Parishes, Guilds, Societies, and Communities have adopted special Allotments in this Cemetery, so that those who have lived and worked together may also rest together. Amongst them are the following, viz. :—

St. Mary, Kensington.
St. Mary Abbot, Kensington.
St. Saviour's (South London Cathedral).
St. Ann's, Westminster.
St. Margaret's, Westminster.
St. Alphage.
St. Martin's, Ludgate Hill.
Christ Church, Blackfriars Road.
Allhallows the Great.
St. Magnus, Fish Street Hill.
St. Alban's, Holborn.
St. Mildred, Bread Street.
St. Michael, Wood Street.
Hanover Chapel, Regent Street.
St. Mary-le-Strand.

The Parsees.
The Roman Catholics.
The Swedish Church.
The Sisterhood of St. John.
St. Joseph's Hospital.
The Order of Reparation.
St. John's House.
The London & South Western Railway.
The Chelsea Hospital Pensioners.
The Commissionaires.
The Dramatic Society.
The Oddfellows.
The Foresters.
Metropolitan Asylums Board.
Bakers.

St. Botolph, Aldersgate Street.

Funeral Train leaves Necropolis Private Station, Westminster Bridge Road, at 11.45 a.m. Sundays, 11.30 a.m.

'List of parishes &c' from a LNC brochure of 1899.

Chapter Five

Operation: Specials and Incidents

'No more beautiful burial-place could have been selected.'
(The Times)

Special Trains: (1) Before the Cemetery Opened

The system of operation described in the previous chapter was the normal service provided by the LNC for those who chose to be buried in the London Necropolis. In addition, there were occasions when the rich or famous chose Brookwood as a final resting place which sometimes warranted a special train - that is, one outside the normal scope of the LNC's service. Broun, in his *Necropolis*, envisaged his large Anglican chapel as a great Victorian Valhalla, a national memorial chapel to the greatest men and women in the kingdom, the 'National Mausoleum'. But the LNC, when it eventually struggled into existence, had little of this grandiose vision; yet special trains were operated with surprising frequency and a representative sample will be described here. The costs of arranging these trains were met by the executors of the deceased, and the standard charge for a 'special' appears to have been £15, excluding fares and the cost of conveying the body by rail.*

The Day Excursion to the Proposed Necropolis (1852)

The first special train ran to the site of the proposed London Necropolis in September 1852, less than three months after the passage of the private Act of Parliament. The train was arranged by the LNC so that representatives from London parishes could visit the site and decide for themselves about the accommodation at Woking. It was also designed to clarify that the proposed site was not the 'low dismal swamp' surrounding Woking station, but the 'elevated plateau' of Hook Heath nearly a mile beyond. The special train also provided proof that the distance involved, some 25 miles from Waterloo, could be covered in about 30 minutes.

The train was advertised as leaving Waterloo at 11.15 am on 14th September, 1852. The train also called at Vauxhall, and between 250-300 'gentlemen, mostly church wardens, overseers, poor-law officers, with a fair sprinkling of undertakers' were on board, the LNC providing free tickets for the excursion. The outward journey took about 45 minutes and the train stopped, incongruously, in the Goldsworth cutting shortly after noon. Incredibly, the visitors were invited to alight from the train (newspaper accounts do not make it clear if a temporary platform was provided) and then climb the side of the cutting by a narrow path previously prepared! Arrived at the top 'they found themselves on an elevated plateau commanding an extensive and variegated

---

* *See Chapter Seven* for more information about the charges for special trains.

view in every direction'. This was the site of Abraham's proposed Anglican section and the location of the National Mausoleum church. Plans of the site were distributed, and by means of coloured flags stuck in the ground at various points, the different parts of the proposed London Necropolis were indicated to the visitors:

> . . . where the entrance was to be, with the station, and the reception-rooms for arrivals and departures – where the lodge, where the church, the dissenting chapel, and (what seems as necessary to an Englishman as either) the hotel – where were the catacombs, and the monumental plateau for the dead – where the walls, the seats, and the alcoves for the living.

At about 2 pm a 'bountiful cold collation' was provided in a pavilion erected for the occasion. This was followed by speeches* and a further opportunity to explore the site. The party left at 5.30 pm, possibly via the existing footbridge near the Brookwood end of Goldsworth cutting, enabling the visitors to cross to the up line; otherwise they must have crossed the main line on foot. The special train arrived back in London shortly after 6 pm. The LNC was charged £30 for this train.

The Ceremony of Consecration (1854)

Over two years later, following the restructuring of the LNC, a special train ran just before the cemetery opened to the public. This conveyed a large number of the shareholders and Directors of the LNC to Woking for the ceremony of consecration. The Directors agreed that tickets should be available from the LNC's offices, free of charge. The Directors of the LSWR were invited to attend the consecration and the dinner afterwards. The special train carrying these guests left Waterloo at 12.30 pm on 7th November, 1854. Necropolis Junction was reached in three-quarters of an hour, after which the train, with driver Joseph Porter in charge,† was propelled through the cemetery grounds to South station. Shortly before 2 pm the Bishop of Winchester (the Right Revd Charles Sumner), attended by his Commissary, Dr Haggard, and the Registrar of the Diocese, Mr Rothery, arrived in his private carriage from Farnham Castle. The Bishop was received by the Chairman of the LNC (Mr Thomas Dakin), the Directors, and the local clergy. The Revd L. Humbert, Curate of St Olave's, Southwark, officiated as chaplain. After robing (probably using the chaplain's rooms in South station for this purpose), the Bishop proceeded to the Anglican chapel where Dr Haggard and Mr Rothery presented the Bishop with a petition and the plans of the cemetery, requesting him to consecrate the chapel and ground. The Bishop of Winchester then entered the chapel and, standing in the centre, recited prayers and the 49th Psalm. The sentence of consecration was

---

* During which Mr Voules (then effectively Chairman of the LNC) explained the reason for the scramble up the embankment was to disprove allegations that the site was damp and waterlogged. But it is difficult to understand why the LNC could not have arranged carriages from Woking station or, even easier, to request that the special train was stopped just beyond the Goldsworth cutting where guests would have avoided the 80 ft climb.
† See below, under the LSWR burial plots, for more information on Joseph Porter.

then read by the Commissary and signed by the Bishop, who gave it to his Registrar requesting him to enrol and preserve it in the Registry. Parts of the 39th Psalm were then sung, followed by further prayers. The Bishop then left the chapel, thereby ending the service.

Rather curiously, only a brief glance was given to the extensive grounds. The area immediately surrounding the chapel and South station had in fact been planted only a few days previously with laurels, bay trees, rhododendrons and cedars. A brief lunch in the station followed, after which the Directors and shareholders returned to London by train. One newspaper account records the train left the cemetery at 2.45 pm and arrived back in London about 4 pm; if correct, both the exploration of the grounds and the lunch must have been extremely hurried! Shortly after 5 pm the Directors and other interested parties sat down to 'an excellent dinner' at 'The Albion', Aldersgate Street, for the LNC's foundation banquet.

Special Trains: (2) After the Cemetery Opened

The Reburial of Human Remains from London Churches (1862 and later)

Brookwood Cemetery is sufficiently large to accommodate human remains from a number of London churches and burial grounds. One of the first major projects occurred in 1862 with the construction of the Charing Cross Railway. Due to the necessity of demolishing many houses to make way for the new railway viaducts, and the areas through which the railway would pass, the Act of Parliament authorising the work contained a number of clauses protecting a number of special interests, including the old St Thomas's Hospital.

Another special interest was Cure's College, which comprised almshouses and a burial ground off Park Street. The College was named after Thomas Cure, a local benefactor in the Tudor period. The Charing Cross Railway was obliged to purchase the whole site and provide new almshouses. Land was acquired in Hamilton Road, West Norwood, and the new almshouses for those displaced from the College were opened in 1863. During 1862 work began on clearing the old burial ground. A good impression of the amount of work involved can be obtained from the following letter sent in October 1862 by the Architect to the works, Edward Habershon, to Samuel Smiles, Secretary of the railway company:

> I have been very careful to keep down the cost or it would have been double from the almost incredible number of bodies buried in the ground. The following short data will give you an idea of the whole:
>
> There were at least 7,950 bodies removed. There were about 5,000 cubic yards of earth removed to the depth of 16 feet amidst an effluvium almost suffocating.
> Finding the number so enormous and that the cost of separate removals would be so great, I did it wholesale and had 220 very large cases made each containing 26 human bodies besides children and these weighed 4¾ cwt. There were 1,035 cwt of human

remains sent in these cases alone. These were conveyed in the night and the Cemetery Company made arrangements for them. Each body has cost us less than three shillings. It was fortunate that such reasonable terms could be made at Woking Cemetery. [*sic*]

A more horrible business you can scarcely imagine; the men could only continue their work by the constant sprinkling of disinfectant powder. Mine was no easy task for the Bishop, the Warden, the parishioners and particularly the relatives have watched the steps taken, and the interviews with people and the correspondence has been great but all are more satisfied than could be expected.

The proximity of the LNC's station must have been another advantage alongside the cost of under 3s. per body removed to Brookwood. However, even this modest charge earned the LNC at least £1,192 10s. 0d. The scale of this task underlines one of the principal reasons why the London Necropolis was opened: it was large enough to accommodate many more undertakings of this nature, and rid London of its plethora of insanitary burial grounds. No further details have been traced about the special trains used to convey the remains down to the cemetery at night, but given the use of 'very large cases', the hearse carriages cannot have been used for this purpose. The parochial authorities later arranged for a special service to be held in the cemetery where the remains were reburied, and some 70 parishioners attended. Today there is little evidence in the St Saviour's burial grounds of this enormous project; but some of the headstones in plots 88 and 90 are identifiable as originating from Cure's College (*see cemetery map inside rear cover*).

Further reburials at Brookwood took place from time to time, which must have made use of the cemetery railway. In chronological order they include human remains from St Margaret's, Westminster (1866); St Antholin, Budge Row (1874-75); All Hallows the Great & Less (1893-96); St Botolph Without, Aldersgate (1893-94); St Magnus the Martyr (1893-94); St Martin's, Ludgate Hill (1893-94); St John, Clerkenwell (1894); St Peter's, Walworth (1894); the Hanover Chapel (1896-97); St Michael, Wood Street (1896-97); the Charterhouse (1898); St Mary-le-Strand (1898); St Mildred, Bread Street (1898); St George the Martyr, Southwark (1899); St Clement Danes (1900); St George's, Botolph Lane (1904); Holy Trinity, Kingsway (1909); St Olave, Tooley Street, Southwark (*c*.1927-28); and St George's, Southwark (1940).*

Revd Alexander Heriot Mackonochie (1825-1887)

The Revd Mackonochie, the first curate of St Alban the Martyr, Holborn, died in an atrocious blizzard whilst walking the Bishop of Argyll's dogs (Righ and Speireag) in the Mamore Forest, near Ballachulish, on Thursday 15th December, 1887. Due to the appalling weather, his body was not found for two days, half buried in the snow and guarded still by the two dogs.

His body was brought first to Kinloch (now Kinlochleven) and thence to the Bishop of Argyll's house in Ballachulish. On Tuesday 20th December, 1887, Mackonochie's coffin of plain Scots pine was taken by steamer to Oban, and thence by overnight train to Euston, arriving in London at 8 am on the 21st. A

---

* This is not an exhaustive list. For instance, the following projects will have used road transport for the removal of human remains: St Swithin, London Stone (1958); St Marylebone (1983); and St Michael's Fish Street Hill (1987).

plain hearse met the train, and proceeded to St Alban's, where his body rested prior to the funeral. This took place on Friday 23rd December at 10 am, with a 'low mass' followed, at 11 am, by a solemn requiem mass, in a very crowded church. Afterwards, at about 11.45 am, a massive procession formed:

> First came the Crucifer, . . . he was supported by two men to relieve him from time to time. Next followed members of the Choir, and after them came some fifty Clergy in cassocks and surplices. Then the hearse, preceded by two Acolytes, bearing lighted tapers in lanterns, cresset fashion. The pall-bearers were the Revs. R.A.J. Suckling, A.H. Stanton, F.F. Russell, G.R. Hogg, H.T. Howes, H.G. Maxwell, E.A. Harris, J.W. Doran, E. Ibbotson, and L.S. Wainwright. Relatives and other principal mourners immediately followed the hearse, and after them came the Parochial Guilds and the general Congregation. . . . Since the days when Puritanism first robbed the Church of her spectacular teaching . . . no such priest's funeral had, probably, been seen in the streets of London. . . . Punctually at one o'clock the solemn cortège started on its way . . . the choir beginning the hymn 'Hark! hark! my soul'. At this time Brooke Street is crowded with spectators . . .

Mackonochie's coffin was beautifully decorated with flowers, and flanked by lighted candles. The procession continued along Brooke Street, High Holborn, Kingsway, the Strand, Waterloo Bridge, and on to the LNC's private station. From there the coffin, accompanied by 478 mourners, travelled by special train down to Brookwood Cemetery. On arrival at South station, the procession was re-formed and made its way through the cemetery grounds to the parish burial ground, which Mackonochie had done so much to secure for St Alban's through its burial society (which still exists). The brief service at the graveside was led by the Revd Arthur Stanton, and the service concluded with the singing of 'Lead, kindly light'. It was a fine winter's afternoon as Mackonochie was laid to rest near the foot of the great memorial cross within the St Alban's ground in plot 46. Members of the Church of England Working Men's Society, at their own request, filled the grave with earth.

Charles Bradlaugh (1833-1891)

Charles Bradlaugh was one of the most controversial public figures in 19th century Britain, who championed such unpopular ideas as atheism, birth control, republicanism, reform, peace and anti-imperialism. He is chiefly remembered for claiming the right of MPs to affirm (rather than swear) the oath when taking their seat in Parliament. Bradlaugh died on 30th January, 1891 and his funeral took place on 3rd February.

The day before, Bradlaugh's coffin was conveyed from his home in St John's Wood to a private mortuary in the York Street station and was watched over day and night by a Marshal of the Secular Society. The coffin was subsequently conveyed to Brookwood on the morning of 3rd February by the normal Necropolis train. Over 5,000 mourners, from all over the country and from all walks of life, turned up and jammed the approach roads to Waterloo in an attempt to attend the funeral. During the early afternoon three special trains, the first of which consisted of 17 carriages, were provided by the LSWR to

accommodate those wishing to travel down to Brookwood. The funeral was notable for the absence of conventional mourning dress (only Mrs Annie Besant arrived in black and heavily veiled) and the lack of any formal ceremony at the graveside. As *The Northampton Mercury* recorded:

> It was a silent funeral, and yet how eloquent ... Thousands came from London, and many came from North and South, East and West, to witness the silent burial of one of England's greatest sons. 'Slowly and sadly they laid him down', with no words of man to break the solemnity of the scene or to mar its impressive significance.

The mourners included the young David Lloyd George (later Prime Minister) and John Morley (Gladstone's great friend and biographer). Most of London's resident Indian population attended because Bradlaugh had been sympathetic to the cause of Indian self-government, and was unofficially known as the 'MP for India'. Amongst this group was the young Mohandas Gandhi, and he witnessed another bizarre aspect of this unusual funeral. As Gandhi was returning from the graveside, and awaiting the return train to London, he overheard a heated argument that took place between a 'champion atheist' and one of the clergymen present. All this probably took place on or near the platform of North station.

Bradlaugh is buried in a family grave in plot 108, just off Holly Avenue. He is buried alongside his wife, sister-in-law, grandson and daughter. His memorial was the first public testimonial to his memory, consisting of a bronze bust by the sculptor Francis Verheyden atop a red granite pedestal designed by W.L. Sugden and made by J.J. Millson of 24 City Road, Manchester. Mr Sugden also designed the decorative cast-iron railings which surround the tomb. It was erected at a cost of £225 (plus extras), a sum raised absolutely spontaneously without a single appeal or request. The monument was completed in early 1893 and the National Secular Society arranged a special train for the convenience of those who wished to inspect it. This was advertised by Bradlaugh's daughter, Hypatia Bradlaugh Bonner, in the pages of *The National Reformer*:

> I have arranged with the Necropolis Company to run a special train to Brookwood on Sunday, March 5th., at cheap fares. The 3rd class return will be 2s., or half the ordinary rate. The train will leave the Necropolis Company's station, Westminster Bridge Road, (at the back of, though not in communication with, the Waterloo terminus of the London and South Western Railway) at 11.30, and call at Clapham Junction a few minutes later. Tickets will be obtainable at the Necropolis Company's station at the time; but those getting in at Clapham Junction can have their tickets supplied by the guard on the train. The Special will leave the Cemetery for the return journey at 2.30. It would be convenient if those who determine to go would send me a post card . . . as I can then acquaint the Company approximately as to how many they will have to provide accommodation for.

This visit was well attended. Mary Reed, one of those who travelled down to Brookwood on this train, subsequently wrote:

> The general verdict seemed in favour of the profile view of the head as seen from the right side; for in that aspect the set of the head and shoulders is most characteristic of

Mr Bradlaugh. . . . And the monument stands out there in unpretending dignity, eight and twenty miles from the great city, and on ground unconsecrated save as Nature herself consecrated it of her best; with the song of birds, the stir of insect life, and the breath and ceaseless murmur of the pines, all around . . . an enduring witness to the men and women that are to come of what manner of man this was, whose like we in our generation shall not see again.

This visit started a custom by the National Secular Society to visit the grave periodically. The inaugural visit was followed in July 1893 by an 'official visit', when the special train left Waterloo (not the private station) at 11.30 am for Brookwood and returning at 4 pm, and this appears to have become the usual timing for the event.

Unfortunately the memorial as it survives is incomplete. During the night of 12th-13th September, 1938, the bust was mysteriously removed. The incident was so timed to embarrass delegates of the International Congress of the World Union of Freethinkers, then convening in London, and who were due to visit the memorial later on the 13th. A total 142 people travelled down on the Necropolis train to pay their respects at Bradlaugh's grave, only to witness the vandalised memorial. It must have taken at least two men to remove the bust, but no trace of it has ever been found.*

Viscount Sherbrooke (1811-1892)

In the following year the death of Viscount Sherbrooke was the occasion for another special train. Sherbrooke, as Robert Lowe, is remembered for his opposition to the Second Reform Bill (1866-67), when he argued the case against democracy. He became Chancellor of the Exchequer (1868-73) in Gladstone's first Government, and was subsequently Home Secretary (1873-74). In 1880 he was created Viscount Sherbrooke and held no further major political post.

Viscount Sherbrooke died at his home in Warlingham, Surrey, on 27th July, 1892. The funeral was held a few days later on 3rd August. That morning, at 8.30 am, the cortège left his home, Sherbrooke House, for the local station. A detachment of police acted as escort, whilst the papier-mâché 'earth-to-earth' coffin,† covered in violet velvet and embellished with a silver cross and tablet, was followed by his widow and other relatives and members of his household in carriages. A large number of villagers and tenants followed on foot. Warlingham station was on the South Eastern Railway, and lay but a few hundred yards from Sherbrooke's home. Prior arrangements had been made with the railway company for the journey to London. The coffin was placed in a carriage (possibly a horsebox, luggage or milk van), whilst the mourners were provided with two saloon coaches. All these vehicles were attached to the 9 am ordinary up train. The extra carriages were detached from the rest of the train upon arrival at Waterloo Junction (now Waterloo East). Here, a LSWR locomotive hauled the coaches over the special single line connecting Waterloo Junction with Waterloo proper, and thence to the LNC's private station. There

---

* Except that an entry in the LNC Ledger Book No. 26 (8th May, 1938) shows that the bust was found and replaced on its pedestal shortly afterwards. What its subsequent fate was remains a mystery.

† A perishable coffin, widely promoted by the LNC for more sanitary burial.

it was connected to other carriages which contained other friends and mourners, who had chosen to join the train in London. Details of the locomotive which took this train to Brookwood are not recorded; because it was a special train, it may well have been hauled by an express engine. The train left the Necropolis station shortly afterwards, and arrived at South station in the cemetery at about 11.30 am.

Preceded by the Revd Neville Sherbrooke, who read the service, the coffin was removed from the train and carried into the Anglican chapel, where the first part of the burial service was conducted. Thence it was borne through the cemetery grounds to St Mark's Avenue, where the remains of Viscount Sherbrooke's first wife rest. *The Times* suggested that 'no more beautiful burial-place could have been selected'. Here an ordinary earth grave had been prepared, the sides of which were concealed by bracken leaves and knots of white dahlias, lilies, roses, chrysanthemums, and geraniums. Beside this grave the burial service was concluded. Among the large number of floral tributes was a beautiful wreath of delicate violet coloured orchids from Lady Sherbrooke. Shortly before noon the mourners and friends were leaving the cemetery in the special train. Viscount Sherbrooke is buried in plot 31 in the cemetery, near the junction of St Mark's Avenue with St George's Avenue.

Friederich Engels (1820-1895)

Friederich Engels was the joint founder, with Karl Marx, of modern communism. They co-operated in writing the *Communist Manifesto* (1848), whilst from 1870 to Marx's death in 1883, Engels spent much of his time assisting Marx with his research and writing of *Das Kapital*. Work on this was only completed in 1894. Engels died in London on 5th August, 1895. In his will, Engels declared his wish to be cremated and his ashes scattered at sea. His funeral service took place on Saturday 10th August in what *The Times* referred to as 'one of the waiting-rooms' in the LNC's York Street station. His family, friends and comrades, around 150 people all told, gathered around his coffin where 'eloquent eulogies on Engels's character and work were delivered' by Mr Justice Moore (one of the executors and joint translator of *Das Kapital*), Hermann Engels (Engels' nephew), Wilhelm Liebknecht (editor of *Vörwarts* and one of the founders of the German Sozialdemokratische Arbeiterpartei), and Paul Lafargue (member of the French Chamber of Deputies and son-in-law of Karl Marx) amongst others. It was perhaps fortunate that due to certain formalities with the death certificate, the journey to Brookwood was delayed, allowing more time for these tributes. Engels' coffin was covered with flowers and wreaths, on the red ribbons of which the socialists of Germany, Austria, France, Britain, Italy, Belgium, Holland, Russia, Poland and Bulgaria expressed gratitude to their teacher and leader, and their profound grief at his passing. The cremation was originally planned to take place at 1.15 pm at Woking, but the delay meant the special train did not leave London until after 3 pm, and did not arrive at North station until after 4 pm. Most of the mourners and all the ladies remained there, and only 12 people proceeded in two carriages to the crematorium. No service took place, and the coffin was transferred from the hearse to the furnace with the minimum of delay. *The Times* reported that 'contrary to the usual practice most of the members of the party were allowed to go inside the crematorium but none of them waited till the cremation was concluded'. Afterwards, Engels' ashes were removed from the crematorium and temporarily deposited somewhere within Brookwood Cemetery, possibly in the Nonconformist chapel. On 27th August the urn was taken to Eastbourne by a few close friends and consigned to the waves about five sea miles off Beachy Head on what proved to be a stormy day.

Eleanor Marx (1855-1898)

Eleanor Marx was the youngest daughter of Karl Marx. She committed suicide in Sydenham on 31st March, 1898. She lived with Dr Edward Aveling, although was not legally married to him. Dr Aveling's second marriage was the immediate cause of Eleanor's death, although this was never mentioned at her inquest. Eleanor's funeral service took place on Tuesday 5th April at the Necropolis station where a large number of mourners gathered around the coffin in what was probably the same room where Friederich Engels' coffin had rested. Her coffin was covered with handsome wreaths from various socialist organisations in Britain and on the continent, and also from close friends. Several short addresses were delivered, but there was considerable ill feeling over the presence of Dr Aveling. Those present, who heard Dr Aveling had attended a football match on the day before the funeral, were shocked by his callousness. Many of those present travelled on the Necropolis train to Brookwood Cemetery, and onward to Woking Crematorium.

Eleanor's ashes were not claimed by Dr Aveling, and for many years were kept in the offices of the Social Democratic Federation in London. In 1920 they were transferred to the headquarters of the Communist Party of Great Britain. The following year, when the police raided the premises, they for some reason removed the ashes. Later the urn was returned and deposited in the Karl Marx Memorial Library in Clerkenwell Green. Eventually, in 1956, when a new family grave was erected in Highgate Cemetery, her ashes were at last laid to rest with her father.

Sir Henry Morton Stanley (1841-1904)

Stanley remains a famous explorer and journalist, perhaps best remembered for finding Dr Livingstone at Ujiji on 10th November, 1871. Stanley died on 9th May, 1904, at No. 2, Richmond Terrace, Whitehall, and was granted what was tantamount to a state funeral in Westminster Abbey on 17th May, just like Dr Livingstone. However, the Dean of Westminster refused to allow the burial of Stanley's mortal remains in the Abbey. The funeral arrangements were undertaken by the LNC and this must have been one of the most prestigious funerals the company ever conducted. Large numbers of people gathered in the neighbourhood of the Abbey to watch the procession pass. At 11.30 am Stanley's coffin was placed on an open funeral carriage drawn by four horses and, escorted by the pall bearers, the funeral procession went to the Abbey by way of Parliament Street, Parliament Square and Broad Sanctuary. At 11.40 am his coffin was taken into the Abbey by the west cloister door, proceeded down the south aisle, passing into the central aisle near the west door. It was then carried up the nave, pausing briefly by Livingstone's grave, and into the choir. The main part of the service began at noon, conducted by the Dean of Westminster, the Sub-Dean, and others. Afterwards, at 12.45 pm, the procession left the Abbey through the west aisle of the north transept and the north door. Stanley's coffin was again placed on the funeral carriage and borne to the LNC's private station by way of Parliament Square, Bridge Street, and Westminster Bridge Road, thus taking Stanley's body to North Lambeth, his former Parliamentary constituency. At the LNC's station a special train was provided to carry his body and the mourners to Brookwood. This train left the private terminus at 2.25 pm and reached North station at 3.30 pm, allowing a very generous timing for the journey. At the station, Stanley's coffin was placed in a hearse, whilst the mourners followed on foot to the cemetery gates, where carriages were waiting to take them to Pirbright Church, just over a mile away. As the cortège passed cottages on the way, and those in the village, all blinds were drawn and every shop was shut as a mark of respect. Near the church, the road was lined with villagers. The simple ceremony at the graveside began at 3.50 pm, and was conducted by the Revd Arthur Krause, Vicar of Pirbright. Those mourners who were returning to London journeyed back to North station, where the special train was waiting. It departed at 4.25 pm and arrived back in London at 5.15 pm.*

Lord Edward Pelham-Clinton (1836-1907)

Lord Edward was the second son of the 5th Duke of Newcastle. He had a distinguished career in the army, and retired in 1880. Between 1881-94 he was Groom-in-Waiting to Queen Victoria, and succeeded Sir John Cowell as Master of the Queen's Household in 1894. Lord Edward was involved with the domestic arrangements for foreign royalty visiting London for the Diamond Jubilee celebrations in 1897. He was at Osborne during the Queen's last illness and, at King Edward VII's express wish, was the only commoner present at the private burial of the Queen in the Royal Mausoleum at Frogmore on 4th February, 1901. At the time of his death, Lord Edward was Groom-in-Waiting to King Edward VII. He died at his London home, 81, Eccleston Square, and the King and Queen, along with the Prince and Princess of Wales, sent messages of deep sympathy to his niece, Mrs Farnham.

Lord Edward's funeral took place on Saturday 13th July, 1907, when a special train left the LNC's station at 1.50 pm. It arrived in good time for the funeral service, which commenced at 3 pm in the cemetery. Canon Morris, of St Gabriel's Church, Warwick Square, officiated. King Edward VII was represented by General Sir Godfrey Clerk, and the Prince and Princess of Wales

---

* The times quoted are taken from the order of service published in *The Times* for 16th May, 1904.

The splendid bronze memorial to Lady Matilda Jane Pelham-Clinton (c.1825-1892) near the Anglican chapel, late 1890s. Note that an engine can just be seen in the shrubs to the left of the chapel. The monument has recently been listed Grade II*.   *Author's Collection*

by the Hon. Sir William Carrington. Twenty-four boys from King Edward's School, Witley, of which Lord Edward was a governor, also attended. At the same time, a memorial service was held in St Gabriel's Church, led by the Revd J.H.J. Ellison, Vicar of Windsor, and Canon Sheppard, Sub-Dean of the Chapels Royal. The special train left the cemetery at 3.55 pm. Lord Edward is buried in plot 4 with his wife, Lady Matilda Jane, who had died in October 1892. After her death, Lord Edward commissioned a splendid bronze statuary group entitled '*Into the Way of Peace*', which has been described as one of the most dramatic of any English cemetery group. In September 2004 this monument was listed Grade II* by the Department of Culture, Media and Sport.

Dugald Drummond (1840-1912)

Dugald Drummond was the LSWR's Mechanical Engineer from mid-1895, and its Chief Mechanical Engineer from 1905. The events surrounding his death were dramatic. In early November Drummond, at the age of 73, severely scalded one of his legs. The leg had to be amputated, and Drummond died at home the day after the operation, on the evening of 7th November, 1912.

His funeral took place on Monday November 11th. A special train conveying the mourners from London left the Necropolis station at 2.30 pm. It was hauled by a 'D15' class 4-4-0, the last locomotive class Drummond designed. The

'D15' class 4-4-0 No. 463 in photographic grey livery. This locomotive hauled Dugald
Drummond's funeral train on 11th November, 1912.   *Author's Collection*

engine used, No. 463, was the first of the class. This train, surely a unique tribute
to a locomotive engineer, stopped at Surbiton *en route* to the cemetery to pick up
the mortal remains of Mr Drummond. A party of engine drivers acted as pall
bearers and carried the coffin from his home 'Morven', on South Bank, to the
train. A van had been provided for the coffin and was full of beautiful wreaths
which, as *The South Western Gazette* commented, 'bore striking testimony to the
respect and esteem in which Mr Drummond was held by his colleagues and
subordinates'. One of these wreaths, given by the locomotive staff at Nine Elms,
was of an engine made from white chrysanthemums with the letters 'L&SWR'
worked in violets on each side. The service was conducted by Canon Skelton,
Anglican chaplain to the LNC, assisted by the Revd J.H.S. Taylor, senior curate
of St Mark's, Surbiton. Amongst the 350 persons present at the funeral, which
included over 200 employees of the LSWR and a number of children from the
LSWR's Servants' Orphanage at Woking (of which Drummond was one of the
original trustees), were his brother Peter Drummond (Locomotive
Superintendent of the Highland Railway, who had moved to the Glasgow &
South Western Railway in 1912), Mr W. Bishop, Mr Jacomb Hood, Mr A.
Szlumper, Mr R. Urie, Mr J. Vickery (representing the General Manager of the
LSWR), Mr Surrey Warner, and Mr George F. West. Drummond's grave is in
plot 38, off Church Avenue, close to the site of South station.

The memorial, consisting of a celtic cross set in a large kerbed plot, has been
sadly neglected in recent years. I decided to launch an appeal for funds through
the South Western Circle, the historical society for the LSWR. This call was
answered by the Co-operative Funeral Service, whose Public Affairs Manager,
Geoffrey Simpson, agreed to undertake the necessary restoration work. This
was successfully completed in November 1994. On Saturday 29th April, 1995, a

The striking headstone commemorating the life of fireman John Spencer, who was accidentally killed on the LSWR in October 1865. *Author*

The grave of Dugald Drummond (1840-1912) in Church Avenue, Brookwood Cemetery. The memorial was fully restored by Co-operative Funeral Services at the end of 1994. *Author*

brief service of re-dedication was held at the graveside. This was attended by some of Mr Drummond's grandchildren and great-grandchildren, representatives from the Woking Homes, the South Western Circle, the Brookwood Cemetery Society, and other interested groups.

The LSWR Burial Plots

The LSWR Company chose Brookwood as a burial ground for its deceased employees, and distinct areas were set aside for the burial of the company's Officers and Servants within the cemetery. Three principal areas were used: the 'L&SWR 1st class' area (plot 47), the 'L&SWR 2nd class' area (plot 48), and an area for Nonconformists adjacent to plots 125 and 134. Other areas were used, but were not exclusively reserved for the LSWR Company.

Amongst the ex-LSWR employees buried at Brookwood are (in plot 47): Henry Bricknell (c.1826-1871), who died 'from injuries received whilst in the performance of his duty at Clapham Junction'; Miles James Chilton (c.1841-1869), for 'several years a fireman on the LSW Railway'; Edwin Furber (c.1828-1871), Inspector, who 'was accidentally killed while in the performance of his duty at Clapham Junction'; Charles Edwin Furber (c.1857-1895), Station Master at Parkstone; Charles Hatcher (c.1828-1892), 'Station Master of North Camp & Ash Vale, SWR'; George Ireland (c.1816-1867), 'formerly of Waterloo Station'; George T. Maynard (c.1844-1916), 'for 50 years in the employ of the LSWR as Signalman, Inspector and Station Master'; James Richard William Maynard (c.1852-1934), 'late Station Master of Wandsworth Town, for 51 years in the service of LSWRyCo.'; John Thomas Middleton (c.1848-1866), 'late of Waterloo Station … this stone was erected by friends of the deceased as a memento of respect'; Samuel Norwood (c.1824-1874), 'late Chief Inspector SWRy'; Joseph Palmer (c.1848-1922), 'for 48 years in the L&SWRly service retiring November 1914 as Chief Inspector, Nine Elms Goods Station'; William Perry (c.1845-1917), 'Inspector at Clapham Junction'; James Turner Smith (1835-1884) 'late Inspector at Waterloo Station L&SWRy'; and George Tubbs (c.1831-1890), a Sergeant in the LSWR police, who was accidentally killed while on duty at the Nine Elms Goods Depot on 8th April, 1890.

Two memorials are worthy of note in this plot. First there is the striking headstone commemorating the life of John Spencer (c.1838-1865), a fireman 'who met his death by accident while engaged as a fireman on the L & SWR at Winchester on 11th October 1865'. This tragic accident took place on the 7.15 pm up train from Southampton and it appears that Spencer climbed onto the rear of the tender to relieve himself and was unaware of the approaching overbridge close to St Cross tunnel. He was killed instantly by the impact with the bridge. His memorial, which is the earliest one in this plot, includes a carving of a Beattie locomotive of the period, *Firebrand*, which is presumably the one upon which Spencer lost his life.

Secondly there is the headstone of the Porter family. Joseph Porter (1822-1885) worked on the LSWR his whole life, starting as a flag boy when the railway was being laid across Wandsworth Common, and ending up as engine

Above: Detail of the Beattie locomotive Firebrand on John Spencer's headstone. *Author*

Right: Joseph Porter (1822-1885), driver of the first train into Brookwood Cemetery.
Courtesy of Derek & Sheila Heasman

inspector at Nine Elms. During his career he befriended Joseph Beattie and, according to family legend, was the driver of the first train that ran into Brookwood Cemetery. This was the special conveying Directors and shareholders of the LNC and LSWR for the ceremony of consecration on 7th November, 1854.

Amongst those buried in plot 48 are: William Gude (c.1852-1938), who served the LSWR for 50 years, latterly as Foreman at Nine Elms goods station, and who was one of the original founders of the London & South Western Railway Servants' Orphanage; William H. Hilditch (c.1843-1908), 'for 23 years Station Superintendent at Waterloo', whose headstone has now sadly collapsed; Albert Holden (c.1841-1905), for '43 years a faithful servant of the L&SWRy'; Andrew Henry Moore (c.1857-1909), 'late Station Master Wimbledon L & SWRy, who passed away 24th July 1909, aged 52, the last of Sir H.M. Stanley's expedition up the Congo in 1879'; and Richard Sims (c.1832-1892) for '40 years Parcel Clerk at Waterloo'.

The plot in the Nonconformist section has very few memorials, but includes James Greetham, 'who lost his life on the LSWR, 4th September 1896'; and William Phillips (c.1830-1888), a locomotive inspector. Also buried here, but in an unmarked grave, is John Stamp (c.1858-1911), a constable in the LSWR police. He died from a heart condition whilst on duty at Esher station on a very hot day in July 1911.

Those buried elsewhere in the cemetery grounds tend to include more senior officials. In addition to Dugald Drummond they include: Thomas Bent (died 1869), 'late Police Superintendent of the London & South Western Railway' (plot 32); Samuel Bircham (1838-1923), Solicitor to the LSWR for nearly 30 years (plot 31); Lewis Crombie (c.1800-1880), Secretary of the LSWR 1853-62 (plot 32); and Charles Tompkins (died 1899), 'late Station Master of Brookwood' (plot 108). William Frederick Godson (1807-1867), who rose from chief booking clerk at Nine Elms to become Superintendent of the Line, and was latterly responsible for the safety of the Royal Train between Gosport and Basingstoke when Queen Victoria travelled from Osborne House to Windsor, is also buried in the cemetery. When Godson died, his body was accompanied to Brookwood by some 400 'brother officers and servants' (plot 32). Edgar William Verrinder (1837-1893) also worked his way up from a junior clerk at Woking to become Superintendent of the Line in 1874. Verrinder was taken ill after supervising one of Queen Victoria's journeys from Windsor to Gosport. He died shortly afterwards, on the afternoon of Sunday 23rd July, 1893. His death was widely reported in the national and local press. At his funeral, two special trains conveyed the Directors, chief officers, and staff of the LSWR from Waterloo to Brookwood. His coffin was carried from the funeral train to the grave in torrential rain by a number of inspectors, between lines of uniformed staff said to be up to six deep in places. In addition to the LSWR dignitaries (which included a host of station masters from as far away as Barnstaple and Torrington), many other railway companies were represented. In all it was estimated that over 3,000 staff attended the funeral (plot 32). Nearby is buried George Turner White (c.1853-1899), who succeeded Verrinder as Superintendent of the Line in 1893 (plot 32).

The Burial of American Servicemen (1942-44, and 1948)

During World War II, the Brookwood American Military Cemetery was extended. This section was originally opened in 1929 as the principal military cemetery in Britain for American casualties from World War I. Burials of Americans who died in England began in April 1942. As many US troops were based in the West Country, a railway service for the conveyance of bodies operated from Devonport to Brookwood. Bogie utility vans were normally used to carry the coffins and these vans were attached to suitable up services as required, normally being coupled next to the engine. The vans returned to Devonport attached to down newspaper trains. It is likely that many of the 946 casualties from 'Operation Tiger' - the secret D-Day rehearsal off Slapton Sands, Devon, where a convoy of landing craft was ambushed by German E-boats - were removed to Brookwood for burial in this way. Similarly, the 19 American servicemen executed at Shepton Mallet Prison for various offences during the war would have been conveyed to Brookwood Cemetery by rail, for subsequent burial in unmarked graves in the isolated 'plot x' behind the American Memorial Chapel. By August 1944 over 3,600 bodies had been laid to rest in the extended American Military Cemetery, in areas now occupied by the Italian prisoners of war, the Russia Memorial, and the Free French. From this date, burials at Brookwood ceased, and a new American Military Cemetery was created at Madingley, just outside Cambridge.

In 1948 the American authorities requested permission to remove the bodies of those servicemen buried between 1942 and 1944, including those conveyed to Brookwood from Devonport, and those buried in 'plot x'. As by this time the cemetery railway had been removed, temporary platforms were erected on the Bisley Camp branch, about a mile from Brookwood station and on the Bisley Camp side of the Cowshot Road level crossing, to facilitate this operation. Under the usual procedures of the American Battle Monuments Commission, the next of kin were able to request the repatriation of the body for burial in America; otherwise, the bodies were transferred to the new Military Cemetery at Madingley. However, the 19 bodies from 'plot x' were moved to a special 'dishonoured' plot in the American Military Cemetery at Oisne-Aisne in France, in a section of the grounds not normally accessible to visitors. There was just one exception to this, the body of Private David Cobb, a 21-year-old black American who was executed on 12th March, 1943. His body was claimed by his mother as early as 22nd March, 1943, which resulted in the subsequent repatriation of his body. This eventually took place on 31st March, 1949 using a padlocked casket. His body was finally laid to rest in April 1949 in an unmarked grave in North Highland Street Cemetery, Dothan, Alabama.

Charles Bradlaugh's memorial in its original state, complete with the bronze bust by Francis Verheyden and the bronze wreath beneath.   *Author's Collection*

Accidents and Incidents

En route to and from Brookwood Cemetery

An accident involving the Necropolis train took place at Surbiton station on the afternoon of Thursday 14th April, 1864. The train was returning to London, having left the cemetery slightly earlier than usual, at 2.25 pm. It comprised three passenger carriages and a brake van, whilst the engine was running tender first due to the absence of a turntable at Brookwood. It passed Surbiton distant signal, about 1,300 yards from the station, at 30 mph (according to the fireman) and at 'not much less than 60 mph' (according to the guard). The driver did not shut off steam until after he passed the distant (which was 'on'); furthermore the home signal was also 'on', but he could not see it clearly because coal dust from the tender flew in his eyes. Almost at the same time the driver noticed there was a horsebox standing on the main line in the station. He told the fireman to apply the tender brake, but the screw thread stripped; the driver then attempted to reverse the engine, but the reversing lever became strained and would not move. The tender hit the horsebox at 20 mph (according to the driver) or 50 mph (according to the guard).

The horsebox was certainly struck with great force: its roof and part of the body were forced back over the tender, bending the weather board and fracturing the gauge glass on the engine. Other debris was pushed for over 600 yards before stopping. The three 'valuable horses' in the horsebox were killed, whilst the platform canopy, which was supported by wooden columns just 4 feet from the platform edge, was also demolished.

The driver, fireman and guard agreed that the distant signal was only partially turned to danger. It was one of the semi-disc signals, then in common use on the LSWR and, as Captain Tyler reported in the aftermath of the accident, 'is not so clearly visible at any time, but especially when it is not properly turned to danger, as a good sized semaphore'. The driver had been driving for 10 years on the LSWR and had 'an excellent character'. He had driven the Necropolis train once or twice a week for some six years. He was probably driving too fast on this occasion, but was disadvantaged by the ambiguous signal, the loss of the tender brake, and the weak reversing lever on his engine. The horsebox had been detached from the noon passenger train from Portsmouth, due at Surbiton at 2.25 pm. However, it reached Surbiton at 2.38 pm when the horsebox was detached. Had the groom been there, the horses would have been unloaded onto the passenger platform, but instead it was about to be pushed back into a siding out of the way of the Necropolis train. This train was undoubtedly running early. It generally passed Surbiton at times varying between 2.58 pm to 3.05 pm; on this occasion it was 2.50 pm (according to the guard's watch) or 2.45 pm (according to the station clock). Captain Tyler concluded that it probably left Brookwood Cemetery at 2.25 pm instead of 2.30 pm. Although the Surbiton station master saw the Necropolis train approaching from a considerable distance, he assumed that the distant signal would be clearly seen. Captain Tyler recommended that greater use should be made of the electric telegraph 'for the safe working of a train', as used on the crowded portions of other lines. In fact only two trains were telegraphed to Surbiton each day: the Portsmouth direct (telegraphed from Woking) and the Exeter Express (telegraphed from Farnborough).

On 12th January, 1867, the driver of the Necropolis train was so drunk that the fireman had to manage the engine on his own for the return journey. The driver was dismissed and the LSWR Company wrote to the LNC commenting on the availability of intoxicating liquors in the refreshment rooms of the cemetery stations. The Secretary of the LNC replied that the driver had not been served on their premises, but had adjourned to a nearby public house while the funeral services were taking place. The Secretary suggested that the LNC should give the train crew a lunch of beer, bread and cheese, which the LSWR agreed to, providing that each man was given only one pint of beer. This custom lasted for many years: driver Bill Mullins, who operated funeral trains in the 1920s, remembered the LNC allowed the train crew goods to the value of 1s. (4d. each). By then, beer was priced at 5d. a pint, so another 1d. was needed. However, Bill Mullins was a teetotaller, and was able to enjoy a cup of tea and a cake with his 4d.! Apart from the train crew it was not unknown for *mourners* to have drinks with them for the journey. On one morning in the 1850s, at the York Street station, two mourners were so drunk that the station caretaker refused to allow them to board the train. Another funeral party used the return trip to consume their drinks, and were found dancing about the carriage by the ticket collector!

Another incident, which only indirectly involved the LNC, may also be mentioned. It occurred in 1878 in connection with the work to enlarge the 'A' signal box outside Waterloo. A girder wedged itself across the approach tracks to the terminus late one day, thus effectively blocking off Waterloo. Due to this, the overnight mail from the West Country had to be stopped on the Westminster Bridge Road overbridge and the passengers conducted across the lines to the LNC's York Street station so they could descend to street level from the railway viaduct.

At 3.22 pm on 22nd March, 1920, as the 2.33 pm train from Brookwood Cemetery was entering the Westminster Bridge Road station, the engine collided with the buffer stop, and caused some damage to the coaches. No complaints were made by passengers on the train. Driver Deller, who was suspended for one day, stated that due to the wet weather the rail surface was bad and the wheels 'picked up' when the vacuum brake was applied. The cost of the repairs to the buffer stop and the coaches amounted to £17 19s. 0d.

During a burglar hunt in the LNC's station on 14th March, 1929, constable David Fleming Ford fell through the plate glass roof over the 3rd class platform and was killed. He was just 22 years old. PC Ford was buried at Brookwood and his funeral procession was watched by thousands of people who lined the route from Kennington Road to Westminster Bridge Road. Senior members of the detective and uniformed forces marched in the procession, along with constables from several divisions, inspectors and sergeants from various parts of the Metropolitan Police, and officers and men from PC Ford's own 'L' Division. The procession included the Metropolitan Police Pipers Band. Owing to the circumstances of PC Ford's death, the LNC waived all funeral charges. The officers and men of the Metropolitan Police paid for the pink granite memorial in plot 107 which includes PC Ford's own police badge carved into the headstone.

In the Cemetery

On 6th May, 1893 Frank Hook, a private of the 20th Hussars then in camp at Pirbright, was knocked down and killed by a train in the Necropolis siding behind Brookwood station. It is not clear from the Minute by the LSWR's Court of Directors whether this was due to the negligence of the railway company in shunting.

On 26th October, 1928 the Necropolis train, hauled by 'M7' 0-4-4-T No. 33 and proceeding at a walking pace from the Anglican section towards North station, collided with a Daimler where the line crossed Western Avenue. The accident happened at 2.17 pm and resulted in the engine's steps being twisted and in the car being badly damaged. There were no injuries. The car contained four Australian ladies (who had been visiting the War Graves section in the cemetery) and their chauffeur; they returned to London on the Necropolis train. The driver of the train requested a replacement engine to be attached at Woking because the steps on No. 33 were touching the coupling rod. The accident was blamed on the chauffeur who was driving too fast at a point where the line was partly obscured on either side by trees and shrubs, and who was contravening the notices displayed at the entrances to the cemetery that 'Motors in the cemetery must proceed at a walking pace'. Subsequently notices were erected at all level crossings on the branch stating 'Special caution: Level Crossing'.

A similar accident occurred at 2.03 pm on Friday 13th May, 1938 when the Necropolis train collided with one of the LNC's lorries driven by a Mr Cheeseman. This happened as the lorry emerged from the company's Masonry Works and, without making due observation, the train (which was being propelled) hit the lorry as it crossed the line on the level crossing - the visibility being poor as tall shrubs and trees flanked the track on both sides at this point. The hearse van, which was leading, rode up over the lorry; the driver fortunately escaped injury. No complaint was made by passengers in the train and arrangements were made for their conveyance by car to Brookwood station from whence they proceeded by ordinary train to Waterloo. Breakdown vehicles were obtained from Guildford which arrived at 3.40 pm, and the van was re-railed at 4.35 pm. The damage incurred to the railway vehicles, from the official accident report, was:

SR Hearse van No. 1425 - derailed with one pair of wheels and buffer locked with Third Brake No. 6521. 3 step boards and 2 step irons broken, end cornice and 1 steam hose pipe damaged.
SR Third Brake No. 6521. (Set 99) - Buffer locked with van No. 1425 - End panels broken behind gangway frame, 1 letter rack displaced and gangway shield broken.

The cost of repairing this damage was £8 4s. 0d. The LNC admitted the accident was due to 'want of care' by its lorry driver and was obliged to purchase another lorry.

In November 1938 an accident occurred when the main timbers of the derrick crane in the masonry works broke, presumably when trying to lift too heavy a load. No-one was injured. John Walker* of the LNC obtained an estimate of £75 from the manufacturers for carrying out the necessary repairs, but the Directors agreed to make enquiries for the purchase 'of a new or second-hand up-to-date crane' to replace the broken one.

* John Baker Walker (died 1943). Walker joined the LNC in 1889 as a clerk and worked for the company for the rest of his life. He was promoted to General Manager in 1897, and became Managing Director from 1919. Walker succeeded Henry Ricardo as Chairman in 1941. He is buried in plot 76.

The accident on Friday 13th May, 1938, when Set 99, being propelled and with hearse van No. 1425 leading, collided with the LNC's lorry. Amazingly the lorry driver escaped alive. On the original print, the legend 'Necropolis Train' can be discerned on the solebar.

Reproduced by permission of Surrey History Service

Chapter Six

Rolling Stock

Hearse Vans

Special hearse vans were used exclusively for the Necropolis train. They were especially built for the LNC, to the company's general specification, and it owned them outright - unlike the passenger stock.

Broun's plan involved the use of large vehicles, with about 50 or 60 coffin 'cells', each provided with its own lock and key. Under his scheme of operation, trains composed of these vans would have travelled down to the 'morgue chapels' at Brookwood during the night or in the early morning. When the revamped LNC came to consider its mode of operation, the company decided to ignore Broun's ideas, which involved the separation of corpses from mourners. Presumably, the LNC felt its use of the railway (instead of the usual form of funeral transport to the place of burial) was radical enough. Further changes to funeral customs might easily prove unpopular and therefore detrimental to trade.*

The Early Hearse Vans

One problem that Broun never seemed to consider was how to accommodate the various sorts of coffins, coffins differentiated not only by class but also religion. The first problem, that of class, was solved by adhering to Broun's 'cell' concept, with different 'compartments' used for the three coffin classes and with each class determined by the LNC's tariff of funerals. Such pecuniary divisions were of great importance in Victorian times, when a funeral was an opportunity for social display, and the degree of expense and ostentation utilised was related by society to the degree of love and respect in which the deceased was held. Death is supposed to be the great leveller, but rank and protocol were preserved and respected by the LNC. To us, these divisions and attitudes, imposed by the age, seem unimportant and many of the consequent expenses unnecessary, especially when one considers that the divisions within the LNC's hearse vans were somewhat nominal. For each coffin, of whatever class, high or low, travelled in similar surroundings - and certainly at the same speed - as the rest of the train. Moreover the deceased were in no way able to appreciate any possible difference in 'comfort' that might be enjoyed by the mourners.

The method of distinguishing between the classes in each hearse van was suggested by William Austin, the Deputy Chairman of the LNC, in 1854:

> That some distinction as to ornament may be made between the central and interior compartments, to correspond with the different classes of funerals, so that coffins of differing classes may be conveyed in the same vehicle.

---

* Some of these issues are discussed further in *Chapter Four*.

Austin went on to describe the LNC's general requirements for these vans as follows:

> It is suggested that in the first instance it will be necessary to provide four vehicles for the conveyance of coffins each divided transversely into twelve compartments six above and six below, each compartment being at least seven feet long that is as long as the interior width of the carriage, the width and depth of each compartment to be that of an ordinary hearse.

The vans were therefore fitted with internal partitions to segregate the different coffins. These partitions were probably set at intervals of every two coffins, so that each van had separate 'compartments', each holding coffins of one class. The vans became in effect - and comparable to - a composite carriage. However it is also possible that each van was used exclusively for one class, since from *Appendices Two* and *Three* we may note that 2nd class was the tariff least used.

The other problem, that of the different religions, was overcome by (theoretically) using half the hearse vans solely for Anglican coffins, and half for Nonconformists. As there was no external difference between them, this was a purely superficial arrangement, ignored at once if only burials in the Anglican (or Nonconformist) section were taking place, or if the number of coffins for one section of the cemetery demanded the use of more hearse carriages. Religious segregation may seem anathema to us, but was natural in the context of mid-Victorian England. However, it is by no means clear where the vans were placed in the train since custom and practice appears inconsistent. From photographic evidence it seems the vans were sometimes placed at the rear of the relevant religious portion of the train. This relegation of the coffin was in complete contrast with the strict order of precedence at a conventional funeral, where the hearse and coffin are given due prominence and respect by being placed at the head of the funeral procession. This formation is confirmed by the 1890s and 1902 photographs of the train (*see pages 92 and 139*). The former shows a hearse van at the end of the train, the latter shows hearses at the end of each part of the Necropolis train. This formation did mean the hearses led the train as it proceeded through the cemetery grounds, assuming the train was being propelled. For the return journey along the branch, the empty hearses would have been at the rear of the train, and at the front for the return journey to London. But other photographs show the hearse vans at the front of the Necropolis train, following the traditional order of precedence for the hearse (*see pages 92 and 96*). On these occasions the hearse vans were at the rear of the train as it proceeded through the cemetery grounds, assuming the train was being propelled. For the return journey along the branch, the empty hearse carriages would have been at the front of the train, and at the end for the return journey to London.

There also remains some uncertainty over the exact number of hearse vans supplied to the LNC in 1854 and shortly afterwards. The surviving records of the company suggest that six 'coffin trucks' were ordered by the LNC in 1854. Two had been ordered, possibly from the LSWR, by the end of October 1854 in readiness for the opening of the cemetery. They cost £20 each, and may be the 'type I' vans described below. A further four vans were ordered from a Mr Bowden in December of the same year in anticipation of increasing traffic, at £16 each. The low prices quoted for all these vans strongly suggests that both batches were conversions of old carriages, although no further details are known about them. William Austin's comments, quoted above, imply that four vans were needed for the first funeral trains, whilst other evidence suggests that only three vans in all were supplied. Surviving records of the LSWR Company show that one second and two third class vans were ordered in July 1854 but, if correct, this implies there was no means of conveying first class coffins. In 1858 an old 3rd was converted into a hearse, but the Stock Committee reported in 1856 and in 1859 that only three hearse vans existed.

Photographic evidence only adds to the uncertainties. In the 1892 view of the York Street station (*see page 134*) there are two hearse vans. The right-hand one is probably a 3rd since its appearance is like an early 3rd class carriage. The left-hand one is similar to that in the *c.*1884 view of the same station (*see page 26*), but the underframes differ. These vans could both be 2nds, or perhaps one is a 1st and the other is a 2nd. Whether these vans were also subdivided into three classes it is impossible to determine. One possible explanation is that the LSWR built and supplied three or four hearse vans in addition to those provided and owned by the LNC. Given the level of business undertaken by the LNC at this time, the existence of seven to ten vans seems most unlikely. Probably the full details will never be known, but any further information would be most welcome.

These vans were certainly of a smaller capacity than those suggested by Broun. The description of the LNC's requirements given by William Austin, and quoted above, suggests a hearse van with a maximum capacity of 12 coffins in two layers. If four vans of this type existed, the total capacity would be 48 coffins; if six vans of this type existed, then a maximum of 72 coffins could be carried.*

But surviving photographic evidence suggests that the hearse vans actually supplied did not conform to this design. It is clear that at least three separate designs existed, probably because each van was built at different times or converted from other stock. The LNC's vans were little more than panelled boxes, internally subdivided, and mounted on a simple four-wheel carriage underframe. A very good description of one of the original hearse vans is provided by a correspondent from *Cassell's Illustrated Family Paper* who travelled on the Necropolis train in 1856:

> The railway carriage appropriated to the dead instantly attracts the eye. It is very massive, and in form somewhat similar to the ordinary luggage-van. Doors open on either side of it, and within we see the several compartments assigned to the use of the dead, ranged one above another; each coffin having a separate receptacle, and secured by straps during transit. The coffins when brought up by the lift are conveyed with noiseless promptitude to the funeral tender.

In fact there are three hearse van styles that may be identified from surviving photographs as follows:

---

* It is known that later in the 19th century some funeral trains contained upwards of 60 coffins. Therefore more than three hearse vans must have been available to the LNC by this time.

Part of the York Street station *c.*1892. This shows the second (deep) awning valance provided after the construction of the new 'A' box, and an interesting selection of stock. The passenger vehicles are probably 19 ft 6 in. firsts of 1859. The hearse vans are very different and are designated types I and II in the text.

P. Wood Collection

Type I Hearse Van (see opposite, right-hand van)

These hearse vans were probably the earliest design used by the LNC. It is of a similar design to early third class carriages, and may have been converted into a 'coffin truck' from a passenger coach. The van appears to be eight panels long, suggesting it had three coffin 'compartments', each with double doors, but with doors at each end of the van and intervening panels beside the central set of doors (*see diagram*). This suggests the van had a total capacity of 12 coffins, assuming there was room for four coffins in each 'compartment'. This design would have been similar to that suggested by William Austin. These vans may have been used either as a third class hearse or as a composite.

Type II Hearse Van (see opposite 60, left-hand van)

This type of hearse is similar in design to second class carriages of the 1850s. The van appears to be just seven panels long, whilst the detail that can just be discerned suggests that each panel comprised a door into each compartment. Assuming these vans were similar to those used later for the Fawkner Cemetery railway,[*] some of these compartments may have been slightly wider than others. These vans would have had a total capacity of 14 coffins, assuming two coffins to each 'compartment' and a central shelf (*see diagram*). These vans may have been used as a first or second class hearse, or as a composite.

Type III Hearse Van (see page 26)

This type of hearse is also seven panels long and is of a similar design to the type II vans described above, except that the underframe is completely different. This type of van may also have been used as a first or second class hearse, or as a composite.

All these vans probably incorporated rollers to assist with the loading and unloading of the coffins from their 'compartments' in the hearse. Strong leather straps were used to secure the coffins whilst in transit. Being used only in conjunction with passenger vehicles, the hearse vans were painted in the relevant passenger livery of the period. These early vans appear to have remained in use until the end of the 19th century, when new stock was eventually provided for the LNC by the LSWR. Such longevity of stock was not uncommon amongst the old railway companies, and indeed such a tradition persisted with British Rail!

The LNC's Last Hearse Vans

The ratification of the 1899 agreement led to the construction of the second and final set of hearse vans. Generally the design followed the principles laid down by Mr Austin in 1854, but they were longer vehicles, having a capacity of eight coffins on each level. These vans also contained three coffin 'shelves' each, instead

* *See Appendix Eight.*

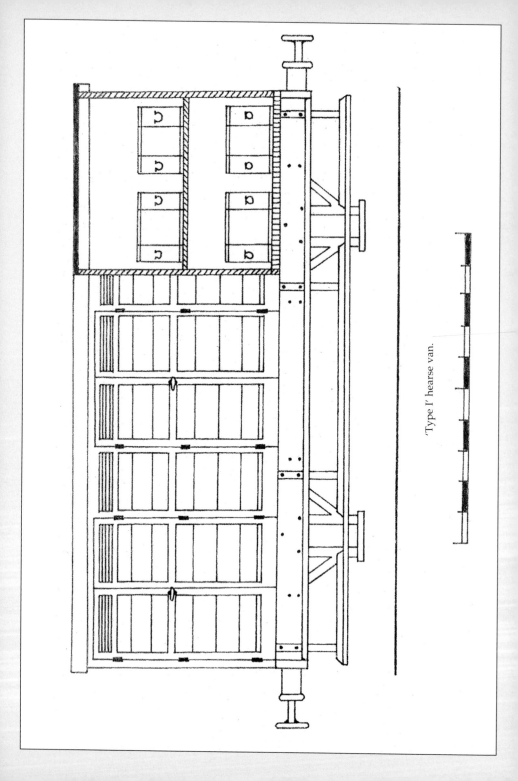

'Type I' hearse van.

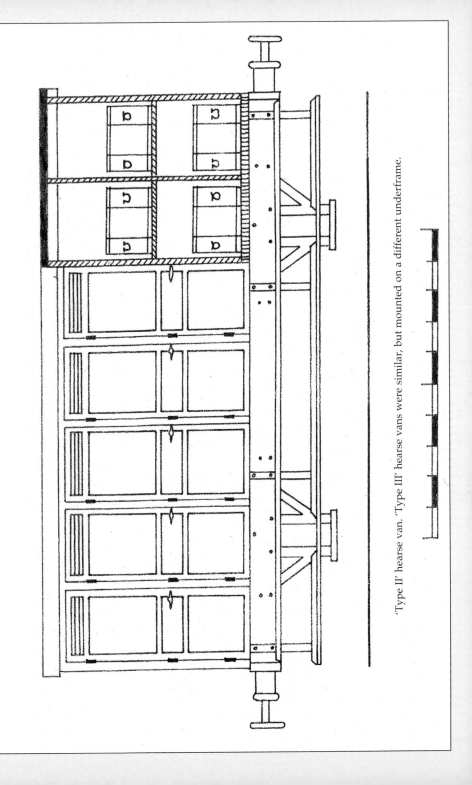

'Type II' hearse van. 'Type III' hearse vans were similar, but mounted on a different underframe.

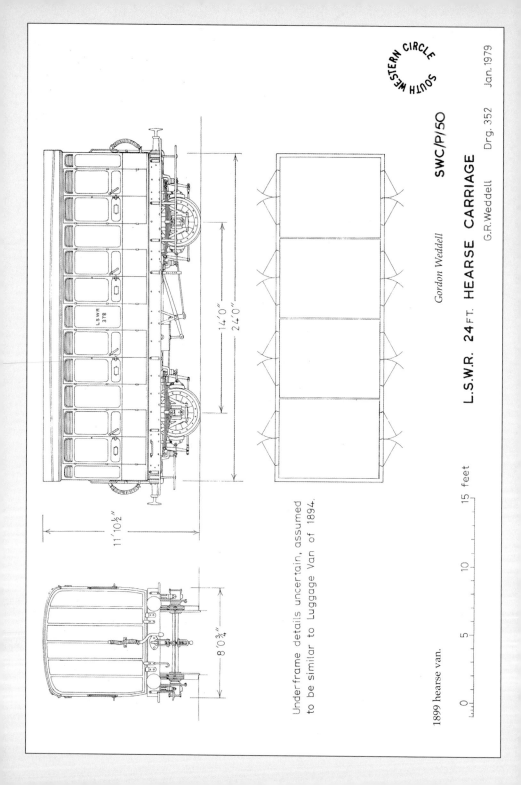

SOUTH WESTERN CIRCLE

SWC/P/50

Drg. 352   Jan. 1979

Gordon Weddell

L.S.W.R. 24 FT. HEARSE CARRIAGE

G.R. Weddell

L.S.W.R.
378

14'0"
24'0"

11'10½"

8'0¾"

Underframe details uncertain, assumed
to be similar to Luggage Van of 1894.

1899 hearse van.

0   5   10   15 feet

The Necropolis train at North station, sometime in the 1890s. The two coaches on the left are Beattie firsts and are oil-lit. The last vehicle is one of the type I hearse vans. *Author's Collection*

Hearse van No. 1426 at Rotherhithe Road in June 1950. The van is in the same livery as when last used in the Necropolis train, except that 'Railway' has been painted over in the eighth panel. Note the card holders in the waist panels of the doors. *D. Cullum*

of two (as has been assumed for the early hearse carriages), thus increasing the total load to 24 coffins per van as compared with 12 or 14 previously. This was important because only two (one nominally Anglican, the other nominally Nonconformist) were built. Each coffin 'shelf' incorporated a number of rollers to assist the loading and unloading of coffins, a feature copied from the original vans. The internal partitions, facilitating the division of coffin classes within the vehicles, were set at two coffin intervals, thus creating four separate sections in the van, each holding six coffins on three different levels. Small metal card holders were provided in the waist panelling of the left-hand compartment doors, a feature which may have been copied from the earlier vans. The card holders allowed the easy identification of the coffins within. The two new vans were built at a cost of £224 6s. 11d. each in December 1899, and numbered 377 and 378.

The only major alterations made to these vans were that the centre partition and shelves were removed from van No. 377 in February 1910, and that all the partitions and shelves were removed from No. 378 in October 1909. These changes necessarily reduced the total number of coffins that might be conveyed in these vans. The vehicles were renumbered 5338 and 5339 respectively in 1912, and again in 1928 (after Grouping) when they became SR numbers 1425 and 1426. In SR days overall green livery was applied to the hearse vans. Lettering was applied at the top of the second ('1426'), sixth ('SOUTHERN'), eighth ('RAILWAY') and twelfth ('1426') panels. It is possible that on occasion the hearse vans were not used in the last year of operation with the second carriage Set 100, because of the generous luggage spaces in the brake ends.

Both vans continued in use until the destruction of the Necropolis train and part of the LNC's terminus in April 1941, an incident which claimed van No. 1425. No. 1426 escaped unscathed and survived until the 1950s before being withdrawn; it was still in SR green livery when photographed at Rotherhithe Road in June 1950 (*see page 139*). It is not known when this van was subsequently scrapped.

Carriage Stock

The passenger stock used for the Necropolis train was not owned by the LNC, unlike the hearse vans, but was on 'permanent loan' from the LSWR. The original reason for this was opposition from LSWR shareholders in 1852, some of whom objected to the railway company's interest in the Necropolis undertaking, alleging that travellers (especially excursionists) would refuse to use the line once they knew that dead bodies were being frequently conveyed by passenger trains. This objection was overcome by reserving a train solely for the Necropolis traffic. However, during his inspection of the Westminster Bridge Road station in 1902, Major Pringle, appointed by the Board of Trade, noted:

> The Railway Company regard the new station as a private one, and are concerned, so I understand, only with the provision of engine power for the special trains which are the property of the Necropolis Company.

This was a simplification of the facts since, as will be described, it was the LNC who made requests to the railway company for new or replacement stock.

I. Beattie stock, 1854 - c.1899

The original stock consisted of Beattie four-wheeled oil-lit stock. This is all that can be definitely ascertained. William Austin, the Deputy Chairman of the LNC, suggested the provision of three first class carriages, four seconds, and three thirds, which were presumably supplied for the original Necropolis train. The train would have varied according to the number of funerals actually furnished on each day.

Old photographs give some clues concerning the early stock used for the Necropolis train. The c.1884 view of the York Street station (*see page 26*) shows the right-hand vehicle as a Beattie 19 ft 10 in. second. Curiously - and rarely - this vehicle has the LSWR's coat of arms on the outside, previously recorded only on first class coaches. (It is also possible the LSWR upgraded the interior of this coach for the LNC to use as a first.)

In the 1892 view (*see page 134*), the passenger vehicles appear to be Beattie 19 ft 6 in. firsts, albeit with different underframes. The coach on the right appears to have a very early type of underframe. This stock must be regarded as typical of that supplied to the LNC by the LSWR during the 19th century. The 1890s view of the Necropolis train at North station (*see page 139*) shows two Beattie firsts and a hearse carriage. Although not clear - due to the small size of the original print - these are probably the same 19 ft 6 in. firsts shown on page 134.

The Beattie stock remained in use until the end of the 19th century. The LNC made continued and increasingly vehement complaints to the LSWR about the 'disgraceful' condition of the stock used for its train. So important was the question of new stock that the LNC insisted it should form one of the clauses in the 1899 agreement, to which reference has already been made. The clause in question made the provision of a new train ('which shall be of a quality and character not inferior to the normal average . . . of the passenger rolling stock used by the Railway Company for its ordinary main line traffic') binding on the LSWR.*

II. The arc roofed set, c.1899 - c.1907

Newer stock therefore replaced the ancient stock soon after this agreement was ratified in May 1899. As the new hearse vans were built in December 1899, it is possible that the new set - which may be called the 'arc roofed set' - was supplied concurrently with the vans. This comprised six-wheeled vehicles of the Adams period, as shown on page 92. The carriages that are known to have been included in this set are as follows:

The arc roofed set, c.1899-c.1907
(A) Brake 3rd *c.*30 ft long, and divided into the guard's and baggage compartment and three 3rd class compartments.
(B) One 1st/2nd Composite *c.*34 ft long and divided into five compartments as follows: 2/1/1/1/2.
(C) One all 3rd (or 2nd) *c.*30 ft long and divided into five 3rd class compartments (or five 2nds).
(D) Brake 3rd, details as (A) above.

* The use of antiquated and uncomfortable stock was also a feature of the Rookwood Cemetery system (Australia), where the early funeral trains have been described as 'quite the worst form of travel of the period'. See David Weston (ed.) *The Sleeping City: The Story of Rookwood Necropolis* (Society of Australian Genealogists, 1989), p.51.

Very probably, other similar carriages of this period were allocated by the LSWR for the exclusive use of the LNC, the actual composition of the train depending on the number of funeral parties and visitors to the cemetery being catered for on each occasion. However, no details of any other vehicles that may have been used are known; nor are any numbers for any of the coaches in the set - save the hearse vans.

The same photograph shows one interesting feature of the Necropolis train: the fourth vehicle is a LSWR 24 ft four-wheel 'Windsor' saloon. As the cemetery burial registers show no important funerals on the date in question, this suggests that a wealthy family party was travelling to Brookwood to visit a grave. The provision of such a vehicle must have been unusual, and the presence of the saloon in the picture should not be taken as evidence the LNC regularly made use of these carriages. This coach differs only in detail from the two LSWR four-wheel semi-saloons which became Nos. 15 and 17 on the Weston, Clevedon & Portishead Railway. Similar vehicles were in the rake of LSWR carriages purchased by the Plymouth Devonport & South Western Railway about 1910, although these saloons may subsequently have gone to the Weston, Clevedon & Portishead Railway.

III. The elliptical roofed set, c.1907 - c.1917

The 'arc roofed set' was replaced by more modern elliptical roofed stock about 1907. Another photograph in this book (*see page 96*) appears to show, in addition to the hearse vans, one bogie coach and three 'modern' six-wheelers. Unfortunately, little else is known about this set.

IV. Set 100, c.1917-1938

The SR (or possibly the LSWR) replaced the existing Necropolis set with 'Set 100', which comprised four ex-LSWR non-corridor bogie carriages as follows:

Set 100, c.1917-1938

(A) 51 ft brake composite, SR No. 6465, originally built in November 1902 as LSWR No. 179 to LSWR diagram No. 1122 (in SR days to diagram No. 405). It was renumbered 3504 in January 1917. For the Necropolis train, the carriage was divided as follows: two 3rds; lst; two lavatories; 1st; two 3rds (converted from 2nds of earlier LSWR days); brake end. The vehicle was withdrawn in July 1938.

(B) 50 ft composite, SR No. 5022, originally built in December 1901 as LSWR No. 107 to LSWR diagram No. 980 (in SR days to diagram No. 273). It was renumbered 2352 in June 1913. For the Necropolis train, the coach was divided as follows: 3rd; lavatory; two 3rds; two lavatories; two 1sts; lavatory; 1st. All the 3rd class compartments had been converted from 2nds. The vehicle was withdrawn in December 1938.

(C) 46 ft 3rd, SR No. 551, originally built in 1901 as LSWR No. 392 to LSWR diagram No. 993 (in SR days to diagram No. 13). It was not renumbered until after Grouping. For the Necropolis train, the carriage consisted of six compartments divided into three pairs, each pair having access to an adjacent lavatory. The vehicle was withdrawn in July 1938.

(D) 51 ft Brake Composite, SR No. 6468, originally built in November 1902 as LSWR No. 218, and renumbered 3507 in January 1916. Other details are the same as for No. 6465. The vehicle was withdrawn in July 1938.

This set remained in use for most of the inter-war period, and was withdrawn only in April 1938.

In 1926 the *Eastern Section Carriage Working Notice* quoted SR No. 7806 as being part of the Necropolis train. This vehicle was a 47 ft 6 in. double saloon, originally built by the Birmingham Railway Carriage & Wagon Works in May 1885 to LSWR diagram No. 41. As built, it was arc-roofed and had 30 first class and 10 third class seats, and was No. 18. It was later renumbered as LSWR No. 4108, and at some stage rebuilt with an elliptical roof. Allocated to SR diagram No. 585, it is not known when and for how long this vehicle remained in the Necropolis train. This interesting carriage, in the same batch as the two LSWR Royal Saloons, was withdrawn in September 1933.

Occasionally Set 100 was reduced to three coaches, one probably being withdrawn for overhaul. At one time, ex-LSWR bogie third No. 186 was noted as replacing Nos. 5022 and 551 mentioned above; latterly the set was recorded with coach No. 5022 replaced by (SR) No. 560, which it retained when the set was superseded by Set 99.

V. Set 99, 1938 - 1939

Set 100 was replaced by Set 99, another four-coach set. It comprised ex-LSWR bogie corridor stock as follows:

Set 99, 1938-1939
(A) 56 ft Brake Composite, SR No. 6521, originally built by the LSWR between 1910-11 as LSWR No. 3519. The coach, as per SR diagram No. 410, was divided into: brake end; two 3rds; two 1sts; two 3rds. All compartments had access to a side corridor and an end lavatory (*see page 144, top*).
(B) 56 ft 3rd, SR. No. 696; the LSWR had originally built coaches of this type between 1904-16. It was originally LSWR No. 890. The carriage, as per SR diagram No. 21, was divided into eight 3rd class compartments, all with access to a side corridor and two end lavatories.
(C) 57ft 3rd, SR No. 708, originally built by the LSWR in 1920 (LSWR No. 875). The coach, as per SR diagram No. 22, was divided into eight compartments, like No. 696 (*see page 144, bottom*).
(D) 56 ft Brake Composite SR No. 6532 (LSWR No. 3621), details as for No. 6521 (*see page 145*).

Set 99 was in use on the Necropolis train by April 1938 and was involved in the accident of 13th May, 1938 in the cemetery (*see Chapter Five*). By September 1939 Set 99 had been withdrawn from use on the Necropolis train and thereafter was used for special traffic (including troop trains) as required. It was probably strengthened to eight vehicles, but in 1941 was noted as comprising SR Nos. 6532, 696, 5106 and 6521. As an eight-coach set it later comprised SR vehicles Nos. 6521, 704, 696, 707, 5135, 5108, 709 and 6532, although this formation did

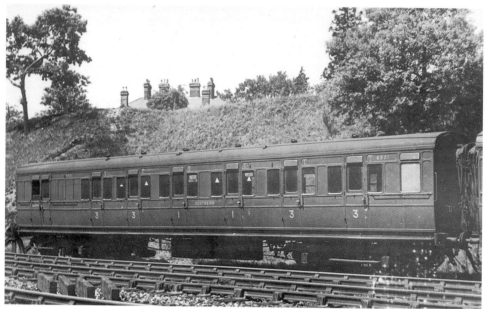

56 ft brake composite, SR No. 6521, previously used in Set 99 (1938-39). Photographed at Hook, May 1948.
D. Cullum

57ft third, SR No. 708, previously used in Set 99 (1938-39). Photographed at Hook, May 1948.
D. Cullum

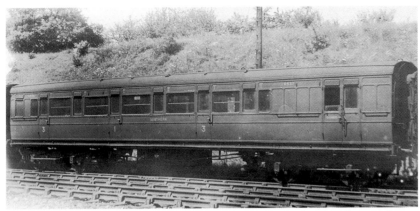

54 ft brake composite, SR No. 6532, previously used in Set 99 (1938-39). Photographed at Hook, May 1948. *D. Cullum*

vary from time to time. Set 99 became a six-coach set sometime in 1954 (comprising Nos. 3165, 696, 707, 5135, 709 and 3175) and was finally withdrawn sometime in 1958.

VI. Set 100, 1939-1941

Set 99 was replaced by a further Set 100, which consisted of ex-South Eastern & Chatham Railway (SECR) Royal Train vehicles as follows:

Set 100, 1939-1941
(A) Saloon brake, SR No. 7914, originally built in 1900 as a 45 ft brake 3rd (SECR No. 2301), but rebuilt in 1902 as an all 1st saloon brake with 12 seats and raised roof-end guard's lookout.
(B) 1st, SR No. 7254, originally built in 1901 as a 44 ft composite (SECR No. 225), but rebuilt in 1902 as an all 1st with 23 seats.
(C) Saloon, SR No. 7918, originally built in 1904 as a 50 ft all 1st saloon (SECR No. 3514). It had 20 seats.
(D) Saloon Brake, SR No. 7918 (SECR No. 3493); the details are the same as for No. 7914, but this coach had only nine seats.

These details describe the vehicles as they were in the Royal Train only. It is not known what alterations were made (if any) for their use on the Necropolis service, although some of the carriages must have been converted for use by third class passengers. This set, with its ornate and tapestried interiors, must have made a magnificent sight. Unfortunately, it was the stock that was damaged and destroyed when the Necropolis terminus was bombed in April 1941 (*see page 146*). As the luggage spaces were particularly generous in the Saloon Brakes, it seems likely that when few funerals were catered for the hearse vans were not used.

One of the ex-SECR birdcage saloon brakes (No. 7914 or 7918) from the second Set 100. It is shown in the Westminster Bridge Road station, probably taken on 17th April, 1941. The vehicle on the extreme right is almost certainly hearse van No. 1426 (*see also page 42*).

R.C. Riley Collection

The remains of the Necropolis train adjacent to the remains of the private station, sometime after 17th April, 1941. The stock has been temporarily berthed in the locomotive facilities adjoining the Westminster Bridge Road station (*see also page 41*).

Reproduced by Permission of London Borough of Lambeth, Archives Department

The immediate aftermath of the air raid, taken from the first class platform, *c.*17th April, 1941. Note that the main building has been completely destroyed, revealing damaged houses along the Westminster Bridge Road. Hearse van No. 1426 is on the extreme right, with the remains of the screen between the two private lines. It is not known why the Maunsell corridor coach was berthed in the station at this time. (*See also page 42.*)

Southern Railway Photographic Unit

The stock used for the Necropolis service, including the hearse vans, had the solebars inscribed 'Necropolis Train'. This practice dated from SR days at least, and probably from the LSWR. It has been confirmed by a photograph of the 1938 accident in the cemetery (*see page 130*).

Locomotives

In addition to the passenger stock, the LSWR also provided the locomotive, crew, and guard for the Necropolis train. Generally speaking, throughout the lifetime of the railway funeral service, any suitable available engine was used to haul the train. No particular locomotive ever appears to have worked the service exclusively until the 1930s. By then, the train was invariably worked by a Drummond 'M7' 0-4-4 tank, and for a long period No. 255 was for some reason almost solely used. Other engines recorded working the Necropolis train between 1938 and 1940 were 'M7' class Nos. 32 and 33. The locomotive working the Necropolis train was on Nine Elms duty 87, which also included the Clapham Junction-Waterloo empty carriage workings.

Chapter Seven

Fares and Tickets

Fares

The Necropolis service was perhaps unique in retaining the same fare structure for 85 years. This was due to the LNC and the LSWR being bound by the LNC's Act of 1852 to certain maximum fares. As *The Undertakers' Journal* noted in 1898:

> Parliament, in the paternal goodness of its heart, has fixed a penny a mile as the ordinary fare for live people. But it has not stopped here, and a visit to the mortuary station of the London and South-Western Railway in the Westminster Bridge-road discloses the Parliamentary tariff for dead ones.

Early Tariffs (1849-1853)

Fares would have been much lower had Broun's scheme been implemented. By proposing to send coffin trains down to Brookwood in the early morning or late evening, he exploited the LSWR's 'off-peak' hours on the busiest portion of its network. This, along with his projected large-capacity hearse vans and the volume of anticipated traffic, undoubtedly resulted in the proposed low cost of conveyance, of 6d. per corpse, irrespective of class or religion. Similarly, by the expected number of mourners and visitors to the Necropolis, ordinary fares would have been a mere 'few shillings' each.

All these charges were revised and increased during the Committee stages of the LNC's Bill. Largely, especially regarding the mourners' fares and those for pauper or artisan coffins, the charges remained at reasonable levels. Much of this was due to the continued confidence both companies had in the success of the Necropolis venture, and the consequent heavy traffic and financial rewards to be gained from the scheme. Indeed, from estimates made at this time, the LSWR was expecting to make some £40,000 a year from its part in the Necropolis project.* *Herepath's Journal* in August 1852 discussed some of these issues and suggested caution:

> And what are the terms on which we are to carry [the] dead? Ridiculously low. I have not the figures here, but we only hope to gain by carrying large numbers at low prices, and I fear we shall only get the dead by killing our live traffic; but at all events the question is one of such vast importance, that the Shareholders ought *not to sanction the engagement* until *they are themselves* satisfied that good will come of it.

An early fares tariff, dated 6th July, 1852, gives the following scale of charges for paupers and artizans:

---

* But *see Appendix Two.*

	£.	s.	d.
PAUPER CLASS			
For the reception, transmission by Railway, and interment of each body in a separate Grave, which shall be buried at the expense of any Union or Parish, including the conveyance and return by Railway of two friends or attendants, and the funeral services at the Cemetery	0	14	0
ARTIZAN CLASS			
For the reception and interment of each body in a separate Grave, and for the funeral services at the Cemetery	0	15	0
To the South-Western Railway Company, for the use and haulage of the carriage and conveyance, according to the number of corpses therein. For each corpse of the Artizan class not to exceed	0	5	0
For the conveyance by Railway to and return from the Cemetery of the Mourners actually attending the funeral, and all necessary attendants thereon, but not exceeding six persons for any one funeral, Second Class, each person, not to exceed	0	3	6
[Total]	[£1	3	6]

These funeral charges appear to have been revised again in November 1853. In the case of paupers, an additional 1s. was payable by the parish to the incumbent, making a total of 15s. payable. This fee appears to have remained standard for paupers buried under contract by the LNC. Children were buried for the reduced charge of 10s. under these contracts. For artizans, the total charge was increased to £1 8s. 2d. as follows:

	£.	s.	d.
ARTIZAN CLASS			
For the burial and transmission of the body by Railway	1	0	0
For each friend to the Cemetery and back	0	2	0
Fee to the Incumbent of the Parish in which the death takes place if the burial takes place in consecrated ground	0	6	2
Total expense of such a burial with one attendant	1	8	2

Charges for better class funerals were published in December 1852 as follows:

	£	s.	d.
SECOND CLASS			
Single grave, same depth [i.e. 7 ft deep], including conveyance of body from the Waterloo or Nine-Elms Stations to Woking, funeral service, and interment	1	0	0
Privilege of placing head and foot stone, 10s. extra.			
FIRST CLASS			
Single grave, in perpetuity, same depth, 6 feet 6 inches by 2 feet 6 inches superficial, including conveyance of the body from the Waterloo or Nine-Elms Stations to Woking, funeral service, and interment, with the privilege of placing head and foot stones without extra payment	2	10	0

Other options included brick graves, vaults, the re-opening of graves, incumbent's fees, etc. At this stage it is clear the railway fares for the conveyance of mourners showed a maximum of six to any one funeral, for second or third class. However adult pauper funerals allowed up to two mourners to accompany the body without extra charge. It should be noted that the limitation on the number of mourners applied only to Artizan (or second) class, and third class funeral parties. These restrictions were later removed under the terms of the 1899 agreement between the LSWR and the LNC (see *Chapter Two*).

The LNC's Tariff (1854-1957)

The fares and funeral charges were set out in the LNC's price lists, although there was a great deal of choice in the accessory fees payable. In 1854 this was a new departure for funeral directors, which *The Spectator* applauded:

[Here] is the promise of a release from the dead weight of funeral charges, the importance of which can scarcely be over-estimated for those very numerous classes who are beneath the wealthy. There is no tax so severe as that for the funeral; there is none which the taxed is so helpless to resist … When a great trading company [the LNC] brings the whole of these arrangements into one uniform plan, the details of which everybody can ascertain, and which is guaranteed … [doubts] will be removed. The survivors will be able to select the class in which the remains shall travel to their last home as easily as living passengers can classify themselves. The survivors will be able to choose the amount of black cloth, the array of feathers, the number of attendants, and the length of the ceremony; but we presume that the humblest will be certain of order, decency, solemnity, and all the essentials of the last 'comfortable lodgings'.

Punch (1854) also commended the idea of a published tariff of fares and funeral fees:

The London Necropolis Company advertises First and Second Class graves, and First, Second, and Third Class Funerals. This sort of nomenclature suggests the remark that Life is a railway, of which the terminus is at the Cemetery. However we are glad to find that the fares - to follow out the style of phraseology - of the Company are very moderate, being £2 10s. for the first class, and £1 for the second, the third not specified.

The fares fixed by the LNC's Act of 1852 were:

Maximum charges for the conveyance of mourners and attendants by rail:

Class	Charge
1st	6s.
2nd	3s. 6d.
3rd	2s.

Maximum charges for the conveyance of bodies by rail:

Class	Charge
Pauper	2s. 6d.
Artisan	5s.
All others	£1

The rates for the conveyance of mourners and attendants are self-explanatory. It is not entirely clear how the fares were paid. However, from surviving evidence during SR days it appears that for relatives and friends travelling to Brookwood for a funeral, the fares were added to the total bill as an additional charge. But for relatives and friends travelling by the Necropolis train to *visit* a grave in the cemetery, it appears the mourners' tickets were paid for by cash prior to the departure of the train. The pauper (later 3rd class) fare was calculated as the lowest possible rate the railway company could offer, for these mourners were carried some 60 miles for only 2s., which works out at under ½d. per mile. In the 1880s, 2s. was equivalent to the single cab fare from the Strand to either Brompton or Kensal Green cemeteries. This helped the LNC quote cheap rates for pauper funerals in its bid to attract custom. Some metropolitan parishes had special contracts with the LNC for the burial of the very poor. Under these arrangements, travel 'warrants' were issued by the Town Clerk or other official to allow up to two 3rd class mourner tickets to be granted to the immediate relatives, who could accompany the deceased to Brookwood. Additional mourners might also attend the funeral, but the family would have to pay the extra fares.

The charges for other classes were far from extortionate and, over the years, became very favourable when compared to the normal railway fares from Waterloo to Woking or Brookwood. Consequently in the latter years of the service, many avid London golfers, suitably disguised as mourners, used to travel by the Necropolis train to play at one of the nearby golf links, and save on their railway fares at the same time.*

The coffin charges require more explanation. The conveyance of corpses by rail has always been expensive compared to all other rates, not least because of the special handling that such 'freight' requires. The LSWR usually charged over £1 per coffin, for carriage in normal horseboxes at this time. In 1858 an instruction to Station Agents listed the usual charges for conveying coffins on the LSWR system as follows:

Corpses conveyed in the Company's hearse carriage†	1s. per mile by ordinary trains
Corpses conveyed in a hearse on a Carriage truck	1s. per mile by ordinary trains
Corpses conveyed in a Horse Box	8d. per mile by ordinary trains
Or in a hearse on a Carriage truck by Parliamentary trains	6d. per mile
The charge to be no less than 8s. in any case.	

However, because the LSWR anticipated a large number of corpses being conveyed by the Necropolis train, it was prepared to offer cheaper rates, especially for those coffins that would not have to be handled so carefully - that is, the pauper coffins. Mr Wyndham Harding, the Secretary of the LSWR, explained the reasoning behind this:

---

* At least unofficially condoned by the LNC since its General Manager, John B. Walker, was closely involved with the foundation of the West Hill Golf Club, which opened in 1909. This was laid out on about 150 acres of land adjacent to the cemetery and known as the 'Cemetery Reserve'. Walker was Captain of the West Hill Golf Club (1922-23 and 1942-43) and its President from 1932-43. For comparison, the standard return fares in 1902/3 from Waterloo to Brookwood were: 1st class 8s., 2nd class 5s. 2d., 3rd class 4s.

† It is not clear if this refers to a hearse carriage owned by the LSWR or one borrowed for the occasion from the LNC.

... we should have to lift by the simplest possible machinery the coffins of the poorest class and put them into a great carriage constructed for the purpose ... If one were to come to the better class, we should have to do it in a different way. We should have to take them up one by one, and to allow the mourners to see the coffin put in if they chose to, and to do it in a more circumspect manner than with regard to the paupers, [being] merely attended by the Parish officers.

Hence, if one could afford to pay, one could receive all the decency and deference one could wish for in the handling of the coffins. Another factor was the supposed distinction between the different classes in the hearse vans, but the main reason for the different charges was the distinction between the three main classes of funerals (and type of grave space offered in the cemetery).*

Originally the 2s. 6d. charge for paupers applied only if more than eight coffins were carried by the Necropolis train, so that the 20s. minimum carriage threshold was passed. However, this issue was not addressed in the 1899 agreement and by this time it is likely that custom and practice was that second or third class coffins would not be sent down to Brookwood on their own. Although of a later date, this is confirmed by the surviving LNC Ticket Book which covers the period 1937-41.

With the opening of Woking Crematorium in 1885, and the LNC being particularly well placed to take full advantage of additional business generated by the Cremation Society, there were some hostile comments in the professional press regarding the higher rates charged by the LSWR to other undertakers for the conveyance of coffins. For instance, in 1892 an anonymous contributor (identified only as 'Dust Remover'!) to The Undertakers' & Funeral Directors' Journal commented:

> Every undertaker who takes a body for cremation from London to Woking by railway has to pay 24s. to the railway company, being the regular rate from Waterloo to Woking station at 1s. per mile. The Necropolis Company undertakes cremations, and convey the body from their station in Westminster Road [sic] to the Brookwood station [sic] by what is familiarly known I believe as their dead meat train, which leaves about 11.30 every morning. Now I am pretty sure they do not pay anything like 24s. to the Railway Co., seeing that they provide a separate grave, including conveyance from Westminster Road, for 20s. The amount paid for carriage would, I suppose, certainly not exceed 5s. Now, while there can be no objection to this arrangement, so far as burials at Brookwood Cemetery are concerned, it is clearly unjust that the undertakers should have to pay 24s. when taking a body for cremation, while the Necropolis, so far as I can see, only pay 5s. or so. Fair competition is surely sharp enough, without any (presumably) unfair dealings of this sort. I think, at all events, the South-Western Railway Co. might be approached upon the subject. If matters are as they seem to be, the company ought, in fairness, either to reduce the charge to the undertakers, or raise it to the Necropolis Co.

'Dust Remover' was mis-informed since none of the bodies for cremation handled by the LNC would have been charged at the artisan rate of 5s. for the simple reason that at this time cremation was the preserve of the rich: therefore each coffin would be charged at 20s. Moreover the special rates for coffins had been fixed by Parliament rather than the LSWR, although it remained true that all other undertakers were being charged an additional 4s. per coffin over the

---

* The three main funeral classes are discussed further in Chapter Four.

LNC's 'preferential rate' from Waterloo to Brookwood. Comparing the 24s. charge with the LSWR's usual tariff for carrying coffins (quoted above), it is clear that other undertakers were charged the standard rate of 1s. per mile. The 20s. funeral quoted by 'Dust Remover' applied only to 2nd class funerals (where the coffin rate would have been 5s.), with no right to erect a memorial without additional fees being payable: nor were there contracts to cremate paupers at this time.

Some bargain fares were offered to intending visitors. In February 1888 the LNC placed advertisements that:

At the instance of the Directors [of the LNC] the South Western Railway Company have made the following abatement in the fares for return tickets between Waterloo and Brookwood by all trains on Sundays:

First Class   8s. reduced to 6s.
Second Class   6s. reduced to 4s.
Third Class   4s. reduced to 2s. 6d.

This meant the special fares charged on the Necropolis train were effectively applied to all ordinary passengers provided they travelled to Brookwood on a Sunday. The slight exception was that second and third class 'special' fares were 6d. more expensive. These 'Special Cheap Day' tickets were still available in 1902-03, every Sunday from Waterloo and Clapham Junction, by any LSWR train. Unfortunately, it is not known how much longer this arrangement lasted, but the cheap Sunday fares were obviously intended to attract more travellers to Brookwood.

The rates and fares were increased five times in the last couple of years of the Necropolis service: July 1939 (general revision), May 1940 (general revision), June 1940 (mourners' fares only), December 1940 (mourners' fares only), and January 1941 (coffin rates only). These changes may be summarised as follows:

	July 1939			May 1940			June 1940			Dec. 1940			Jan. 1941		
	£	s.	d.	£	s.	d.	£	s.	d.	£	s.	d.	£	s.	d.
Mourners, 1st class return		6	4		6	11		7	0		7	5		7	5
Mourners, 3rd class return		2	1		2	3		2	4		2	5		2	5
Corpses, Pauper		2	8		2	11		2	11		2	11		3	1
Corpses, Artisan		5	3		5	9		5	9		5	9		6	2
Each other corpse	1	1	0	1	3	1	1	3	1	1	3	1	1	4	6

For comparison, in May 1946 the ordinary rates from Waterloo to Brookwood were: corpses £1 13s 1d.; 3rd class passengers, 5s. 10d. (monthly return) or 4s. 3d. (single). Doubtless these increases were necessitated by the rising costs of providing facilities for the LNC and general price increases during wartime.

As noted in Chapter Four, after the destruction of the Necropolis private station in April 1941, funerals were conducted as required from time to time using platforms 11 or 12 at Waterloo for the remainder of World War II. These appear to have followed the tariff of January 1941 and the long-standing arrangements between both companies for the conveyance of funerals by railway. But these special rates did not apply to visitors to the cemetery, who previously could use the Necropolis train at these reduced rates. On their part the LNC received many enquiries concerning the availability of reduced travel for visitors to the cemetery using ordinary trains. Mr Miller, the LNC's Secretary, tried on several occasions to alter the SR's view on this. He enquired if 'facility could be granted' to issue tickets from the LNC's offices so that mourners and visitors could travel from Waterloo to Brookwood at the same rates as the existing arrangements. He referred to the frequent enquiries about the cheap tickets since 'many people would visit the Cemetery who otherwise could not make the journey ... strict instructions would be given for these tickets to be issued to mourners attending funerals or to those actually visiting graves within the Cemetery only.' Some examples of comments received by the LNC during the latter part of 1941 include 'the ordinary fare will preclude my frequent visits', 'I was greatly distressed last week to find that [the Necropolis train] no longer existed', and whether 'there is any way of getting to Brookwood cemetery by a Cheap Train for Visitors, as usual'.

In June 1941 Mr Miller suggested the LNC be issued with a supply of mourners' tickets at the 'old rate, viz: 2/5 Third Class and 7/5 First Class' to be used only by the 11.57 am departure from Waterloo 'which is about the same time the Necropolis train left the Private Station'. Getting nowhere, Mr Miller referred the matter to his Directors. After their Board meeting on 30th June, 1941 he wrote to Mr Perts (the SR's Commercial Superintendent at Waterloo) on 16th July:

> [The Directors] very much regret that you are unwilling to reconsider your decision not to allow the issue of visitors' tickets to Brookwood Cemetery - except at full ordinary fares - as this decision will undoubtedly have a serious effect on our business.
> Your Company is under an obligation to run our train and provide for visitors by that train at a 3rd Class return fare of 2s. 0d.,* the tickets being available to return by an ordinary train from Brookwood the same day. It is on that understanding that graves have been purchased in our Cemetery, and it is not reasonable to now expect grave-owners to pay 5s. 7d. because our Station and train has been destroyed by enemy action.
> Ordinary passengers to Woking (only three and a half miles short of Brookwood) can get a day ticket for 4s. 0d. yet, for those extra three and a half miles you want an additional 1s. 7d. The only day tickets you issue to Brookwood are Saturday and Sunday at 4s. 7d. - neither day being convenient for ordinary visitors.

Mr Perts' reply noted that the SR was under *no* obligation to extend the cheap fares offered by the funeral train to visitors to Brookwood 'conveyed from London by the advertised service of ordinary trains', whilst Mr Miller's further suggestion of a special 3rd class return fare for visitors to the cemetery of 3s. 6d. was also declined. It is difficult to escape the conclusion that had the SR acted differently at this time over visitors' fares, the effects of the loss of the funeral train on the LNC might have been considerably reduced. Moreover this decision rests uneasily with the London West Divisional Superintendent's declaration (5th June, 1941) that 'it is our desire to assist your Company in every way possible', or with the 1899 agreement between both companies which officially removed the restriction on the number of mourners or visitors

---

* Mr Miller was quoting the pre-war fare. From December 1940 the actual fare was 2s. 5d.

travelling on the Necropolis train. On the other hand, the SR was operating its extensive network of services under severe wartime constraints and disruptions, and may have been reluctant to lose further revenue on its ordinary services.

From time to time after the war, as noted in Chapter Four, funerals were conducted by ordinary trains down to Brookwood. At a meeting held in the Traffic Manager's Office on 13th May, 1946, it was agreed that 'the charging arrangements could remain undisturbed for the present [i.e.: January 1941 tariff] ... and be reviewed at a later date in the light of the traffic then passing'.

These rates may be compared with those operating on British Rail until 1988. The transport of a coffin by rail was somewhat difficult as BR required it to travel in a separate vehicle throughout. As Brookwood station is served solely by electric multiple units and does not deal with goods traffic, the coffin would have to be conveyed to Woking and thenceforward by road to the cemetery. If a special van was attached to a goods train from Waterloo, the cost would have been approximately £300 (including cleaning the van and extra staff required for shunting etc.). Alternatively a special train would have to be chartered from Waterloo to Woking, at a cost of over £2,000. However as from 28th March, 1988 BR no longer carried coffins.*

Remarkably, Mr Miller returned to the issue of cheap fares to Brookwood Cemetery at the end of 1956, 15 years after his original exchange of letters with the SR. In the summer of 1957 he met with a representative from the Southern Region Commercial Department to discuss holding a stock of day excursion tickets. These would be valid for travel any day by trains departing from Waterloo up to and including the 2.57 pm. It was proposed to operate this as an experiment for one year from 1st October 1957 at the special fare of 7s. 6d. However, the Directors of the LNC were unenthusiastic, and felt the 'so very little difference' between the proposed day excursion fare and the usual return fare of 9s. 4d. would not attract people to using the railway. This implies that by this time, most visitors were coming to Brookwood Cemetery by road rather than rail, and non-car owners were presumably visiting by bus or coach.

---

* I am indebted to Mr D. Latimer of Red Star Parcels (North) for supplying me with the above information. The prices quoted were those applying in 1988. (See also C.J. Polson and T.K. Marshall *The Disposal of the Dead* third ed. (English Universities Press Ltd, 1975), pp. 376-79.) Since the third edition of this book, we have witnessed not only the privatisation of Britain's rail services, but also a remarkable shift in precedent with three major Royal funerals, those of Diana, Princess of Wales (died 1997), Princess Margaret (died 2002) and that of HM Queen Elizabeth the Queen Mother (died 2002). In all cases the Royal coffins were transported by motor hearse rather than rail, presumably setting a trend for future Royal funerals. One significant exception to the transport of coffins by road since 1988 was the funeral of railwayman and trade unionist Jimmy Knapp (died 2001), whose coffin was conveyed by rail from Euston to Glasgow. *See Appendix Six* for further information on these four funerals.

Special Trains

As noted in Chapter Five, the LNC also offered the use of special or exclusive funeral trains. These were usually reserved for the rich or famous and were deemed 'special' since they operated outside the normal scope of the LNC's service. Some examples of these trains are described in Chapter Five. The standard charge for a 'special' appears to have been £15, excluding fares and the cost of conveying the body by rail.

Assuming the LNC was charged in full the LSWR's usual rate for special trains, and taking Brookwood Cemetery to be 25 miles from Waterloo, it would appear this rate was levied at 6s. a mile. This may be compared with the rates offered by other railway companies for providing special trains for personal use (such as Lord Salisbury's specials from King's Cross to Hatfield) or more sombre tasks:*

	Other Companies' Charges for Special Trains	
Company	*Rate*	*Notes*
Great Eastern Railway	5s. per mile	Minimum charge £3.
Great Northern Railway	5s. per mile (one way)	Minimum charge £3.
	7s. 6d. (return)	Fares for passengers, &c, extra.
Great Western Railway	5s. per mile	Minimum charge £3.
		Fares for passengers, &c, extra.
London & North Western	5s. per mile (one way)	Minimum charge £3.
Railway	7s. 6d. per mile (return)	Fares for passengers, &c, extra.
London Brighton &	7s. mile†/10s. mile#	Minimum charge £5† and £10#.
South Coast Railway		Passengers charged 1st class fares.
London Chatham &	7s. per mile (one way)	Minimum charge £5.
Dover Railway	10s. 6d per mile (return)	Fares for passengers, &c, extra.
Midland Railway	5s. per mile (one way)	Minimum charge £3.
	7s. 6d. per mile (return)	Fares for passengers, &c, extra.
South Eastern Railway	7s. per mile	Minimum charge £3. Mileage calculated from the nearest engine shed. Passengers charged 1st class fares.

However at some time during or after World War I, the cost of providing special funeral trains was reduced to £10 10s. 0d. A late example of this charge was the funeral train provided for Sir Nowroji Saklatvala on Monday 25th July, 1938. On this occasion the train carried 155 mourners (all travelling 1st class at a total cost of £46 10s. 0d.) along with the coffin (which also travelled 1st class at a cost of £1). The total cost of providing this train was £122 18s. 4d., including the cost of the funeral and the railway fares. Sometimes the £10 10s. 0d. fee was shared by two or more private funerals using the same train. For instance, Stanley Spooner's funeral on Saturday 6th April, 1940 included a charge of £5 5s. 0d. 'to part cost of Special Train (as agreed)'; whilst the cost of the special train for Emma Austen-Leigh's funeral on Monday 29th January, 1940 was similarly shared with another 1st class funeral on the same day.

The LNC's fares may be compared with those applied on other railway funeral services and the following table provides a useful summary of these. The main point to note from this table is that corpses often travelled free of charge in Australia!

---

* Source: J.H. Kenyon records; no date, but assumed to be *c*.1895. I am very grateful to Brian Parsons for providing details of these charges.
† Between 6 am and 10 pm.
# Between 10 pm and 6 am.

Fares Charged by Other Railway Funeral Services

Railway Funeral Service	Mourners			Coffins		
	1st	2nd	3rd	1st	2nd	3rd
Great Northern Cemetery, London	1s. 3d.	1s. 0d.	Not issued	6s.	6s.	6s.
Fawkner Cemetery, Melbourne, Australia	1s. 3d.	9d.	Not Issued	Free (except if forwarded via country stations)		
Springvale Necropolis, Melbourne, Australia				10s.*	10s.	Free
Woronora Cemetery, Sutherland, Australia	2s. 3d.	1s. 5d.	Usually Free	Free		

Tickets

Special tickets for mourners and corpses were provided for those using the Necropolis train. They were issued from the LNC's private ticket office and were of standard Edmondson style. Unfortunately only sparse details are known of LSWR issues because the LNC was particularly diligent in the collection of these tickets. In the late 19th century, *The Undertakers' Journal* noted that mourners' tickets were collected at the cemetery stations. In the SR Working Timetables, their collection was authorised to take place as the train left the cemetery. The railway photographer Mr H.C. Casserley, who travelled on the train in May 1930, was obliged to surrender both halves of his ticket before he could leave the Westminster Bridge Road station, at a time when the purchase of an additional ticket to keep was not an option. Consequently, examples are now rare. The fares were never quoted on the tickets, possibly because they had been fixed by special agreement between the LNC and LSWR.

LSWR tickets

The mourners' tickets were always issued as returns. The LSWR issue bore the legend:

Available by Necropolis
Train only.

on each half of the ticket. The return portion of the ticket was boldly overprinted with a red St Andrew's cross, which denoted the special fare. This may have been added to assist the ticket collectors at Waterloo for, after the opening of Brookwood (Necropolis) station in 1864, many mourners preferred to travel back to London by a train that left Brookwood later than the Necropolis train. This was not officially sanctioned by the LSWR until 1899, when the agreement between the LNC and the railway company made the return half valid on any train returning to Clapham Junction, Vauxhall, or Waterloo from Brookwood. The tickets were issued in standard LSWR colours, that is: first class: white, second class: blue, third class: pink.

* After 1922 coffins were charged at the following rates, 1st or 2nd class: 12s. (adult) and 6s. (child).

Left: LSWR second class mourner's return half. The bold St Andrew's cross denoted the special fare. This is the only known example of a LSWR Necropolis ticket.

The Bodleian Library: John Johnson Collection

Above and left: SR first, second and third class coffin tickets. The first was issued sometime between August 1936 and June 1937, the second between October 1934 and June 1937, and the third between March 1936 and June 1937.

Birmingham Central Reference Library: W.H. Bett Collection

Above SR third class mourner's outward half, dated 21st May, 1925. Note the variant heading to the ticket: 'SOUTHERN RLY'.

E. Foster Collection

Right: SR first and third class mourner tickets, headed 'SOUTHERN RAILWAY'. Note the large 'SA' overprint on the outward (*upper*) portions, and the bold 'M' printed in the lower right-hand corner of the return halves.

C.R. Gordon Stuart Collection

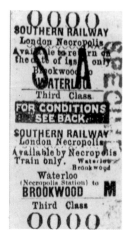

The coffin tickets were issued only as singles. They were literally one-way tickets, and it is quite possible the Necropolis train provided the origin of the phrase 'a one-way ticket'. No details of LSWR tickets are known but comparing early SR examples, which were similarly printed to the LSWR tickets, it seems likely they were designed as follows:

L & SWR [or South Western Ry.]
LONDON NECROPOLIS
COFFIN TICKET
WATERLOO to
BROOKWOOD

followed by the class of the ticket. They were issued in the same colours as the mourners' tickets.

A curious development occurred with the Necropolis tickets following the abolition of second class on the LSWR, which took place on 22nd July, 1918. This was extended to the mourners using the Necropolis train, who henceforward had to choose between two classes only, but not to the deceased! - for coffin tickets continued to be issued in three classes.*

Undoubtedly the reason was that the LNC's tariff of funeral charges continued to subdivide the cost of grave spaces and the coffin transit charges into three classes - a privilege now denied to the living.†

SR tickets

Mourners' tickets in SR days were only issued in two classes. Their design also changed. The outward (lower) half was inscribed:

SOUTHERN RAILWAY
London Necropolis
Available by Necropolis
Train only.

whilst the lower right-hand corner of this part of the ticket had a black 'M' printed there, which presumably stood for 'mourner'. The return half was similarly printed, but instead of the 'M', it was overprinted 'S A' in large, bold type. This stood for 'Special Arrangement', and explained the special fare and nature of the ticket as the red St Andrew's cross had in LSWR days. The tickets were still valid on any train returning to London, and they reminded mourners that they were 'Available to return on the date of issue only'. The ticket colours were: first class: white, third class: green.

From the evidence presented in *Appendix Three*, it is clear that occasional mourner single tickets were issued. However there are just two instances noted in the Ticket Book from mid-1937 through to April 1941, both issued during 1938, which strongly suggests that only the outward portion of the mourner's ticket would be issued on these occasions. Certainly there is no evidence

---

* As no examples of LSWR coffin tickets have come to light, it has been assumed the ticket colours remained the same even after the abolition of 2nd class.
† For a more detailed description of the three classes of funeral, *see Chapter Four*.

suggesting that mourner singles were also printed and supplied to the LNC, although any further information on this would be welcome.

First class tickets were issued in batches of between 500 and 2,000 tickets during the period 1922-1938. Stock quantities ordered by the LNC during this time were:

Date Ordered	First class Mourner Tickets Quantity Supplied	Ticket Numbers
August 1922	1,000	5500-6499
August? 1923	1,000	6500-7499
July 1924	1,000	7500-8499
June 1925	1,500	8500-9999
June 1927	1,500	0000-1499
September 1928	2,000	1500-3499
February 1932	1,000	3500-4499
August 1933	1,000	4500-5499
February 1936	500	5500-5999
September 1936	500	6000-6499
July 1938	500	6500-6999
Total	11,500	

On 25th June, 1937 the opening stock number for first class mourner tickets was 5965, whilst the very last first class mourner ticket issued on Tuesday 18th March, 1941 (which was *not* the last train) was No. 6610, leaving 389 unused. The total number of these tickets used between August 1922 and 18th March, 1941 was therefore 11,111. Further information about these ticket issues may be found in *Appendix Three*.

Third class mourner tickets were always issued in batches of 5,000 during the period 1922-1939. Stock quantities ordered by the LNC during this time were:

Date Ordered	Third class Mourner Tickets Quantity Supplied	Ticket Numbers
August 1922	5,000	5000-9999
July 1923	5,000	0000-4999
April 1924	5,000	5000-9999
January 1925	5,000	0000-4999
October 1925	5,000	5000-9999
July 1926	5,000	0000-4999
June 1927	5,000	5000-9999
April 1928	5,000	0000-4999
December 1928	5,000	5000-9999
October 1929	5,000	0000-4999
September 1930	5,000	5000-9999
August 1931	5,000	0000-4999
August 1932	5,000	5000-9999
September 1933	5,000	0000-4999
November 1934	5,000	5000-9999
July 1935	5,000	0000-4999
April 1937	5,000	5000-9999
July 1938	5,000	0000-4999
December 1939	5,000	5000-9999
Total	95,000	

On 25th June, 1937 the opening stock number for third class mourner tickets was 5250, whilst the very last third class mourner ticket issued on 11th April, 1941 was No. 7622, leaving 2,377 unused. The total number of these tickets used between August 1922 and 11th April, 1941 was therefore 92,623. From these figures it appears that during the period August 1922 to April 1941 a total of 103,734 mourners and visitors travelled to Brookwood Cemetery on the Necropolis train.

The SR coffin tickets were very similar to the LSWR type, described above, but they were of course headed 'SOUTHERN RAILWAY'. As explained previously, three classes of these tickets continued to be issued, and their colours were: first class: white; second class: light or pale blue; third class: green. The first class coffin tickets were issued in batches of either 500 or 250 during the period 1922-1941. Stock quantities ordered by the LNC during this time were:

| | First class Coffin Tickets | |
Date Ordered	Quantity Supplied	Ticket Numbers
May 1922	500	6750-7249
February 1923	250	7250-7499
July 1923	250	7500-7749
April 1925	250	7750-7999
May 1926	250	8000-8249
May 1927	250	8250-8499
February 1928	250	8500-8749
June 1928	500	8750-9249
June 1931	500	9250-9749
April 1934	250	9750-9999
July 1935	250	0000-0249
August 1936	250	0250-0499
July 1937	250	0500-0749
July 1938	250	0750-0999
February 1941	250	1000-1249
Total	4,500	

On 25th June, 1937 the opening stock number for first class coffin tickets was 0362, whilst the very last first class coffin ticket issued on 11th April, 1941 was No. 0930, leaving 319 unused. The total number of these tickets used between May 1922 and 11th April, 1941 was therefore 4,181.

The second class coffin tickets were the least used of all those issued by the LNC. They were usually produced in batches of between 500 and 250 tickets during the period 1927-1939. Stock quantities ordered by the LNC during this time were:

| | Second class Coffin Tickets | |
Date Ordered	Quantity Supplied	Ticket Numbers
January 1927	500	8500-8999
January 1929	500	9000-9499
April 1932	250	9500-9749
October 1934	250	9750-9999
June 1937	250	0000-0249
December 1939	250	0250-0499
Total	2,000	

On 25th June, 1937 the opening stock number for second class coffin tickets was 9969, whilst the very last 2nd class coffin ticket issued on 11th April, 1941 was No. 0280, leaving 219 unused. The total number of these tickets used between January 1927 and 11th April, 1941 was therefore 1,781.

The third class coffin tickets were usually produced in batches of between 500 and 2,000 tickets during the period 1922-1937. Stock quantities ordered by the LNC during this time were:

	Third class Coffin Tickets	
Date Ordered	*Quantity Supplied*	*Ticket Numbers*
January 1922	1,500	6500-7999
July 1923	1,000	8000-8999
August 1924	1,000	9000-9999
April 1925	1,000	0000-0999
September 1925	2,000	1000-2999
July 1927	2,000	3000-4999
May 1929	2,000	5000-6999
March 1936	500	7000-7499
November 1937	500	7500-7999
Total	11,500	

On 25th June, 1937 the opening stock number for third class coffin tickets was 7188, whilst the very last third class coffin ticket issued on Tuesday 8th April, 1941 (which was *not* the last train) was No. 7538, leaving 461 unused. The total number of these tickets used between January 1922 and 8th April, 1941 was therefore 11,039. From these figures it appears that during the period January 1922 to April 1941 a total of 17,001 coffins of all classes were carried down to Brookwood Cemetery on the Necropolis train.

Chapter Eight

Conclusion

'London may send all its dead to Woking for centuries to come.'
(LNC brochure)

As the Necropolis train left the private terminus at 11.40 am on Good Friday, 11th April, 1941, no-one could have known that it marked the end of an era. For this train, carrying 17 third class mourners and two coffins, proved to be the final departure from this station. It marked the end of a railway funeral service that had performed a unique undertaking for Londoners - and others - for nearly 90 years.*

Unlike a conventional railway service, which is invariably established for purely economic reasons, the Necropolis train was also founded on grounds of vital social reform. The inauguration of this railway funeral service was a direct response to an urgent need to reform the repugnant and expensive system of burial that was prevalent in London and other major cities of the period. As *The Morning Chronicle* reported in 1854:

> Amongst the various uses of railways, it was an ingenious and happy idea to include that of making them conduce at once to the comfort and health of the living, and the orderly and decent performance of the last obsequies for the departed, by removing public cemeteries to a sufficient distance from the precincts of crowded cities.

In the same year, *Punch* commented:

> We wish success to this undertaking, which is the most reasonable that we have ever heard of, and will, we hope, prove the means of saving many a poor family bereaved of its bread-winner, the waste of much money, in addition to that loss, on a foolish and useless exhibition of manners and customs, rendered compulsory by the usage of a society which calls itself civilised, but is in this respect no better than the most barbarous description of natives.

Whilst *The Times* noted, in its coverage of the opening of the London Necropolis:

> A very few years ago the idea of founding a cemetery for the metropolis which should be more than 20 miles distant from it would have been looked upon as an absurdity. Yesterday, however, saw the practical embodiment of this idea ... and it was fitting enough that the largest city in the world should have, as it will now have, the largest cemetery in the world. When, however, the spot selected is found to be 24 miles distant from the metropolis, it will be asked how cheapness of transit and a reduction upon the ordinary cost of burial can be attained? The answer of the directors is contained in their scale of fees, for which they claim extreme moderation.

---

* This train carried a Chelsea Pensioner and a member of the LNC amongst the passengers, and one 1st and one 2nd class coffin. One of the coffins contained the mortal remains of Chelsea Pensioner Edward Irish (*c.*1868-1941) of the Bedfordshire Regiment whose body appears to be the last identifiable one carried on the Necropolis train.

When Brookwood Cemetery opened in 1854 it was the largest cemetery in the world, and the railway was the only available form of transport that could cheaply and conveniently convey coffins and mourners from London to Brookwood. This remained true for many years, and many thousands of Londoners - and others - were carried to their final resting place by this train. Yet despite the longevity of its railway funeral service, the LNC failed to attract the numbers of burials the cemetery was designed to accommodate. In discussing the merits of out of town burial grounds and the use of tramways or railways to connect them to city centres, *The Undertakers' Journal* commented in 1897 that:

> One only success can be mentioned ... The London Necropolis is at such a distance [from London] that a railway service is unavoidable; this Company, however, found it so impossible for many years after they started to induce the public who had choice of cemeteries to patronise them, that they had to lay themselves out to bury the paupers of all the parishes which they could get hold of as being near to their London terminus in the Westminster Bridge Road, and it has been with them the work of a generation to make a funeral connection of their own in London in order to get a fair measure of support for that train. To this day their success in this is so limited, despite the beauty and suitability of their extensive cemetery, that they are largely indebted to those who patronise cremation for passengers for their daily train.

Even in its years of slow decline after World War I (when it was derided as 'the dead meat train' or, more coarsely, as 'the stiff's express'), still it represented a Victorian bid for more sanitary burial. Eventually the rise of motorised transport and more convenient methods of disposal succeeded in vanquishing this novel use of railway transport.

Although the Necropolis scheme was not the only railway funeral service in the world,* it was undoubtedly the best known and most enduring of them all. Hopefully this book will have fulfilled its purpose by augmenting what is known of the Necropolis service, generating a wider interest and sympathy with one of the most bizarre of British branch lines.

---

* *See Appendix Seven* for brief details of other examples of railway funeral services.

Selected timings of the Necropolis Train

Timings for some typical years are given in the table below: the details shown after 1900 should be considered as timetable 'paths' retained for the Necropolis train. In reality, it ran less often than these tables suggest.

KEY TO LETTERS

W - Weekdays only (includes Saturdays)   X - For water, if necessary
S - Sundays only   M-F - Mondays to Fridays only
T - Tuesdays only   Sa - Saturdays only
F - Fridays only   * - Departs South Station 2.15 pm

Down

1857 (August)

		W	S
Waterloo (Necropolis)	dep.	11.20	11.20
Necropolis Junction	arr.	12.20	12.20

1860

Waterloo (Necropolis)	dep.	11.35	11.20
Necropolis Junction	arr.	12.25	12.20

1866 (December)

Waterloo (Necropolis)	dep.	11.35	11.20
Brookwood (Necropolis)	arr.	12.25	12.20

1870

Waterloo (Necropolis)	dep.	11.50	11.30
Brookwood (Necropolis)	arr.	12.44	12.30

1880 (March)

Waterloo (Necropolis)	dep.	11.50	11.30
Brookwood (Necropolis)	arr.	12.47	12.27

1890 (January)

Waterloo (Necropolis)	dep.	11.50	11.30
Clapham Junction (T, F)	dep.	12.00	-
Brookwood (Necropolis)	arr.	12.47	12.27

1900 (January-April)

Waterloo (Necropolis)	dep.	11.55	11.30
Clapham Junction	dep.	-	11.40
Walton (X)	dep.	12.31	12.05
Brookwood (Necropolis)	arr.	12.52	12.27

Up

1857 (August)

		W	S
Necropolis Junction	dep.	2.30*	2.30*
Waterloo (Necropolis)	arr.	3.30	3.30

1860

Necropolis Junction	dep.	2.30	2.30
Waterloo (Necropolis)	arr.	3.30	3.30

1866 (December)

Brookwood (Necropolis)	dep.	2.30*	2.30*
Waterloo (Necropolis)	arr.	3.30	3.30

1870

Brookwood (Necropolis)	dep.	2.30	2.30
Vauxhall	arr.	-	3.26
	dep.	-	3.28
Waterloo (Necropolis)	arr.	3.32	3.33

1880 (March)

Brookwood (Necropolis)	dep.	2.35	2.30
Woking (X)	dep.	2.45	-
Waterloo (Necropolis)	arr.	3.35	3.30

1890 (January)

Brookwood (Necropolis)	dep.	2.35	2.30*
Clapham Junction (T, F)	dep.	3.24	-
Waterloo (Necropolis)	arr.	3.35	3.30

1900 (January-April)

Brookwood (Necropolis)	dep.	2.35	2.35
Clapham Junction	arr.	-	3.19
	dep.	-	3.20
Vauxhall	arr.	3.19	3.26
	dep.	3.21	3.29
Waterloo (Necropolis)	arr.	3.26	3.34

1910 (June-September)

		W				W
Waterloo (Necropolis)	*dep.*	11.52	Brookwood (Necropolis)	*dep.*	2.30*
Brookwood (Necropolis)	*arr.*	12.43	Woking Junction (X)	*arr.*	2.36
				dep.	2.38
			Vauxhall	*arr.*	3.15
				dep.	3.17
			Waterloo (Necropolis)	*arr.*	3.22

1920 (October)

Waterloo (Necropolis)	*dep.*	11.52	Brookwood (Necropolis)	*dep.*	2.35
Brookwood (Necropolis)	*arr.*	12.41	Waterloo (Necropolis)	*arr.*	3.20

1930-1 (6th July-4th July)

Waterloo (Necropolis)	*dep.*	11.42	Brookwood (Necropolis)	*dep.*	1.42
Brookwood (Necropolis)	*arr.*	12.41	Waterloo (Necropolis)	*arr.*	2.20

1939 (July)

		M-F	Sa			M-F	Sa
Waterloo (Necropolis)	*dep.*	11.44	11.54	Brookwood (Necropolis) *dep.*		2.13	2.17
Brookwood (Necropolis) *arr.*		12.21	12.52	Waterloo (Necropolis) *arr.*		2.53	2.55

(Sa 8th July to 23rd September only, then follows M-F service.)

Vignette of train in the Nonconformist section.

Appendix Two

Operating Costs for the Necropolis Train: 1854-1941*

From copies of the LNC's annual *Reports of the Directors* it is possible to chart the costs to the company of operating the Necropolis train and hence the fees paid to the LSWR and the SR for running the service. It is remarkable how modest these sums were, especially when it is remembered that the LSWR was anticipating (in 1852) to make some £40,000 a year once the cemetery opened. These figures tell a very different story and suggest the train continued to operate for so long because of the statutory obligation of the railway company to run these trains as long as the LNC offered it the traffic. For comparison the receipts from burials are also included, but it should be noted that these figures include items other than burials (from 1886 onwards) and funerals *not* conducted by railway.

Years	Total cost of carriage per LSWR/SR	Average cost per year of carriage per LSWR/SR	Total receipts from funerals	Average receipts per year from funerals
	£	£	£	£
1854-1863	10,553	1,172	41,457	4,606
1864-1873	13,537	1,354	64,630	6,463
1874-1883	11,966	1,197	74,655	7,466
1884-1893	12,976	1,298	90,864 †	9,086 †
1894-1903	16,671	1,667	185,648 #	18,565 #
1904-1913	14,322	1,432	202,716	20,272
1914-1923	13,811	1,381	301,284	30,128
1924-1933	11,911	1,191	369,156	36,916
1934-1941§	4,935	705	*Figures not available*	

Notes

* The figures are extracted from the LNC's annual *Report of the Directors*, with the exception of the carriage per SR between 1934-41 which are partly from the LNC Ticket Book (1937-41) and partly estimated (1935-37).

† From 1886 the figures for funeral receipts include general undertaking, statuary and masonry work, keeping graves in order, etc.

The increased receipts from funerals shown in the figures after 1894 are due to an increased level of undertaking conducted by the LNC (including the manufacture of coffins, and cremations offered via the Cremation Society) consequent to the opening of a showroom for statuary and masonry work in the cemetery.

§ From 1935 the costs of operating the Necropolis train were not listed separately in the annual reports. Instead this figure was included in the general expenses for undertaking and running the cemetery. The change underlined the steady decline in the fees paid to the SR. The individual year figures were: 1929: £1,227; 1930: £978; 1931: £904; 1932: £1,016; 1933: £858; and 1934: £798. The figures from 1935 are partly calculated from the LNC Ticket Book, which covers the last six months of 1937 through to April 1941. The figures used are 1934: £798 (actual); 1935: £788 (estimated); 1936: £778 (estimated); 1937: £764 (estimated from half-year figures); 1938: £682; 1939: £576; 1940: £432; and 1941 £117 (January to 11th April).

Appendix Three

Summary of Mourner and Coffin Tickets Issued:
1922-1941*

From recently rediscovered records now in the Surrey History Centre, it is possible to summarise the mourner and coffin tickets issued between 1922 and 1941. These have been tabulated and listed in two parts. The first, covering the period 1922-1937, attempts to list the annual number of tickets issued calculated from the returns in the *LSWR/SR Requisitions & Receipt Book*. The second table covers the period July 1937 to April 1941 and is based on the actual tickets issued during this period and recorded in the *LNC Ticket Book*.

The *LSWR/SR Requisitions & Receipt Book* records the dates when batches of new tickets were ordered and supplied, and the number of tickets ordered. Sometimes there are notes recording the last ticket number in the existing stock at 121 Westminster Bridge Road, and sometimes a record of the number of unused LNC tickets in stock. Unfortunately not all these details are recorded for each entry, meaning that precise figures cannot be calculated (or in the case of the second class coffin tickets for the period 1922-26, cannot be calculated at all since the first SR batch of these tickets was not ordered until as late as January 1927). Therefore the figures quoted in the first table should be approached with some caution; nevertheless it shows a slow decline in the use of the Necropolis train during this period. The actual total ticket issues for the period 1922-41 (taken from the tables in Chapter Seven) have been quoted with the known ticket issues from 1937-41 (extracted from Table Two below) deducted from them to provide comparative figures.

The second table is based on the entries found in the last *LNC Ticket Book*. This (and presumably others like it, which apparently have not survived) was used to record the sale of tickets actually used on the Necropolis train. Since the entries (usually) record the precise numbers and quantities of tickets issued, it is possible to tabulate the monthly issues of tickets from July 1937 to the very last funeral train in April 1941. The entries record the total numbers of tickets issued on each train, with a further breakdown of tickets issued for LNC staff, for trade representatives, for those issued to members of the Royal Hospital Chelsea, and those added to funeral accounts. Information about the latter usually includes the name of the deceased and sometimes the grave number.

These figures also show a continuing decline in the use of the Necropolis train, complicated by the onset of war and the effects of enemy action on the service (for instance the period from September to December 1940). Put together it is hoped these tables help indicate the usage of the private train over 20 years. From the evidence presented in *Appendix Two* (giving the costs of operating the train) this forms what will probably be the closest we can get to evaluating its operation during this period. Since the heaviest usage of the Necropolis train appears to be the period 1894-1903 (average cost of carriage £1,667), it is regrettable that further documentary evidence from this period is lacking. However, these tables suggest that at its peak, during 1894-1903, the funeral trains may have been carrying well over 9,000 mourners and over 2,000 coffins a year. We shall not see its like again.

---

* Extracted from the *LSWR/SR Requisition & Receipt Book for Tickets* and the *LNC Ticket Book* held in the Surrey History Centre.

Table One
Estimated Usage of the Necropolis Train: 1922-1937

Year	Mourners 1st	3rd	Total	Coffins 1st	2nd	3rd	Total
1922	828	5,460	6,288	564?	?	1,322	1,886
1923	960	5,730	6,690	252	?	999	1,251
1924	1,056	5,370	6,426	252	?	1,566	1,818
1925	880	5,160	6,040	243	?	1,566	1,809
1926	780	5,838	6,618	264	?	1,152	1,416
1927	1,053	4,689	5,742	244	264	1,110	1,618
1928	988	6,802	7,790	279	264	1,068	1,611
1929	468	5,865	6,333	192	144	564	900
1930	468	5,336	5,804	192	144	312	648
1931	468	5,018	5,486	199	144	312	655
1932	611	4,850	5,461	204	117	312	633
1933	549	4,580	5,129	204	108	312	624
1934	444	4,176	4,620	186	105	312	603
1935	444	4,014	4,458	192	96	312	600
1936	422	4,152	4,574	199	96	232	527
1937	336	4,170	4,506	180	109	233	522
Estimated Totals	10,755	81,213	91,965	3,846	1,591	11,684	17,121
Actual total tickets issued (to 1941)*	11,111	92,623	103,734	4,181	1,781	11,039	17,001
Total tickets issued 1922-1937 (less Table Two)†	10,470.5	80,278.5	90,749	3,614	1,480	10,692	15,786

Table Two
Actual Usage

1937	No. of trains	Mourners 1st	3rd	Total	Coffins 1st	2nd	3rd	Total
July	9	24	388	412	13	16	25	54
Aug	9	5	489	494	13	10	0	23
Sept	8	4	359	363	9	6	5	20
Oct	9	7	356	363	20	11	4	35
Nov	9	53	254	307	14	7	29	50
Dec	9	19	362	381	16	12	62	90
Total	53	112	2,208	2,320	85	62	125	272

* *See Chapter Seven* for further details of these figures.
† Figures calculated from the actual total figures from the row above (i.e. figures from the tables in Chapter Seven), less the known totals from 1937-41 from Table Two (for which see below).

Table Two (continued)
Actual Usage

1938		Mourners*				Coffins		
	No. of trains	1st	3rd	Total	1st	2nd	3rd	Total
Jan	8	32	204	236	15	8	15	38
Feb	8	3	229	232	21	4	8	33
Mar	10	21	314	335	17	6	16	39
April	11	17	378	395	14	2	18	34
May	9	8	293	301	9	8	21	38
June	8	17	320	337	8	6	4	18
July	10	189.5	504	693.5	9	2	18	29
Aug	9	5	409	414	11	2	7	20
Sept	9	6	477	483	12	1	4	17
Oct	8	6	304.5	310.5	9	7	2	18
Nov	9	16	326	342	13	4	8	25
Dec	8	11	283	294	11	7	8	26
Total	107	331.5	4,041.5	4,373	149	57	129	335

1939								
Jan	10	34	220	254	16	9	6	31
Feb	8	6	245	251	18	3	2	23
Mar	10	7	311	318	19	11	3	33
April	9	7	372	379	11	5	0	16
May	9	13	281	294	18	2	0	20
June	9	17	380	397	11	9	2	22
July	8	4	315	319	5	7	0	12
Aug	9	8	359	367	11	6	2	19
Sept	9	9	227	236	17	1	3	21
Oct	10	4	227	231	11	18	6	35
Nov	8	4	202	206	11	8	25	44
Dec	9	9	220	229	16	5	9	30
Total	108	122	3,359	3,481	164	84	58	306

1940								
Jan	10	16	210	226	20	14	0	34
Feb	7	4	138	142	16	5	0	21
Mar	9	5	309	314	15	8	3	26
April	10	7	289	296	20	2	0	22
May	9	1	308	309	13	6	3	22
June	8	4	265	269	10	5	22	37
July	9	1	349	350	11	6	2	19
Aug	9	17	297	314	12	7	0	19
Sept	2	2	39	41	4	0	0	4
Oct	2	0	27	27	5	1	0	6
Nov	0	0	0	0	0	0	0	0
Dec	2	0	39	39	4	2	0	6
Total	77	57	2,270	2,327	130	56	30	216

* Note the two instances of singles issued during this period. The author assumes that only outward portions of mourner returns were issued for these two journeys, since there is no further evidence suggesting that SR mourner single tickets were issued.

Table Two (continued)
Actual Usage

1941		Mourners			Coffins			
	No. of trains	1st	3rd	Total	1st	2nd	3rd	Total
Jan	7	4	89	93	11	19	2	32
Feb	8	7	114	121	15	10	0	25
Mar	7	7	116	123	9	10	2	21
April	3	0	90	90	4	3	1	8
Total	25	18	409	427	39	42	5	86

Total Actual Usage of								
the Necropolis train (1937-1941)	640.5	12,344.5	12,985	567	301	347	1,215	

Author's Collection

Appendix Four

BR Coffin Tickets

The discovery of a BR third class coffin ticket dated 12th November, 1952 has resulted in some interesting correspondence. It was first illustrated in the second edition. The two main questions arising are: is it genuine and, if so, was it issued for legitimate use?

Pending the discovery of examples of other classes of tickets for coffins and mourners, it seems most likely that the ticket is a demonstration print made at the Dorking printing works of the Southern Region. Mr L. Dench of the Transport Ticket Collecting Society admitted, in the Society's *Journal*, that he obtained an identical example (except for the heading, which was 'SOUTHERN RAILWAY') during a visit to the Dorking works in the late 1950s. On that occasion, a member of the staff picked up some pieces of a ticket plate and printed a 'Southern Railway' coffin ticket on green card.

Would such tickets have been issued in 1952? Chapter Four describes how the SR anticipated 'no difficulty' in conveying by ordinary services any funeral traffic that might be offered to them by the LNC. Local recollection suggests that this did happen until the late 1950s. Unfortunately during this period the cemetery records do not link funeral details with particular coffins being sent by rail (or road) from London to Brookwood. Several funerals recorded in the burial registers do have the note 'remains removed to Brookwood [date]', which at least hints at the possible removal from London by rail. It would be very difficult to determine the level of such a service, but it seems unlikely that a stock of coffin tickets would have been prepared and printed *c.*1948-49 (from the ticket heading 'BRITISH RAILWAYS (S)') for such a low usage of 11 tickets up to the end of 1952. Any such traffic in coffins is more likely to have been handled through goods or parcels waybills and conveyed by covered carriage vans or similar vehicles.

In conclusion, it seems more likely that this ticket is an interesting demonstration print. However, further research may determine whether such tickets were issued for legitimate traffic, although the cemetery records and the absence of examples of other classes of coffin and mourners tickets suggests that this evidence may not be forthcoming.

BR third class coffin ticket coloured grey-green and dated 12th November, 1952. Note the similarity of this printing with the SR first class coffin ticket (*see page 158*).

A.L. Hillman Collection

Appendix Five

The London Necropolis in Literature

Brookwood Cemetery, Britain's biggest burial ground, is mentioned in a number of novels and memoirs. For instance **Eric Newby**, in his autobiography *A Traveller's Life* (London, HarperCollins, 1982), records a conversation with his father as they left Waterloo for Swanage in the summer of 1927:

> ... as we picked our way among the points, past a platform marked Brookwood [more accurately, The London Necropolis], from which my father told me special funeral trains set out for what was England's largest cemetery, some thirty miles away in the country.
> 'Why', I asked, 'did they take dead people all that way when they could be buried in a cemetery where their houses were? Didn't they have cemeteries?' We had cemeteries near us in Barnes, as I well knew.
> 'Brookwood', my father replied, 'is for well-off people', which although he seemed to think this a sufficient answer to my question, did not really answer it.

Sir Winston Churchill, in his memoirs *My Early Life* (London, 1930; also Mandarin Books, 1990), unfortunately mixed up the Necropolis train with an early morning newspaper train:

> We had to catch the last train back to Sandhurst or be guilty of dereliction of duty. This train, which still starts from Waterloo shortly after midnight, conveys the daily crop of corpses to the London Necropolis. It ran only as far as Frimley near Aldershot which it reached at three o'clock in the morning, leaving us to drive eight or ten miles to the Royal Military College.

Basil Copper's gothic thriller *Necropolis* (USA, 1980) uses the cemetery as a central component in the plot. The activities of the LNC are used as the background for an entirely imaginary crime set in the Victorian period. In his prefatory note, the author explains:

> For plot purposes a number of changes have been made, notably relating to procedures at Brookwood and the layout of the cemetery; ... Similarly the rolling, undulating countryside beyond Pirbright has been transferred to the locale of Brookwood for the purposes of the story.
> While the period has been carefully evoked, there is no point in looking for exactitude of geographical detail or railway practices and time-tabling; these, together with locations and places, have been altered to suit the demands of the plot. But those seeking a genuinely romantic spot should visit Brookwood and its Glades of Remembrance, as I did. They will not be disappointed.

Mr Copper ingeniously weaves a plot which involves a series of bank robberies, the Necropolis train, and Brookwood Cemetery. I do not wish to spoil readers' enjoyment of discovering the plot for themselves, but the references to the train make fascinating reading.

Without giving too much away, the story begins with the exhumation of Mr Tredegar Meredith at Brookwood. This is arranged through Clyde Beatty since Meredith's daughter is suspicious of the cause of her father's death. Curiously, a similar exhumation took place in November 1889. In this case, the brothers of Ernest Weldon made representations to the Home Office for an exhumation so the exact cause of death could be determined. Weldon was only 29, and was the third husband of his wife Violet. The exhumation took place on Saturday 21st September when his coffin was placed in the mortuary (probably the large waiting room of South station). The post-mortem took place there on Monday 23rd, whilst the inquest opened in the cemetery on 24th. It was then adjourned pending further analysis of the internal organs. At the Brookwood Hotel on 6th November, the jury returned a verdict of death from natural causes.

In Chapter Seventeen the LNC's operations are brought to the reader's attention when Clyde Beatty, a private investigator, discusses a planned journey on the funeral train with his friend Dr John Rossington:

'Brookwood is a strange place ... Which is why I propose to travel on the funeral train this morning.'
He glanced quickly at his watch.
'Funeral train?' Rossington repeated.
Beatty smiled thinly.
'It certainly engaged my attention also ... So large is Brookwood that the London Necropolis Company operate their own private railway to and from the cemetery, with two stations within the walls. Every day a special funeral train leaves the Waterloo-road Station in London from its own platform for Brookwood, carrying coffins and mourners together with clergy and priests. It travels nonstop to Woking, taking the different denominations to one of the two stations within the walls. I saw it at Waterloo-road last night. It is painted white. A wag on the platforms told me it is popularly called 'The Ghost Train.'

In Chapter Eighteen Beatty's journey to Brookwood is described. Here are some extracts:

It was a quiet, hushed platform to which his footsteps led him. In the roadway beyond, black-caparisoned horses snorted and pawed the ground; caskets were being unloaded from hearses and brought down the concourse; black-garbed undertakers' mutes were huddled like flies round their charges. A pall of gloom almost visibly descended on Beatty as he tendered his ticket to the downcast attendant at the gate which separated this platform from the seething life of one of London's greatest termini.
. . . There were a great many clergymen about, Beatty noticed; conversing in groups or ministering to their charges. The coffins were being loaded now, into the rear compartments of the train which was drawn up on his right. . . .
The Ghost Train was an extraordinary sight. Both the engine and all the carriages were painted a dull white; this, combined with the sunshine struggling in through the roof overhead, gave it an ethereal, insubstantial atmosphere about it. In the winter-time, in deep countryside and with the mist curling round, it would look as phantomlike as any imagining of a Gothick novella.
. . . Carriage doors were closing; it wanted but a few minutes of departure. Beatty squeezed past a group of women in heavy mourning, their faces half-hidden behind thick veils. Muffled sobbing filled the air. A priest had his arms round an elderly woman's shoulders. He was halfway down the train now, searching the compartments for an empty carriage. People wanted to be alone in their grief; it was a natural sentiment.
. . . Scalding steam hissed and spluttered as the pistons started turning [sic]; porters and station staff stood rigidly to attention as the carriages were set in motion. The station-master had his top hat off and stood erect, his head bowed in salute. It was a strange and impressive ceremony, this leave-taking of souls, as the coffins of these departed Londoners set out on their last journey from the city they had known so well, Beatty thought.

His companions were silent, each occupied with his own thoughts as the all-white train gathered speed, snaking in a long curve out of Waterloo-road terminus. A ragged plume of steam, a final despairing whistle under the high-arched roof, and then they were in the cold sunlight of the open air. Once again the Ghost Train was Woking-bound.

. . . [Beatty] looked up again, this time at the advertisements in the spaces on the carriage wall opposite. They were all concerned with the activities of stone-masons, undertakers and casket-makers. Beatty realised that there would be little point and some impropriety in advertising more frivolous activities on such a train.

The engine was slowing a little now; they were passing through a large station. The station-master in top-hat and tail-coat was drawn up in salute, his staff standing to attention in a long file along the platform. The white-painted train, the engine with its tall smoke-stack whistling a low chord, rumbled steadily through, the bearded faces of the station personnel lowered toward the ground.

Beatty wondered again at the enormous respect his countrymen had for death; this must be a daily ritual observed at all major stations the train passed. It would make an interesting thesis. They were in open countryside again, the engine picking up speed. Beatty noticed a group of old farm workers at a level-crossing; they had their hats off and were standing stiff and frozen, like some rustic frieze. . . .

. . . A few moments later, with a hissing of steam and a shuddering of brakes, they were running alongside a high wall. Great banks of evergreens and bare trees were about them. There was a blur of faces on the platform; so dark was it now that gas-lamps were lit beneath the station canopy. Beatty saw the large notice in gold lettering, CHURCH OF ENGLAND, slide past the window. The Ghost Train had arrived at its destination.

In Chapter Nineteen, Beatty meets Inspector Munson of the Surrey Constabulary as prearranged on the Church of England platform.

[Beatty] got down into the freezing air ... Railway officials were saluting, and the noise of slamming carriage doors sounded loudly down the platform. Coffins were already being unloaded from one of the rear compartments with smooth efficiency ...

... Beatty followed [Munson] as he strode down the platform, brushing past railway-men and black-garbed ministers. To the investigator's astonishment the Inspector pushed open a glass-panelled door. The murmur of voices came out to meet them. Beatty blinked in the warm gaslight, looking incredulously at the long buffet counter, the shelves full of bottles, the fire blazing cheerfully in the enamelled grate. A warm, cherry-coloured carpet stretched out underfoot.

'It's early in the day, but you'll not say no to a whisky', Munson said.

He pushed his way up to the bar, chuckling at Beatty's expression.

'Oh, the Necropolis Company thought of everything', he said. 'They've not forgotten the comfort of the living. There's a buffet on each station at Brookwood. That's the best thing about it.'

... Beatty turned, glass in hand, as the thunder of the engine sounded; the rumble of wheels followed, and steam obscured the buffet windows. The blanched length of the Ghost Train passed out of sight ...

Later on in the plot, Beatty again travels to Brookwood. This time he explores the train in more detail:

Beatty finished the paper and put it down on the seat at his elbow. The two clerics were still engaged in fierce controversy ... He picked up his case and stepped over the two men's feet with a mumbled apology; he opened the door and closed it behind him again.

The corridor was empty. The train lurched forward, and Beatty went slowly back down the carriage, scrutinising the compartments carefully. He took his time, taking pains to avoid revealing his own features …

He passed through into the next car. The air was thick with cigar smoke; sober-looking men with beards, some wearing silk hats, were engaged in animated conversation. It was such a contrast with the rest of the train that Beatty was, for a moment, slightly startled.

Then he realised that these were the last two compartments before those containing the coffins. They were mostly undertakers and their employees in here; hence the jovial atmosphere. Death was an everyday matter to these people; they were professionals, and today was no different from any other. Outside, among the mourners, they would be grave and discreet. Here, in private, they were free to unbutton, joke, and talk shop.

… He went on down to the last coach, … It was darker in here, and Beatty waited for a moment in order to allow his eyes to adjust. There was an overpowering, sickly perfume of flowers. As he moved forward he saw the wreaths and sprays of blooms stacked along the floor and vibrating slowly with the movement of the train …

The coffins were resting on special oak stands set along the sides of the carriage and in rows down the centre, making aisles along which Beatty walked in the semigloom, his eyes passing quickly over the silent ranks of caskets. He carried his case under his arm now; pale oblongs of mist shone in the windows at the sides of the carriage, and the roar of the train intensified as they passed under a bridge.

… He passed through into the last carriage; there would be nothing beyond that but the guard's van. The next was a replica of the first: the coffins on their stands set out in aisles, more flowers, the same sickly perfume.

It was darker here as some of the window blinds appeared to be drawn. Beatty went down the central aisle, almost instinctively. He quickly examined the serried rows of caskets. He stopped near the end, where the shadow was thickest. The silver handles and name-plates of the oak coffins shimmered softly in the dim light.

And there we leave Clyde Beatty to pursue his criminals and solve the case.

The novelist **Andrew Martin** has also used the Necropolis train as a theme in his murder mystery *The Necropolis Railway*, first published in 2002. In a prefatory note, Martin states that the railway funeral service 'provides part of the backdrop to this story, but it should be stressed that no events such as those described here ever took place, nor did any people such as those presented here ever exist'.

Martin's mystery is set in 1903. A chance encounter with Rowland Smith (a senior railway official), leads Jim Stringer (a railway porter from Robin Hood's Bay), to move from Yorkshire to London. He hopes to work his way up the LSWR to drive express trains. When Stringer arrives at Waterloo, he discovers a world of garish pubs and brothels surrounded by towering factories, a world which reverberates with the din of trains passing by on the viaducts overhead. Stringer is set to work cleaning engines at Nine Elms and soon finds that his duties are confined to the 'half link' Necropolis railway. For some reason the men he works with take an instant dislike to him. Stringer discovers that his predecessor met a grim fate, and he starts to wonder what exactly happened to him. The main part of the novel concentrates on Stringer playing the detective. He discovers that several people connected with the Necropolis railway died suspiciously, and eventually solves the mystery behind this.

In Chapter Seven Stringer is introduced to the LNC and its workings, whilst the following chapter finds him visiting the private station for the first time. On this occasion two hearses and two coaches (both incorrectly painted black) are provided for the following day's funerals. When Stringer naively believes the bodies are already on the train, driver Rose replies curtly 'we don't run the stiffs *in*to the Necropolis station, we run them out.' The funeral trains are hauled by the fictitious 'Bampton tanks', and driver Rose deserves a severe reprimand or fine for deliberately shutting off steam late thereby giving the funeral set 'a bit of a whack' against the buffers.*

Given time to look around the station, Stringer is conveniently able to locate and look through the LNC's Minute Books, yet nobody seems to notice him doing so.

In Chapter Fifteen, Stringer gets his first trip out to the cemetery, with the train looking 'more than ever like cripples from a bygone age'. At Brookwood station 'a new, wide, blank station', the tank runs round the train and Stringer follows it on foot, noting as he does so that the cemetery was 'like the Yorkshire Moors squashed flat'. North station is described as 'unreal'. Like Basil Copper, Andrew Martin incorrectly describes the hearse vans as being manned by a guard, on this occasion by the character 'Saturday Night Mack'. Moving onto South station, Stringer then explores the grounds before returning to the bar.

In Chapter Nineteen, Stringer assists with another funeral train, and in Chapter Twenty-Four he visits the deserted London terminus on Christmas Day where the curiously accessible Minute Books suggest that the LNC is selling off land. In Chapter Twenty-Five Stringer makes a more memorable journey down to Brookwood, but describing that would spoil part of the plot.

The Necropolis Railway was published to wide critical acclaim. Unlike Basil Copper's *Necropolis*, there are few set piece descriptions of the cemetery and one wonders if anyone reading the book would be inspired to visit Brookwood, whilst at least one reviewer found Jim Stringer 'rather boring'. Personally I found the novel disappointing and unconvincing regarding details of the LNC, but it has clearly succeeded as a period detective novel.

---

* Compare this fictional cavalier driving with the real driver Deller's experience after hitting the buffers in the private station on a wet day in 1920. Deller was suspended for one day without pay (*see Chapter Five*).

Appendix Six

Road or Rail? Four Recent Funerals

As noted in Chapter Seven, there has been a significant change in precedent with three major Royal funerals, none of which involved the use of the railway for the carriage of the coffin. These are the funerals of HRH Diana, Princess of Wales (died 1997), HRH Princess Margaret (died 2002), and that of HM Queen Elizabeth the Queen Mother (died 2002). In striking contrast, the funeral of railwayman and trade unionist Jimmy Knapp (died 2001) resulted in his coffin being carried by train. This was the first railway funeral on a British main line since that of Lord Mountbatten in September 1979. Jimmy Knapp's funeral train is all the more significant as an exception to the end of this traffic since 1988, and all the more remarkable for a commoner.

HRH Diana, Princess of Wales (1961-1997)

Diana, Princess of Wales was killed in a car accident in Paris on 31st August, 1997. Her mortal remains were returned to RAF Northolt by an aircraft of the Queen's Flight later the same day. From there her coffin was taken to Fulham mortuary before being transferred to the Chapel Royal, St James's Palace, on Monday 1st September. On the evening of 5th September her coffin was taken by motor hearse to Kensington Palace, where it rested overnight in the Princess's apartments. The main part of her funeral service took place on 6th September when the coffin was carried on a gun carriage in procession from Kensington Palace to Westminster Abbey. At the end of the service, her coffin was taken by motor hearse to Althorp House, Northants, accompanied only by two funeral directors and a security guard. Meanwhile the principal mourners, including the Prince of Wales, Prince William, Prince Harry and the Spencer family, travelled in the Royal Train. This was hauled by the two class '47s' dedicated to the Royal Train, Nos. 47798 *Prince William* and 47799 *Prince Henry*. The Royal Train departed from Euston station at 12.35 pm and travelled north to Long Buckby, Northamptonshire, arriving there at 2.06 pm. The mourners then transferred to waiting cars for the short journey to Althorp House and the private funeral arrangements whereby the Princess of Wales's coffin was buried on an island in a lake within the Althorp estate. Meanwhile the Royal Train continued to Nuneaton, where the locomotives ran round before returning to Wolverton. The Princess of Wales's funeral arrangements are interesting in that the Royal Train was not entirely dispensed with, although her coffin made its journey north by motor hearse, separated from the principal mourners but not the public.

HRH Princess Margaret (1930-2002)

Princess Margaret died at Kensington Palace in the early morning of 9th February, 2002. Her coffin was moved to St James's Palace on 11th February so that family and friends could pay their respects. In the late afternoon of 14th February her coffin was driven by motor hearse to Windsor Castle in readiness for a private service in St George's Chapel the next day. The coffin was placed in the nave of the chapel where it rested overnight. The private funeral service took place in the chapel choir on the following day, precisely 50 years after her father, King George VI, was laid to rest. At the end of the service, her coffin was carried through the West Door and taken by motor hearse to Slough Crematorium. Her ashes were subsequently interred in the tomb of King George

VI in the Royal chantry dedicated to his memory within St George's Chapel. Apart from the use of the motor hearse, rather than the Royal Train, her funeral was remarkable for the choice of Slough Crematorium (described in *The Times* as 'a plain municipal crematorium'), but it should be noted that the Princess, who desired a private funeral, had planned all these arrangements in advance.

HRH Queen Elizabeth the Queen Mother (1900-2002)

The Queen Mother died peacefully in her sleep on Saturday 30th March, 2002 at Royal Lodge, Windsor. Her coffin was moved to the Royal Chapel of All Saints, Windsor Great Park, on 31st March. On 2nd April it was taken by car to the Queen's Chapel, St James's Palace. On Friday 5th April the coffin was taken by ceremonial procession to Westminster Hall for the lying-in-state. The Queen Mother's funeral took place on Tuesday 9th April, 2002. The coffin was drawn by gun carriage in ceremonial procession from Westminster Hall to Westminster Abbey. After the service in the Abbey her coffin was taken by motor hearse to Windsor Castle. Later, members of the Royal Family attended the private interment of her coffin in the Royal chantry dedicated to King George VI within St George's Chapel. The funeral arrangements of the Queen Mother, a senior member of the Royal Family, strongly suggests that all future Royal funerals are likely to be conveyed by road rather than rail.*

Jimmy Knapp (1940-2001)

Jimmy Knapp died on 13th August, 2001, after a long battle against cancer. The first part of his funeral service took place on 20th August in the church of Our Lady Queen of Peace, Chiswick High Road, West London. The coffin was draped with the banner of the Rail Maritime & Transport Workers' Union West of Scotland District. Afterwards the coffin was taken by motor hearse to Euston station. It was met by a guard of honour comprising members of the RMT Union, other trade unionists and fellow railwaymen. The coffin was transferred to the Virgin Trains' Driving Van Trailer No. 82142 for the journey to Glasgow. The DVT luggage area had been internally lined in black by the undertakers, whilst an additional 1st class carriage was attached to the train formation for the use of family and mourners. The train was hauled by class '87' No. 87033 *Thane of Fife*. The final part of his funeral service took place on 22nd August at Hurlford Church, near Kilmarnock, where he was buried next to his mother. Jimmy Knapp's funeral arrangements are remarkable, not only for involving the railway to convey his coffin from London to Glasgow, but also that this was arranged for a commoner. Clearly the rich and titled prefer the car and the crematorium to the funeral train and earth burial.

---

* The funeral of the last Queen Consort, HM Queen Mary (1867-1953), followed a similar pattern, although the arrangements for her funeral were curtailed due to the precedence given to the planning of the Queen's Coronation on 2nd June, 1953. Queen Mary died peacefully in her sleep at Marlborough House on 24th March, 1953. Her coffin was moved to the Queen's Chapel on 27th March where it rested until carried in ceremonial procession to Westminster Hall on 29th March. Her coffin lay-in-state until 31st March when it was moved privately by motor hearse to the Albert Memorial Chapel, Windsor Castle, awaiting burial in St George's Chapel later the same day. The Royal Train left Paddington station at 9.15 am to convey the principal mourners from London to Windsor, and returned immediately after the funeral service was over.

Appendix Seven

Other Cemetery Railway Services

The LNC pioneered railway funerals, and it is not surprising to discover that a number of other cemeteries used the railway as an alternative method of receiving funeral parties. These notes are not intended to be a comprehensive survey of this topic and are limited to systems with railways running into, or with platforms at the perimeter of, the cemetery served by funeral trains. Hopefully these brief notes will give the reader an idea of the range of services offered elsewhere, and how the essential elements of the LNC's system of railway funerals were copied. Remarkably, at least five of these railway funeral services were based in southern Australia. Details of the hearse vans used for these services (where known) are described in *Appendix Eight*. Sources of information may be located in the *Bibliography*, and I am very grateful to David Weatherill for supplying for information on the Australian cemeteries, and to Brian Parsons and Chris Molyneux for information on the Cape Town service. A table summarising the various charges (where known) may be found in Chapter Seven.

Great Northern Cemetery, Colney Hatch, London (1861-1863)

This was the only other dedicated standard gauge railway funeral service in the British Isles. These funeral trains operated from a substantial private station at Belle Isle (just outside King's Cross) to the Great Northern Cemetery at Colney Hatch. A siding led from New Southgate to another private station on the perimeter of the cemetery which in 1861 was much closer to the main line. The funeral trains were operated by the Great Northern Railway (GNR) and only ran between 1861-63 and possibly for a period during the cholera epidemic of 1866. The station at King's Cross was acquired by the GNR in 1876 as a necessary prelude to the widening of the approaches to the terminus; however the remnants of the funeral station survived until 1962. The railway company also purchased the siding at Colney Hatch, whilst the Great Northern Cemetery was permitted to sell the virtually unused western section of its cemetery (that part closest to the main line) under a private Act of Parliament of 1876. However, much of the site remained as it was until World War I when part of the former western cemetery was sold for a factory site. After exhumations had taken place, the remaining former cemetery land was redeveloped for housing under private legislation passed in 1968.

Maitland Road Cemetery, Cape Town, South Africa *(operational dates not known)*

This service operated from Cape Town to Maitland Road Cemetery, otherwise known as Woltemade Cemetery. The cemetery is 120 hectares in size, but very long and narrow and is bordered by Voortrekker Road on one side, and the main railway line on the other. There were four stations along the length of the cemetery, named Woltemade 1, Woltemade 2, Woltemade 3, and Woltemade 4.* The funeral train stopped at each cemetery station in turn, discharging its coffins, funeral staff and mourners. They would be met by cemetery staff, and the coffin(s) would be moved through the cemetery grounds using hand biers. There were at least two chapels near Woltemade 1, one Roman Catholic and one Anglican, but both have fallen into disrepair and are no longer used. The cemetery is divided into denominational allotments up to the crematorium. The cemetery includes areas reserved for Greeks, Jews (now full), and a Dutch Reformed Section.

* Woltemade, whose full name was Wolraad Woltemade, was a hero who saved many people from drowning in Table Bay.

New Melbourne General Cemetery, Fawkner, Australia (1906-1939)

The New Melbourne General Cemetery (now known as Fawkner Cemetery) opened in 1906 to provide additional burial space for the city. The cemetery was laid out next to the railway from Melbourne to Somerton, and had a branch line describing a semi-circle along the edge of the grounds, which served two further cemetery stations. The funeral trains were suburban stopping trains, and special fares applied for funeral parties. The trains usually ran on weekdays at 2.33 pm (returning from the cemetery at 4.23 pm), and on Sundays at 2.50 pm (returning at 4.33 pm). The journey took just over 30 minutes each way. The trains left Melbourne Flinders Street No. 10 east end platform. At the cemetery, the coffins were unloaded onto four-wheel hand biers and then onto a two-wheel horse-drawn cart which took the coffin to the graveside. Meanwhile the engine ran round its train in readiness for the return journey. In its final years, the trains ran Sundays only, leaving Flinders Street at 2 pm, with the last train running in 1939. One of the hearse carriages used on this service has been restored from three surviving bodies, and is now on display within the cemetery grounds (*see page 184*).

Rookwood Cemetery, Sydney, Australia (1867-1948)

Rookwood Cemetery was opened in 1867 and was extended in 1881. At 777 acres, it is the largest Victorian cemetery in the world. Rookwood's railway system was closely based on the LNC's service, with a substantial special station (referred to as a 'Receiving House') built of sandstone in Regent Street. At the cemetery, there was a trailing connection from Haslem's Creek station (now called Lidcombe) running into the necropolis and the mortuary station. This was another substantial sandstone structure 104 ft by 45 ft, with a high pitched roof carried on 14 columns and buttressed side walls. As originally built the station had a gothic arch 46 ft high and 40 ft wide decorated with two stone angels, one on each side of the arch. This opening allowed the funeral trains to enter the station. A platform was provided on each side of the single line, whilst coffins could be removed from the hearse carriages under complete cover. Funeral trains usually left Sydney at 9.15 am and 3 pm with the hearse carriages at the rear of the train. The trains were reversed into the cemetery from Haslem's Creek and, after the completion of funerals, were hauled back to Haslem's Creek where the engine ran round the train before returning to Sydney.

Haslem's Creek station was renamed Rookwood in 1876, and in 1887 a platform was provided on the main line for the cemetery and called Necropolis. In 1890 the mortuary station was re-named Rookwood Cemetery. After the major extensions to the cemetery in 1881, the Cemetery Trustees arranged for the cemetery railway to be extended in 1897. This involved the opening out of the end wall in the original cemetery station, to allow the railway to be extended. The new station was called 'mortuary terminus', and was provided with a run-round loop, whilst a new loop siding was provided near the main line, to avoid funeral trains being propelled through the cemetery. A further platform was provided for the Roman Catholic sections in 1901 and lay between the existing two stations. In 1908 the cemetery railway was extended again, with a run-round loop at the end. The stations were then designated Cemetery stations 1-4.

In 1914 the main line station at Rookwood was renamed Lidcombe, whilst the platform serving the cemetery was then called Rookwood, and was available for main line trains to serve the necropolis. With the four cemetery stations and use of run-round loops, it was possible to accommodate up to four funeral trains on busy days. Over the years the rail traffic declined and latterly trains ran on Saturdays and Sundays only, until the trains were finally withdrawn from 3rd April, 1948. The original stone station building caught fire and its roof was destroyed in the early 1950s. The derelict structure was finally purchased in 1957 by the Vestry of All Saints Church of England, was carefully dismantled, and became the new church of All Saints, North Ainslie, Canberra, dedicated in 1959. This, and the 'Receiving House' in Sydney are all that remain of this once extensive cemetery railway system.

Sandgate Cemetery, Newcastle, New South Wales, Australia (1880-1985)

Sandgate Cemetery opened in 1880 to serve the Newcastle district. A branch line from the Northern Line was built into the cemetery, terminating at a centrally located mortuary platform. A special receiving station was built at Honeysuckle, Newcastle, NSW, especially for this service. Regular funeral trains ran from here to the cemetery using hearse cars similar to those used at Rookwood and Woronora cemeteries. Being situated near the Hunter River, funerals could also be received by boat or barge. The original railway layout included a centrally placed siding with connecting spurs in each direction with the main line. One of the spurs was later removed. Subsequent extensions to the cemetery meant that grave sites became more and more remote from the mortuary platform, and from the 1930s greater use was made of motor hearses. However rail access continued to be available until 1985, and the old platform is preserved within the cemetery grounds.

Springvale Necropolis, Victoria, Australia (1904-1950)

The Necropolis at Springvale opened in 1904 to serve Melbourne. A railway link was provided from Spring Vale station, over the Dandenong Road, and into the cemetery where a mortuary platform was provided. The original intention was that the private railway would encircle the initial cemetery area of 108 acres but this, along with the proposed elaborate city mortuary station, was never completed. Coffins and mourners could be picked up at stations along the route, particularly Hawksburn and Malvern where mortuary accommodation was provided. By the 1920s the funeral trains were irregular and inconvenient for many potential visitors, and were combined with general passenger services. Although the line was electrified in 1922, which reduced the journey time, this did little to offset the increased use of motor hearses. Falling patronage of the railway funeral service was not helped with the introduction of charges for coffins introduced after World War I. The last funeral train ran in October 1950 and the line was formally closed in December 1951.

Woronora Cemetery, Sutherland, New South Wales, Australia (1895-1944)

Woronora Cemetery was opened in 1895. A short railway linking the cemetery with Sutherland station was opened in July 1900. The special trains began their journey from platforms 12-19 at Sydney Central station and picked up coffins and mourners at different stations along the route. Two small mortuary sheds were provided at Sydenham and Kogarah stations to store the coffins until the train arrived; both these stations were close to local hospitals. Funeral trains would bring up to eight coffins to the cemetery platform, which boasted a line of palm trees. They were then loaded onto a four-wheel cart which would transport them to the graveside. About 50 minutes was allowed for the funeral services to take place, and the guard of the train would ring a warning bell approximately 10 minutes before the departure of the train. Later, electric train services departed from platforms 22 or 23 at Central station and passengers would have to change at Sutherland for the short trip by rail motor into the cemetery. Funeral trains continued to use the railway until August 1944, although the line did not finally close until May 1947.

Other Companies' Hearse Vans

The LNC pioneered the design of railway hearse carriages. This Appendix provides some notes on the hearses provided by other companies, some of whom provided no dedicated railway funeral service. These notes are not intended to be a comprehensive survey of this topic but representative of some of the designs used. Often the hearse carriages provided were converted from existing stock rather than special builds. Other sources are listed in the *Bibliography*, and I am very grateful to David Weatherill and Steve Hayes for further information.

Railways at Home and Overseas

Festiniog Railway

The Festiniog Railway operated a single hearse van which is still preserved in the museum at Porthmadoc. It was originally built as a type '2' quarryman's coach in 1875 and was converted into a hearse van between 1885-86. The van would have been very useful before road improvements in the area. For families living in otherwise isolated communities further up the line, the hearse van provided the easiest means of transporting coffins down to Minfford Cemetery. People from Penrhyn and Minfford who worked at Blaenau Festiniog would also wish to be buried in their home town. The hearse van remained in use until the late 1920s and remains a remarkable piece of rolling stock.

Operating on a narrow gauge system the coffin was placed in line with the track and was loaded and unloaded from double end doors. The coffin rested on three rollers located on the floor of the van, which would also have assisted with the insertion and removal of the coffin. Metal rings low down on the inside framing of the vehicle suggest the coffin may have been further secured by straps or ropes. The roof incorporates four Grecian urns, one at each corner, and a circular ventilator in the centre. Further ventilation was provided by a perforated section forming the top plank of the central panel in the side of the vehicle. The van was painted black but it is not known what number it carried since it was not included in the detailed list of rolling stock that was compiled in 1887.*

Great Northern Railway

Funeral trains served the Great Northern Cemetery between 1861-63 and possibly for a period during 1866. It appears that only one hearse van was ever provided, and it is not known if it was specially constructed for this service or another vehicle was converted to carry coffins. The van may have been based on a GNR 'transhipment van', although it is not known if these were the original design, or whether the transhipment vans evolved from the hearse carriage. The design was very similar to the LNC's hearse vans, with four double door 'compartments', each containing two coffins on two levels, with a total capacity of eight coffins.†

* J.I.C. Boyd *The Festiniog Railway* Volume 2 (Oakwood Press, 1975).
† See Martin Dawes *The End of the Line: The Story of the Railway Service to the Great Northern London Cemetery* (Barnet & District Local History Society, 2003).

Midland Railway

The Midland Railway appears to have built two series of hearse carriages. The first, about which very little is known, was ordered in February 1862, when Lot 4059 followed a request from the General Manager for a 'corpse van' to be constructed in place of a carriage truck. This was followed by another van in March 1869, under Lot 5930. The second series of vans were sanctioned in January 1888 when four were ordered to Lot 99 and Diagram 424, and these probably replaced both the earlier Kirtley vans. The new vans had a 10 ft wheelbase and the bodies were 16 ft 7 in. long and 8 ft wide. Lacy and Dow described them as 'neat and attractive in appearance' and outwardly they looked like small parcels vans. The corpse vans had two coffin compartments accessed by two sets of double doors each side. The internal arrangements of the vans are not known but, assuming there was a central shelf provided, these vans may have accommodated up to four (or eight) coffins each. An official photograph exists showing van No. 21 as built. All four vehicles were transferred into London Midland & Scottish Railway ownership and were renumbered 1840-1843 in 1923. Although the exact dates of withdrawal are not known, they had all gone by 1933.*

New Melbourne General Cemetery, Fawkner, Australia

Equally interesting were the 'hearse cars' provided for the New Melbourne General Cemetery, now known as Fawkner Cemetery. Six 'mortuary carriages' were constructed at the Newport railway workshops in 1902-03. These had a wheelbase of 10 ft 6 in. with van bodies 16 ft 6 in. long and 8 ft wide. They were originally numbered C4-C9 inclusive, but the coding was changed to 'J' in 1908. There were seven compartments for coffins on two levels, each compartment having its own individual door for access, except the wider central compartments (3 ft 1 in. wide) which had double doors. This wider compartment also had a 'flower tray' above the coffins shelves for storing wreaths and flowers. The doors were alternately louvred or panelled, the wider central compartment having panelled doors only. In 1912 two of these hearse cars were cut up and the remaining four were made into longer vehicles, 25 ft 9 in. long and mounted on a six-wheel underframe. These cars now accommodated up to 20 coffins each, with one wider double door compartment in each. They were renumbered J7-J10, and two were

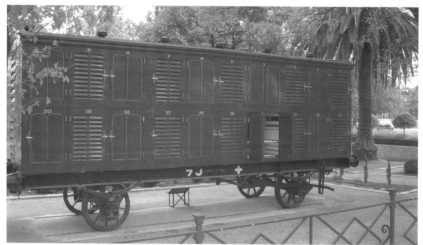

Preserved hearse van in Fawkner Cemetery, Australia.   *Courtesy of Steve Hayes*

* R.E. Lacy and George Dow *Midland Railway Carriages* Volumes 1-2 (Wild Swan, 1984-86).

assigned to the Springvale Cemetery line. Although the final funeral trains ran in 1939, in 1990 it was discovered that three of the vans survived in various states on a farm. The Fawkner Cemetery authorities decided to acquire these remains and use them to restore one of the mortuary cars to its 1912 condition. This was completed in April 1993 and the carriage forms the centrepiece to a memorial garden within the cemetery.

Rookwood Cemetery, Sydney, Australia

Special hearse carriages were provided of two main types. The early design (1865) was for low four-wheel vans that carried up to five coffins on two levels, allowing a maximum capacity of 10 coffins. When the compartment doors were open, each coffin shelf could be extended outwards to assist with the loading and unloading of the coffins. A double roof assisted in keeping the compartments cool, whilst louvres were placed in the middle of the coach ends. Further examples of these vans were provided in the 1880s.

In 1914, the last of the four-wheel vans was removed from revenue earning service. They were replaced by longer 42 ft bogie vehicles with 15 double-deck compartments and a total capacity of up to 30 coffins. A double roof assisted in keeping the compartments cool, whilst louvres were placed in the centre of the coach ends and in the doors of the three central compartments. At Rookwood, the hearse carriages were usually attached to the rear of the funeral train.*

Sandgate Cemetery, Newcastle, New South Wales, Australia

This service was provided with similar vehicles to those described under the entry for Rookwood Cemetery.

Springvale Necropolis, Victoria, Australia

This service was provided with similar vehicles to those described under the entry for the New Melbourne General (Fawkner) Cemetery.

Woronora Cemetery, Sutherland, News South Wales, Australia

This service was provided with similar vehicles to those described under the entry for Rookwood Cemetery.

Tramways at Home and Overseas

Calumet & South Chicago Railway (and connecting lines)

Two 'funeral cars' or trams were provided for hire in the early 1900s. They were available from any point on the Calumet & South Chicago Railway, the Chicago City Railway, or the Whiting & East Chicago Electric Railway to and from the following cemeteries: Oakwood, Mount Greenwood, Mount Olivet, and Mount Hope. *The Undertakers' Journal* provided the following description of these majestic vehicles:

---

* David Cooke et al *Coaching Stock of the New South Wales Railways* (Eveleigh Press, 1999).

'Elmlawn' funeral car or tram of the International Railway Company, Buffalo, New York. Built in 1895 and destroyed by fire in 1915. This is almost identical in design to the funeral trams used on the Calumet & South Chicago Railway. The long window is over the 'cabinet' for the casket or coffin, which is loaded via the door panel immediately below the window. *Author's Collection*

Each car is 43 ft long and has seats for 34 passengers. The interior is divided into two sections, one for the casket and pall-bearers, the other for the mourners and friends. The casket is carried in a longitudinal cabinet or vault extending on one side of the space allotted to the pall-bearers. Access to the cabinet is had through a door on the outside made to hinge downward and held horizontally, when opened, by silvered chains. By a simple system of rollers the casket is placed in position just as in a hearse. The top of the casket cabinet is about three feet above the floor in the interior of the car, and forms a suitable place for the display of floral emblems. The pall-bearers' section has a longitudinal seat, extending along one side and giving seating accommodation for six persons. The mourners' compartment has six cross seats on each side and one longitudinal seat in each corner, and gives seating room for 28 persons.

It is not known for how long these trams were used for funerals. The fare appears to have been £2 5s. 0d. for the hire of the funeral car.

Great Orme Tramway

Llandudno Urban District Council requested the Great Orme Tramway to convey corpses to the St Tudno Cemetery at reasonable fixed charges and in 'a decent and seemly manner'. The company charged 2s. 6d. for the coffin plus normal fares for the mourners. It appears that one of the company's four-wheel vans (otherwise known as 'jockey cars', and usually used to take coke up to the boiler house) was used to transport the coffins.*

Paris Municipal Funeral Cars

When the cemetery at Vincennes was deemed full, a new burial ground was provided three miles further outside Paris. This was felt to be too great a distance for 'ordinary' funeral processions, and the authorities therefore provided a special 'coffin tramcars' and constructed a tramline to the gates of the new cemetery. The car was divided into four compartments: one for the driver, one for the pall-bearers, one for the clergy, and one for the mourners containing 24 seats. One side of the vehicle contained an aperture into which the undertakers could slide the coffin. Floral wreaths could be placed in an opening above. A similar car was usually coupled to the coffin tram which contained the rest of those assisting at the ceremony. The coffin cars were painted dark green and underwent trials in January 1912 before going into service. The journey of three miles was covered in about 10 minutes.

* R.C. Anderson *Great Orme Tramway: The First 80 Years* (Light Rail Transit Association, n.d.).

Appendix Nine

The Brookwood Cemetery Society

The Brookwood Cemetery Society was established in April 1992 to promote a wider interest in the Cemetery and its history. The Society's aims include:

- ensuring the long-term future of the Cemetery
- assisting with maintenance, clearance and renovation work
- ensuring that the Cemetery remains a valuable haven for a wide variety of flora and fauna
- helping relatives locate graves in the Cemetery

The Brookwood Cemetery Society organises a regular programme of events during the year. This includes regular guided walks through the grounds, usually on the first Sunday in the month, and also at other times; regular clearance sessions in the grounds; an Open Day, usually in June; Society Lectures by visiting speakers which cover some aspect of the history of cemeteries or undertaking, or about people buried at Brookwood. The Society also arranges visits to other cemeteries, graveyards and crematoria. In addition, members of the Brookwood Cemetery Society give talks to local organisations about the Cemetery and the work of the Society; it also publishes leaflets and booklets on the Cemetery.

Membership is open to anyone interested in the work of the Society. Benefits of membership include:

- access to the Society's microfilm set of the burial registers, 1854-1976
- a regular Newsletter (*The Brookwood Express*) giving up-to-date information about the Society's activities
- the opportunity to assist in recording details of those buried at Brookwood
- reduced admission to Society Lectures

If you would like to know more about the Society, please visit its Website at www.tbcs.org.uk

Bibliography

(I) Primary Sources

(a) Manuscript sources
(i) Records of the LNC
Miscellaneous surviving records of the company including minute books, copies of agreements, draft agreements, letters, reports, receipt books, burial registers, brochures, etc. Consulted at the Cemetery Office, Brookwood Cemetery (1978-9).
(ii) Parliamentary records
a. Minutes of evidence of the Select Committee of the House of Lords, 1852, Vol. 4.
b. Minutes of evidence of the Select Committee of the House of Commons, group DD 1852, Vol. 40. Consulted at the House of Lords' Records Office.

(b) Printed Parliamentary Papers and Acts of Parliament

1842 Vol. X	*Report from the Select Committee on the Improvement of Health in Towns: Effect of the Interment of Bodies in Towns.*
1843 Vol. XII	*A Supplementary Report on the Results of a Special Inquiry into the Practice of Interments in Towns.*

1850 Vol. II   *A Bill for Promoting Extramural Interments.*
1850 Vol. XXI *Report on a General Scheme for Extramural Sepulture.*
1850   *Metropolitan Interments Act* (13 & 14 Vict., c.lii)
1852   *London Necropolis & National Mausoleum Act* (15 & 16 Vict., c. cxlix)
1852   *Metropolitan Interments Amendment Act* (15 & 16 Vict., c.lxxxv)
1854   *Woking Commoners Act* (17 & 18 Vict., c. ix)
1855   *London Necropolis & National Mausoleum Amendment Act* (18 & 19 Vict., c. clxiii)
1864   *London Necropolis & National Mausoleum Amendment Act* (27 & 28 Vict., c. lxii)
1869   *London Necropolis & National Mausoleum Amendment Act* (32 Vict., c. iii)
1946   *London Necropolis Act* (9 & 10 Geo. 6, c. xviii)
1956   *London Necropolis Act* (4 & 5 Eliz. 2, c. lxviii)
1975   *The Brookwood Cemetery Act 1975* (c. xxxv)

(c) Books, pamphlets, etc.

Anon.   *Extramural Burial: the Three Schemes* (London, 1850; this pamphlet is probably by Sir R. Broun).

The London Necropolis & National Mausoleum (Woking Cemetery), Brookwood, Surrey (London, 1887).

The London Necropolis & National Mausoleum (Woking Cemetery), Brookwood, Surrey (London, 1887).

The London Necropolis (London, c.1899).

The London Necropolis (London, c.1902).

The London Necropolis (London, c.1904).

Broun, Sir R. *Extramural Sepulture: Synopsis of the London Necropolis and National Mausoleum at Woking* (London, 1851).

Darwin, B.   *The Glades of Remembrance, Brookwood* (Brookwood, c.1950).

Loudon, J.C. *On the Laying Out, Planting, and Managing of Cemeteries, and on the Improvement of Churchyards.* (London, 1843; also reprinted Redhill, 1981).

Walker, G.A. *Gatherings from Grave Yards* (London, 1839).

Practical Suggestions for the Establishment of National Cemeteries (London, 1849).

(d) Newspapers and periodicals

Builder	*Surrey Advertiser*
Daily Telegraph	*Surrey Standard*
Era	*Surrey Times*
Globe	*Times*
Illustrated London News	*Undertakers' & Funeral Directors' Journal*
Leisure Hour	*Undertakers' Journal*
South Western Gazette	*Westminster Review*
Spectator	*Woking News & Mail*

(II) Other sources

(a) Books

Ariés, Phillipe *The Hour of Our Death* (Penguin Books, 1981).

Brooks, Chris *Mortal Remains: the History and Present State of the Victorian and Edwardian Cemetery* (Wheaton / The Victorian Society, 1989).

Clarke, John M. *An Introduction to Brookwood Cemetery* (2nd ed., The Brookwood Cemetery Society, 2002).

London's Necropolis: A Guide to Brookwood Cemetery (Sutton Publishing, 2004).

Connor, J.E. *London's Disused Stations: Volume 5: The London & South Western Railway* (Connor & Butler, 2005).

Copper, Basil *Necropolis* (Arkham House Publishers, Inc., 1980; also Sphere Books, 1981).

Course, Edwin *The Railways of Southern England* Vols 1 and 3 (Batsford Books, 1973 and 1976).

Curl, James S. *A Celebration of Death* (Constable, 1980; also fully revised and reissued as *Death and Architecture* by Sutton Publishing, 2002).

The Victorian Celebration of Death (David & Charles, 1972; also fully revised and updated edition Sutton Publishing, 2000).

Darwin, Bernard *War on the Line: the Story of the Southern Railway in War-time* (Southern Railway Publications, 1946; also reprinted by Middleton Press, 1984).

Dawes, Martin C. *The End of the Line: The Story of the Railway Service to the Great Northern London Cemetery* (Barnet & District Local History Society, 2003).

Ellis, C. Hamilton   *Four Main Lines* (George Allen & Unwin, 1950).
                      The South Western Railway: Its Mechanical History and Background (George Allen & Unwin, 1956).
Faulkner, J.N. and   *The LSWR in the Twentieth Century* (David & Charles, 1988).
  Williams, R.A.
Fay, S.   *A Royal Road: Being a History of the London & South Western Railway from 1825 to the Present Time* (London, 1882; also reprinted by E.P. Publishing, 1973).
Jackson, Alan A.   *London's Termini* 2nd ed. (David & Charles, 1985).
Jupp, Peter C.   *From Dust to Ashes: Cremation and the British Way of Death* (Palgrave Macmillan, 2006).
Kidner, R.W.   *Carriage Stock of Minor Standard Gauge Railways* (Oakwood Press, 1978).
                      Southern Railway Branch Line Trains (Oakwood Press, 1984).
Kingston, Patrick   *Royal Trains* (David & Charles, 1985).
Litten, Julian   *The English Way of Death: the Common Funeral Since 1450* (Robert Hale, 1991).
Marshall, John   *A Biographical Dictionary of Railway Engineers* (David & Charles, 1978).
Martin, Andrew   *The Necropolis Railway* (Faber & Faber, 2002).
Nock, O.S.   *The London & South Western Railway* (Ian Allan, 1965).
Parsons, Brian   *Committed to the Cleansing Flame: The Development of Cremation in Nineteenth Century England* (Spire Books, 2005).
                      The London Way of Death (Sutton Publishing, 2001).
Pryer, G.A. and   *Track Layout Diagrams of the Southern Railway and B.R. S.R., Section*
  Paul, A.V.   *S7: North Hampshire* (R.A. Cooke, 1982).
Sansom, William   *Westminster in War* (Faber & Faber, 1947; also reprinted as *The Blitz: Westminster at War* by Oxford University Press, 1990).
Sekon, G.A.   *The London & South Western Railway: Half a Century of Railway Progress* (London, 1896; also reprinted by Avon Anglia, 1989).
Simmons, Jack   *The Victorian Railway* (Thames & Hudson, 1991).
Small, Ken   *The Forgotten Dead* (Bloomsbury, 1988).
Wakeford, Iain   *Woking 150: the History of Woking and its Railway* (Mayford & Woking District History Society, 1987).
Weddell, G.R.   *LSWR Carriages, Volume 1: 1838-1900* (Wild Swan, 1992).
                      LSWR Carriages, Volume 3: Non-Passenger Carriage Stock (KRB Publications, 2005).
Whiteman, J.R.   *Victorian Woking* (Surrey Archaeological Society, no date).
  and S.E.
Williams, R.A.   *The London & South Western Railway, Volume 1: the Formative Years* (David & Charles, 1968).

(b) Articles
Alexis, Fr.   'The St Edward Brotherhood' in *Necropolis News* Vol.2 (1996), pp.3-13.
Casserley, H.C.   'Brookwood Mourner' in *The Railway Magazine*, Vol. 119 (1973), pp. 198-9.
Chivers, C. and   'Aspects of Old Waterloo' in *The South Western Circular*, Vol. 7 (1986-8),
  Woods, Phil   pp. 2-22.
Clarke, John M.   'Brookwood Necropolis Railway' in *The South Western Circular*, Vol. 5 (1981-2), pp. 118-144.
                      'The Development of London's Cemeteries: a Brief Survey' in the *Genealogists' Magazine*, Vol. 26 (1998), pp. 9-13.
                      'Necropolis Line - comments' in *The South Western Circular*, Vol. 6 (1983-5), pp. 196-200.
                      Necropolis Trail No.1: the Cemetery Railway (The Brookwood Cemetery Society, 1993).
                      'Staff of the L&SWR Co. Buried at Brookwood' in *The South Western Circular*, Vol. 7 (1986-8), pp. 56-65.
                      'Two Railway Funerals' in *The South Western Circular*, Vol. 5 (1981-2), pp. 260-61.
Dendy, George   'Last Orders Please! Memories of Brookwood Cemetery' in *Necropolis News* Vol. 1 (1995), pp. 6-8.
Foote, F.   Letter in *The South Western Circular*, Vol. 6 (1983-5), pp. 124, 117.
                      'LSWR Hearse Van' in *The Model Railway Constructor*, Vol. 46 (1980), p. 304.
Hopewell, York   'Some Little-known Railway Stations' in *The Railway Magazine*, Vol. VIII (1901), pp. 119-24.
Kidner, R.W.   'LSWR Hearse Van' in *The Model Railway Constructor*, Vol. 46 (1980), p. 51.
Lister, M.D.   'Via Necropolis Junction' in *The Railway Magazine*, Vol. 119 (1973), pp. 74-6.

Livesy, H.M.   'LSWR Funeral Train' in *The Model Railway Constructor*, Vol. 46 (1980), p. 147.

Miller, K.H.   'LSWR Hearse Carriage' in *The Model Railway Constructor*, Vol. 46 (1979), p. 723.

Parsons, Brian   'From Welbeck to Woking: William Garstin and the First Cremations' in *Pharos International*, Vol. 71 (2005), pp. 3-8.

Rowley, Alan   'Two Railway Paintings' in *Railway World*, Vol. 36 (1975), pp. 159-61.

Russell, E.S.   'The Brookwood Cemetery Railway' in *The Railway Magazine*, Vol. 88 (1942), p. 104.

Wade, G.A.   'Railway Stations in Unusual Places' in *The Railway Magazine*, Vol. XIV (1904), p. 123-4.

Weddell, G.R.   'LSWR 24 ft Hearse Carriage' in *The Model Railway Constructor*, Vol. 46 (1979), pp. 581-2.

Wilkinson, T.W.   'Burying London' in George R. Sims (ed.) *Living London* (Cassells, 1901-1903; also reprinted in 4 vols. by The Village Press as *Edwardian London*, 1990).

Index

Dates of death indicate the person is either buried at Brookwood or their funeral was conducted by the LNC